Download Forms on Nolo.com

To download the forms, go to this book's companion page at:

 www.nolo.com/back-of-book/LLCH.html

Checking the companion page is also a good way
to stay informed on topics related to this book.

More Resources
from Nolo.com

Legal Forms, Books, & Software
Hundreds of do-it-yourself products—all written in plain English,
approved, and updated by our in-house legal editors.

Legal Articles
Get informed with thousands of free articles on everyday legal
topics. Our articles are accurate, up to date, and reader friendly.

Find a Lawyer
Want to talk to a lawyer? Use Nolo to find a lawyer who can
help you with your case.

Nolo's LLC Handbook

A Complete Legal Guide to Creating and Operating Your LLC

Attorney Glen Secor

FIRST EDITION	OCTOBER 2024
Editor	JANET PORTMAN
Book Design	SUSAN PUTNEY
Production	SUSAN PUTNEY
Proofreading	IRENE BARNARD
Index	VICTORIA BAKER
Printing	SHERIDAN

Names: Secor, Glen, author.
Title: Nolo's LLC handbook : a complete legal guide to creating and operating your LLC / Attorney Glen Secor.
Other titles: Nolo's Limited Liability Company handbook
Description: 1st edition. | El Segundo : Nolo, 2024. | Includes index.
Identifiers: LCCN 2024013114 | ISBN 9781413332230 (paperback) | ISBN 9781413332247 (ebook)
Subjects: LCSH: Limited partnership--United States. | Limited partnership--United States--Forms.
Classification: LCC KF1380 .S44 2024 | DDC 346.73/0682--dc23/eng/20240325
LC record available at https://lccn.loc.gov/2024013114

Please note

Accurate, plain-English legal information can help you solve many of your own legal problems. But this text is not a substitute for personalized advice from a knowledgeable lawyer. If you want the help of a trained professional—and we'll always point out situations in which we think that's a good idea—consult an attorney licensed to practice in your state.

MH Sub I, LLC dba Nolo, 909 N. Pacific Coast Hwy, 11th Fl, El Segundo, CA 90245

About the Author

Glen Secor joined Nolo as a Legal Editor in 2022, focusing on small business, intellectual property, and nonprofits.

Glen earned his J.D. from Suffolk University Law, where he graduated with honors and was an editor for the *Suffolk Transnational Law Review*, and his LL.M from Harvard Law School, where he focused on intellectual property and cyberlaw. He taught copyright courses at University of New Hampshire School of Law for nine years and has taught business law courses in other programs.

Glen spent most of his legal career as an in-house counsel, first for a leading library bookselling company and then for a nonprofit education research company. He also spent years in private practice, focusing on startup and early-stage companies, copyright and trademark matters, and nonprofits.

Dedication

This book is dedicated to my always supportive wife, Rosheen, my superb editor, Janet Portman, and all my LLC clients over the years.

Table of Contents

Your LLC Legal Companion

L imited liability companies (LLCs) are the ideal entity for many single-owner and multi-owner small businesses. This book is aimed at business owners who have decided that an LLC is right for their business (more on that below). You've chosen to establish an LLC because you know it will provide you with pass-through taxation (like a partnership), along with the limited liability protection of a corporation. You might have heard that LLCs are simpler to set up and operate than a corporation, which is true in most cases.

This guide gives you the legal information and documents you need to start, operate, and dissolve your LLC. It's designed for do-it-yourself business owners who want to be able to handle basic legal tasks and documents on their own, as well as for folks who work with an attorney and want to be better informed clients. The more informed you are, the more efficiently you can work with an attorney, thereby saving consultation time and expense. But our primary goal here is to enable you to handle the tasks we cover on your own.

We hope that this book will be a true "companion" for you as you form and begin to run your business. You'll find that many of its forms will be very handy as your business grows and changes. Some parts of the book might not ever be relevant (like the discussion on dissolution). But you'll know that the information is there, accessible, clear, and succinct.

Who Is This Book For?

With so many books about LLCs to choose from, why choose *Nolo's LLC Handbook*? We're a bit biased, of course, but we think this book is unique because of its strong focus on:

Multi-Owner (Multi-Member) LLCs

Our focus in this book is on LLCs with two or more owners. Nolo provides an excellent resource for single-owner LLCs, *Nolo's Guide to Single-Member LLCs*, by David M. Steingold.

Owners Who Have Already Decided on an LLC

This book is designed for business owners who have already decided to operate as an LLC, whether they're starting a new business or converting an existing business to an LLC. If you're still trying to decide whether an LLC is right for you, we recommend *LLC or Corporation: Choose the Right Form for Your Business*, by Anthony Mancuso (also from Nolo). Then, if you choose to go with an LLC, come back to this book.

What You'll Find Inside

Nolo's LLC Handbook is not a comprehensive book about all things LLC. Instead, this book is very specifically about the forms and agreements you need to start and legally maintain your LLC. We've organized it in five parts:

Part A: Forming Your LLC
Part B: Operating Agreements
Part C: Buyout Agreements and Ownership Transfers
Part D: Maintaining Your LLC: Legal and Tax Compliance
Part E: Dissolving Your LLC

Each part includes sample forms and agreements, along with explanations of the decisions you need to make to complete them. Blank forms and agreements are provided in Appendix C and can be downloaded from the companion page for this book on the Nolo website. A complete list of forms and agreements, along with a link to the online companion page, is included in Appendix A.

In terms of tax topics, our focus is on the forms you need to file (or can elect to file) when you form your company, along with your partnership income tax return and your employment tax returns. To understand the ins and outs of LLC taxation (and small business taxation, generally), we recommend *Tax Savvy for Small Business*, by Stephen Fishman (Nolo).

We do not take up employment law, contracts (other than the specific agreements included in this book), leases, licenses, or other legal topics not related to the formation and maintenance of your LLC. Nolo offers a wide range of small business legal guides, which you can find at www.nolo.com.

Terminology

LLCs are relatively straightforward as business entities go, but LLC terminology can be confusing. Here are a few key phrases that we use throughout the book:

- **Members:** LLC owners are called "members." Some writers refer to LLC owners as partners, because LLCs are usually taxed as partnerships and LLCs operate much like partnerships. But LLCs are not partnerships, and we refer to LLC owners as members.

- **Managers:** We think of a manager as a person in a business with responsibility for managing some part of the business—operations, marketing, HR, etc. In many companies, the managers work under the executives. In the LLC world, "manager" has a more specific and legally significant meaning. A manager in an LLC is a person appointed by the members to run the business (or, when no managers are designated by the members, management is vested in all the members). We discuss managers and management in Chapters 1–4 on forming your LLC and in even more depth in Chapters 5–7 on operating agreements.

- **Operating agreement:** An LLC operating agreement is an agreement between the members that spells out their rights and responsibilities as owners, as well as basic rules on how the LLC should be run (operated). You might see LLC operating agreements referred to as partnership agreements. Operating agreements and partnership agreements are very similar, but we refer to the LLC agreement as the operating agreement.

- **Membership interest:** A member's ownership stake in the LLC is called an "interest." An interest is stated as a percentage of all interests. Four equal co-owners of an LLC owns a 25% interest each. Normally, each owner in this scenario would be entitled to 25% of the profits of the company. Some LLCs state their ownership interests in units, with each unit equaling 1% of the whole (so, each 25% owner in our example would own 25 units). Most LLCs use percentage interests instead of units.

- **Secretary of state:** Every state has an office that registers business entities (including corporations and LLCs). Most states refer to this office as the secretary of state, but others call it the department of commerce, corporations division, or a similar term. We refer to this office as the secretary of state.

 FORMS
Accessing state government and IRS forms in this book.
State government forms used to illustrate particular legal and tax filings are available on your state's appropriate state agency website. The IRS forms are available at www.irs.gov.

Get Customizable Agreements Online

You can download agreements from this book's companion page on the Nolo website at:

www.nolo.com/back-of-book/LLCH.html

See Appendix A for a complete list.

P A R T

A

Forming Your LLC

Preliminary Decisions: Registered Agent and Type of Management

L imited liability companies are very easy to form. You file a simple registration form with your state, and your LLC is born. We cover the registration form, called articles of organization (articles) in Chapter 3.

But before you sit down to complete and file your articles, you need to make two preliminary decisions:

- Who will be the registered agent for the company—the person or business who will receive official notices?
- How will the company be managed: by the owners directly (member-management), or by managers appointed by the owners (manager-managed)?

When you file your articles, you will name a registered agent and indicate whether your LLC will have designated managers. Your choice of management structure will also be reflected in your operating agreement (see Chapter 6 on member-managed LLC operating agreements and Chapter 7 on manager-managed operating agreements).

Decision 1: Registered Agent

Every state requires LLCs to have a registered agent. A registered agent is a person or business located within the state who can be served with papers should the business be sued or receive tax deficiency notices from the state. Some states refer to the registered agent as the statutory agent or resident agent, but we'll stick to calling them registered agents.

The registered agent can be an individual or a business, so long as the individual or business has a physical street address in the state. Many LLCs designate one of the owners (members) as the registered agent, using the LLC's business address as the address for the registered agent. You can also use the in-state home address of the designated member, but doing so has its downsides. The address of your registered agent is a matter of public record, so using a member's home address will likely result in that member receiving lots of unsolicited mail from companies wanting to sell goods and services to the LLC.

Some states allow an LLC to be its own registered agent, although most states do not.

Paid Registered Agent Services

Companies and some law firms will act as your registered agent—for a fee, of course. Many LLC formation services (which we cover at the end of Chapter 3) will include a year of free or discounted registered agent service when you form your LLC through them. But you can use a paid registered agent service even if you file your own articles. If you're worried that important legal and tax documents could get lost or mishandled if delivered to your business address, a paid registered agent service can be a good option at a reasonable price.

As we discuss in Chapter 9, you must notify the state immediately when you change your registered agent or when the registered agent's address changes. In short, you must provide the state with the name of your registered agent with a current address at all times.

Decision 2: Management Structure

You have two options for managing your LLC: the members can manage it directly (a member-managed LLC), or they can appoint one or more managers to do so (a manager-managed LLC). When you file your articles, you need to indicate whether your LLC will have designated managers. If you don't designate one or more managers, the law presumes that your LLC is managed by all the members (member-managed).

Why Have Managers?

LLCs are simpler to operate than corporations, because ownership and management of a corporation are separate roles. The owners (shareholders) elect directors, who are responsible for the overall management of the corporation. (The directors appoint officers to run the company on a day-to-day basis, but our point here is that ownership in a corporation is separate from management, even if the same people are shareholders, directors, and officers.) Corporations are required by law to have directors and officers.

LLCs are not required by law to have managers who are separate from the owners. The members can run the company directly, without appointing managers. In fact, when all members will be active in the company, most LLCs choose not to designate managers (and choose instead to be member-managed).

> **EXAMPLE 1:** Constance, Carmen, Chris, and Carly are forming a candle company, 4C Candle Company LLC (4C Candles). Each member will own 25% of the company, and each will be active in the business. They decide not to appoint managers, so the four members will be responsible for managing the company and will vote on any significant business decisions. 4C Candles is a member-managed LLC.

When some members will be active in the company but some will not, the members can appoint the active members to be managers. The managers will run the company, while the members who are not active will have their financial stake but not participate in management.

> **EXAMPLE 2:** Now let's assume that Constance, Chris, and Carly will be active in 4C Candles, while Carmen will invest in the LLC but not be active in it (Carmen is a passive owner). The four members agree to appoint Constance, Chris, and Carly as managers. Assuming that they vote according to their ownership interests, Constance, Chris, and Carly each have a one-third vote on management decisions. Carmen will receive her share (25%) of 4C Candles profits and losses, but will not have a say in the day-to-day management of the company. In this scenario, 4C Candles is a manager-managed LLC.

Example 2 demonstrates the most common reason why LLC owners choose to have the company be manager-managed: Not all owners will participate in management. In such a scenario, the LLC operates similar to a limited partnership. In a limited partnership, the general partners manage the business, while limited partners are passive owners. (Unlike in an LLC, though, where all members have limited liability, in a limited partnership only the limited partners have limited liability; the personal assets of general partners are at risk if the business can't pay its debts.)

Sometimes, owners in a scenario like Example 1, with all members being active, will still choose to appoint managers. In the case of 4C Candles, why would the members separate ownership and management when the same people occupy both roles? Perhaps the members foresee a day when one or more of them might not be active in the company. Or they might want different rules for making decisions at the management level and the ownership level.

> EXAMPLE 3: Each of the four members of 4C Candles will be a 25% owner. But Carmen and Carly have more business management experience and the four members agree that Carmen and Carly should have more management authority than Constance and Chris. The four agree that 4C Candles will have managers (be manager-managed) and that Carmen and Carly will each have a 30% management vote, with Constance and Chris each having a 20% management vote.

In the examples above, only members were appointed as managers. Nonmembers can be LLC managers, as well.

> EXAMPLE 4: Assume that Constance, Carmen, Chris, and Carly are member-managers. Each wants to spend their time working with clients, and none of them has run any kind of business before. They hire Fiona to be director of operations and appoint her as the fifth manager. Fiona is not a member, but she has a vote in manager-level decisions and she can represent the company and do business with third parties as a manager. (This scenario is uncommon among small LLCs, where managers are usually members.)

Again, if you have managers, you need to name them in your Articles of Organization. So, before you sit down to file your articles, decide whether your LLC will be member-managed or manager-managed. If you don't name managers in your articles, your LLC is presumed to be managed by all the members (member-managed).

The information above is an overview of how member-managed and manager-managed LLCs work. For a better sense of how these differently run LLCs actually work, review the member-managed LLC operating agreement in Chapter 6 and the manager-managed operating agreement in Chapter 7. The management provisions in each operating agreement, along with our explanations, demonstrate how decisions are made under each structure.

Changing Your Management Structure

What if your LLC starts out being member-managed or manager-managed and later on you want to change the structure by having or eliminating managers? You can make the change by filing amended articles with the state. Some states require a unanimous vote of the members to amend articles. We discuss amended articles in Chapter 9. You would also need to amend your operating agreement to reflect the change in management structure. ●

Name Reservations and Searches

FORMS IN THIS CHAPTER

Accessing state government forms in this chapter. State government forms used to illustrate particular legal and tax filings are available on your state's appropriate state agency website.

t's undoubtedly important to you that your business have the name you'd like it to have. But you can't use a name that's already taken, or even one that is very close to yours. This chapter explains how to look for existing business names and reserve your name before you file your articles (not all businesses will need to do this advance step; see below).

In all states except Alabama and Florida, you have the option of filing a "Reservation of Name" form (or similarly titled form) before you file your articles. (Florida does not extend that option, and Alabama actually requires you to reserve the name.) If you don't file a separate name registration, your secretary of state's office will evaluate your business name when you file your articles. If your requested name is not available (see below), the office will reject your articles. If your requested name is available and your articles are approved, the name is yours.

What Is a Name Reservation and Why Do It?

A name reservation places a temporary hold on your desired business name. When you file a name reservation request, the secretary of state's office will determine whether the name is available. If it is, you will have exclusive rights to the name for a certain period (in most states, between 60 and 120 days). During that time, if anyone else seeks to reserve a name or register a business with a name identical or even similar to your reserved name, their name reservation request or articles will be rejected. As long as you file your articles within the exclusive time period, that business name is yours.

If you're ready to file your articles and start your LLC today, don't bother filing a name reservation request first. The secretary of state will determine name availability when they review your articles. On the other hand, filing a separate name reservation makes sense if you:

- are sure you want the business name
- aren't ready to file articles

- expect to file articles within the reservation period, and
- are concerned that someone might swoop in and take the name before you file articles.

As discussed below, the name reservation process is very simple. But before you try to reserve or register a specific name, do your homework.

Check Whether the Name Is Available

Before you try to reserve a business name or file articles with your desired name, try to find out whether anyone is already using that name. Your search for potentially conflicting names should include:

- your state's databases of registered businesses and reserved names
- the federal trademark database (and your state's trademark database), and
- a database of domain names.

We discuss each search below. Before you start, though, do a simple internet search on your name. Enter your business name or parts of your business name and see what the search engine coughs up. This search won't necessarily tell you whether a name is available, but it can give you an idea of whether anyone is already using your desired business name.

> **EXAMPLE:** Originally, Constance, Carmen, Chris, and Carly wanted to call their company Lighthouse Candles. But when they did an internet search for the name, they found a few companies in other states already named "Lighthouse Candle Company" or something similar, along with other companies selling lighthouse-shaped candles. Even though they could probably register Lighthouse Candles LLC in their state, they wanted a more original name and decided to explore their backup name, 4C Candles. A web search for "4C Candles" yields few results and none that would discourage them from pursuing the name.

How Similar Is Too Similar When It Comes to Business Names?

Chris does a business name search for "4C Candles" on his secretary of state's website. He reads that a new business name can't be identical to the name of an existing business, or so similar to the name of an existing business that the new business is likely to be mistaken for the existing business.

Chris's search for "4C Candles" uncovers lots of businesses with "4C" in their names, but no "4C Candles," and no businesses with both "4C" and "Candles" in their names. Based on these results, Chris and his cofounders should be able to name their company 4C Candles LLC.

Let's say instead that Chris's search results show that a business already exists in the state under the name 4C Candles & Gifts Company LLC. Is "4C Candles" so similar to "4C Candles & Gifts" that it can't be registered? Assuming that Chris and his cofounders still want to name their company 4C Candles LLC despite the existence of 4C Candles & Gifts LLC, they could submit a name reservation request for 4C Candles LLC, or they could go straight to filing articles with that name. Either way, the secretary of state will determine whether the two names are so similar that one business is likely to be mistaken for the other.

If the office decides that 4C Candles is so similar to 4C Candles & Gifts that the public is likely to confuse the two companies, the state will reject the 4C Candles LLC name reservation request or articles, and Chris and his cofounders will need to find another name. If the secretary of state determines that the names are not too similar, Chris and his cofounders will be able to reserve or register their name.

Searching Your State's Database of Registered Businesses

Your secretary of state maintains a public, searchable database of businesses that have registered in the state. Go to the secretary of state's website and find the business search tool (or do an internet search for "business name search for [the name of your state])." Once on your secretary of state's search page, enter your desired name in the search field and see what the database pulls up. If it appears that no company in the database has your desired name or one very close to it, you can feel comfortable reserving or registering it. If you find another business already using your desired name, and if that business is still active (see below), you'll probably need to vary your name or pick another name altogether.

Most states also maintain a name *reservation* database where you can check names that have been reserved but not yet registered. Check your secretary of state's site for such a database.

Trademark Searches

The United States Patent and Trademark Office (USPTO), the agency that registers federal trademarks, defines a trademark as "any word, phrase, symbol, design, or a combination of these things that identifies your goods or services. It's how customers recognize you in the marketplace and distinguish you from your competitors."

A trademark can be registered or unregistered. An unregistered trademark, also known as a common law trademark, is established by using the mark in a particular state. You would find this type of trademark through an internet search for the name, or through your own observation of the mark in use (such as in TV commercials). A trademark can also be registered at the state level, although state trademarks provide limited protection and most businesses don't register their marks with the state. When people speak of a registered trademark, they are almost always referring to a federal trademark.

Even when no existing registered business has a name that would conflict with your business name, another company could be using the name as a brand in your state and other states that you want to sell in. In other words, someone else might already own a trademark in your business name.

For example, let's say that you wanted to call your company "Quick Books Software LLC." Even if no company is registered in your state under the name "Quick Books" or a similar name, and even if the secretary of state approved articles for your company as Quick Books Software LLC, you'd almost certainly hear from the Intuit Corporation, owner of the QuickBooks trademark, demanding that you cease and desist from using the QuickBooks name. And keep in mind that the issue of confusion runs two ways: You, too, wouldn't want customers confusing the Intuit product for yours, and buying the Intuit product instead.

In addition to staying out of trouble with existing trademark owners, you might also want to trademark your business name once you're up and running. If your name is similar to an existing trademark, you might get turned down by the USPTO. You should always do a federal trademark search (or pay an attorney or search service to do it for you) before you go to the considerable effort and expense of applying for a federal trademark.

The type of trademark search recommended here isn't as extensive as one you might conduct when actually registering a trademark, but it will give you an idea of potentially conflicting marks that are already registered by others).

Doing a Basic Trademark Search

For business naming purposes, you can do a simple trademark search on the USPTO website, using their cloud-based search system. You can access the system and get helpful instructions on using it at the USPTO website (USPTO.gov, under the "Trademarks" tab, click the "Search Our Trademark Database" link).

Interpreting Trademark Search Results

Don't panic if your USPTO search results include one or more trade-marks similar to or even the same as your desired business name. For the most part, a registered trademark applies only to one or more specific classes of goods or services, and the USPTO examiners will reject similar names only when they belong to goods or services in the same class. The examiners are attempting to prevent customer confusion, which is not likely when a name is used for very different products or services.

For example, suppose you'd like to trademark your new marketing company "Dove Marketing Group LLC." You discover that "DOVE" is a registered trademark of Mars, Incorporated in Class 30 (as in Dove chocolates). The name is also registered by Conopco, Inc. in Class 3 (as in Dove soap). Neither mark would pose a barrier to naming your business Dove Marketing Group. On the other hand, you'd be unwise to start the Dove Chocolate Company or the Dove Soap Company. Even if your secretary of state registered the name, you'd likely hear from Mars, Incorporated (or Conopco, Inc., in the case of Dove Soap Company), demanding that you stop using the name.

If your search uncovers an existing trademark that might present problems for your desired business name, or for your own trademark registration (should you want to pursue one), consider consulting a business or trademark attorney. An ounce of prevention here could be worth many pounds of cure, especially if you were to discover later that you have to change the name of your business, or the USPTO decides to block you from registering your own trademarks.

RESOURCE

Nolo's *Trademark: Legal Care for Your Business & Product Name*, by Stephen Fishman, is an excellent resource for understanding the ins and outs of trademarks. The book explains how to pick a trademarkable business name, do a trademark search, and register a trademark. And you'll find lots of free information on trademarks and business names in the "Patent, Copyright & Trademark" area of Nolo.com.

State Registered Trademarks

All states also allow you to trademark your business name at the individual state level. State trademarks tend to be of limited value because they offer protection only within the state's borders, and they are not widely used. Nevertheless, your state's database of registered trademarks is one more place to look to see if anyone is already using your desired business name in your state.

The USPTO maintains a list of state trademark information links on their website (at USPTO.gov, search for "state trademark information").

Domain Name Searches

Assuming that your business will have a website and that you'll want your domain name to match (or at least approximate) the name of your business, you'll want to do a domain name search before you settle on the business name. You can search domain names for free with a domain registration company such as Domains.com, GoDaddy, Bluehost, or Squarespace Domains. Many domain registration companies also offer web hosting and website building services, but you don't need to commit to such a service, or even to register your domain name through that company, to do a free domain search. And you need to do your search with only one company, as they all pull from the same central domain registry.

EXAMPLE: Carmen visits the Domains.com site and enters a search for "4C Candles." The results show that 4ccandles.com is taken, but 4ccandles.net and 4c-candles.com are available. Carmen and the other founders agree that, while they would have preferred 4ccandles.com, they'd be happy with 4c-candles.com (or even 4ccandles.net). Knowing that they can get a domain they want, they proceed with the business name 4C Candles LLC. In fact, they purchase the 4c-candles.com domain, just to be safe.

Filing a Name Reservation

The name reservation process is easy and relatively inexpensive ($10–$50 in most states). Find the form—Application for Name Reservation (or a similar name)—on your secretary of state's website (the New Hampshire name reservation form is included below). You might be able to complete and submit the form online, or you might need to download, complete, and submit it. You'll need to provide very basic information:

- the name and contact information of the person or (existing) business applying for the name, and
- the desired business name (some states allow you to specify a second choice if your first choice is not available).

That's it. Submit the form with the fee, then wait to hear whether the secretary of state has approved the application and reserved the name for you. (Most states turn name reservation requests around in a few business days.)

EXAMPLE: The 4C Candles founders want to sort out a few details before filing articles, but they want to lock in the name 4C Candles LLC. Constance files an Application for Name Reservation for 4C Candles LLC, and the application is approved, giving them rights to the name as long as they file articles within the 60-day reservation period.

Application for Reservation of Name

State of New Hampshire

Form 1

APPLICATION FOR RESERVATION OF NAME
FOR:
CORPORATION, LIMITED LIABILITY COMPANY, LIMITED LIABILITY PARTNERSHIP,
LIMITED PARTNERSHIP, NEW HAMPSHIRE INVESTMENT TRUST OR FOUNDATION

The undersigned applies for reservation of the following name for a period of one hundred twenty days:

1) Application for reservation of name for:

_____

2) Name being reserved under (please check one box only): (Note 1)

☐ RSA 293-A:4.02 - Corporation under RSA 293-A:4.01

☐ RSA 304-C:27 - Limited Liability Company under RSA 304-C:32 or RSA 304-C:177

☐ RSA 304-A:46 - **NEW HAMPSHIRE** Limited Liability Partnership under RSA 304-A:45

☐ RSA 304-A:46 - **FOREIGN** Limited Liability Partnership under RSA 304-A:50

☐ RSA 304-B:3 - Limited Partnership under RSA 304-B:2

☐ RSA 293-B:17 II & III - New Hampshire Investment Trusts under RSA 293-B:17

☐ RSA 564-F:4-402 - Foundation under RSA 564-F:4-401

3) Nature of business **(required)**:

_____

_____

4) Applicant information:

_____
(Print name of applicant)

_____
(No.) _ (Street)   (City/Town)   (State)   (Zip Code)

_____   _____
(Authorized Signature)   (Email address)

_____   _____
(Print or type name)   (Phone number)

_____   Date signed: _____
(Title)

DISCLAIMER: All documents filed with the Corporation Division become public records and will be available for public inspection in either tangible or electronic form.

**Mailing Address - Corporation Division, NH Dept. of State, 107 N Main St, Rm 204, Concord, NH 03301-4989
Physical Location - State House Annex, 3rd Floor, Rm 317, 25 Capitol St, Concord, NH**

Form 1 (8/2018)

"Doing Business As" (DBA) Names

A "doing business as" (DBA) name, also known as a "fictitious business name" or "trade name," is not evidence of a legal entity (unlike "LLC," which tells everyone that the business has registered with the state). Rather, it's a name under which an individual or company is doing business. Many sole proprietors use a DBA (for example, Pat Smith operates as Smith Plumbing). But LLCs and corporations use DBAs, as well.

> EXAMPLE: Let's say that Carly, Carmen, Chris, and Constance want to start additional businesses together, unrelated to candles, but they don't want to set up a separate LLC for each business. They could form 4C Candles LLC and then pursue other businesses under other "doing business as" (DBA) names. For example, "4C Candles LLC DBA 4C Chocolates" or "4C Candles LLC DBA Purple Puppy Essential Oils." Or, they could name the company Foreseeable Future Group LLC (assuming that the name is available in their state) and then operate as "Foreseeable Future Group LLC DBA 4C Candles" and "Foreseeable Future Group LLC DBA Purple Puppy Essential Oils." For marketing purposes only, they would refer to their ventures as 4C Chocolates and Purple Puppy Essential Oils.

DBA names are generally registered at the city or county level, not at the state level. So, multiple companies in multiple cities or counties within a state could be using the same DBA name.

Name Restrictions on LLCs

Certain businesses cannot operate as LLCs, including banks and insurance companies. Accordingly, states prohibit LLCs from having words such as "bank," "insurance company," or "trust company" in their name. Most states also prohibit words that imply the company is a government entity, such as "Federal" or "United States."

Registering Your LLC: Articles of Organization

FORMS IN THIS CHAPTER

Accessing state government forms in this chapter. State government forms used to illustrate particular legal and tax filings are available on your state's appropriate state agency website.

Once you've identified a registered agent, decided whether to be member-managed or manager-managed, and settled on a name (and possibly reserved it), you're ready to create your LLC by filing a formation document with your secretary of state. Most states refer to this document as articles of organization, but many call it a certificate of formation or a certificate of organization. We refer to it as articles.

Converting an Existing Business Entity to an LLC

Perhaps you're not starting your LLC from scratch, but are instead looking to convert an existing corporation to an LLC, or an LLC registered in one state to an LLC registered in a different state. Most states have procedures to accomplish such conversions. We don't cover conversions to LLCs in this book (but we discuss converting an LLC to a corporation in Chapter 9). You can find information on converting a corporation to an LLC or moving an LLC's registration from one state to another on your secretary of state's website. We encourage you to consult an attorney if you need additional guidance or assistance. Consider including a tax professional in the conversation as well, because the tax implications of converting can be complicated.

Completing and Filing Your Articles

Articles of organization is a simple form that you can complete online or download from your secretary of state's website. We've included below a simple, representative formation document from New Hampshire (certificate of formation), and refer to it as we explain common elements of all articles. The required information on the form varies from state to state, but most state articles include the following items:

- **LLC name.** As we noted in Chapter 2, if you haven't reserved your business name before filing your articles, your articles serve as a request for that name. If your business name is available and your articles meet all other requirements, the secretary of state will approve the articles and the name will be yours for the life of the LLC.

All states require the business name to include one of the following designations: limited liability company, L.L.C., LLC, or a similar term (for example, 4C Candles LLC).

- **Business address.** Most states require a physical street address for your LLC. If the company doesn't have its own dedicated space, the address can be that of a virtual office or coworking space. You can also use your registered agent's address or the home address of a member or manager. Be aware that your articles are a public record and that all sorts of marketers monitor new business formations. So, if you use your home address, you can expect to receive lots of junk mail there. Your home address will also be exposed to anyone searching for your company in your state's company database.

  If your LLC's mailing address is different from its street address, you might be required to provide both addresses.

- **Business purpose.** You'll need to provide a short description of what your business does. States vary in terms of what they require and allow for the statement of business purpose. Some require a specifically enumerated purpose (such as the type of product or service the company will offer), while others allow for a more general statement of purpose, such as:

  The purpose of the limited liability company is to engage in any lawful act or activity for which a limited liability company may be organized under the [state name] Limited Liability Company Act.

  California, in fact, requires that you use open-ended language like the above, in your articles. New Hampshire, on the other hand, forbids an "any lawful purpose" statement. Review the instructions that accompany your state's form for guidance on the section of the form.

- **Registered agent.** Your registered agent accepts official notices on behalf of your company (see Chapter 1 for more information). Some states, such as Maryland and Massachusetts, require the registered agent to sign the articles as an indication of consent to serve as registered agent.

New Hampshire Certificate of Formation

Filing fee: $100.00
Use black print or type.

Form LLC-1
RSA 304-C:31

CERTIFICATE OF FORMATION
NEW HAMPSHIRE LIMITED LIABILITY COMPANY

THE UNDERSIGNED, under the New Hampshire Limited Liability Company Laws submits the following certificate of formation:

FIRST: The name of the limited liability company is _____

_____.

Principal Business Information:

Principal Office Address: _____
(no. & street)   (city/town)   (state)   (zip code)

Principal Mailing Address (if different): _____
(no. & street)   (city/town)   (state)   (zip code)

Business Phone: _____

Business Email: _____

____ Please check if you would prefer to receive the courtesy Annual Report Reminder by email.

SECOND: Describe the nature of the primary business or purposes (and if known, list the NAICS Code and Sub Code): _____

_____

_____.

THIRD: The name of the limited liability company's registered agent is:

_____.

The complete address of its registered office (agent's business address) is:

_____.
(no. & street)   (city/town)   (state)   (zip code)

FOURTH: The management of the limited liability company _____ vested in a manager or managers.

Form LLC-1

New Hampshire Certificate of Formation (page 2)

CERTIFICATE OF FORMATION OF A
NEW HAMPSHIRE LIMITED LIABILITY COMPANY

Form LLC-1
(Cont.)

MANAGER / MEMBER INFORMATION
(List all Managers and/or Members you wish to be placed on record)

NAME	BUSINESS ADDRESS	TITLE

*Signature: _____

Print or type name: _____

Title: _____
(Enter "manager" or "member")

Date signed: _____

Note: The sale or offer for sale of membership interests of the limited liability company will comply with the requirements of the New Hampshire Uniform Securities Act (RSA 421-B). The membership interests of the limited liability company: 1) have been registered or when offered will be registered under RSA 421-B; 2) are exempted or when offered will be exempted under RSA 421-B; 3) are or will be offered in a transaction exempted from registration under RSA 421-B; 4) are not securities under RSA 421-B; OR 5) are federal covered securities under RSA 421-B. The statement above shall not by itself constitute a registration or a notice of exemption from registration of securities within the meaning of sections 448 and 461(i)(3) of the United States Internal Revenue Code and the regulation promulgated thereunder.

* The document shall be signed by a "manager" and if there is no manager, by a "member" or see RSA 304-C:28 V for alternative signatures.

DISCLAIMER: All documents filed with the Corporation Division become public records and will be available for public inspection in either tangible or electronic form.

Mailing Address - Corporation Division, NH Dept. of State, 107 N Main St, Rm 204, Concord, NH 03301-4989
Physical Location - State House Annex, 3rd Floor, Rm 317, 25 Capitol St, Concord, NH

Form LLC-1 (10/2018)

- **Duration of the LLC.** State laws presume that LLCs have a perpetual life, but some states allow an LLC to have a fixed term (a specific future dissolution date). Many states are getting away from the fixed-term option and don't include this item on their articles.
- **Management.** Your LLC will be either member-managed or manager-managed (see Chapter 1). On the New Hampshire form above, you would fill in the "FOURTH" item by indicating that management "is" or "is not" vested in a manager or managers ("is" for manager-managed, or "is not" for member-managed).
- **Manager/Member names and business addresses.** Some states require you to include in the articles the name and business address (normally the LLC's address) of each manager (or member if there are no managers). In other states, this information is optional, and in still others, not sought at all.
- **Organizer's name and signature.** The person filing the articles (a member or manager, or their authorized agent) must sign the articles. As previously noted, some states require the registered agent to also sign the articles.

How to File

Most states encourage you to file articles on the secretary of state's website, using their online form. You can instead download and complete the form on your computer or by hand, and then mail it in or deliver it in person, but if you file that way, processing times can be longer as compared to online filing. Whatever method you use to file your articles, the form must be accompanied by a registration fee. The registration fee is generally nonrefundable (although, as noted below, it can be applied to a resubmission of articles after an initial rejection by the secretary of state).

You do not file your operating agreement with your articles. Your operating agreement is an internal document that is never filed with the state.

Some States Require You to Have (But Not File) an Operating Agreement

Only five states (California, Delaware, Maine, Missouri, and New York) require an LLC to have an operating agreement. Even in those states, the operating agreement is not filed with the state, but is instead kept wherever the company keeps its business records. None of the five states has a mechanism for auditing LLCs to see whether they have operating agreements, and LLCs do not face prescribed penalties for not having an operating agreement. Nevertheless, while we strongly advise every multi-member LLC in every state to have a written operating agreement, our recommendation takes on added urgency in the five states that require an operating agreement by law.

If the secretary of state's office accepts your articles, your LLC is formed (comes into legal existence) on the date of acceptance. Some states allow you to specify a later start date in your articles, but most filers want the quickest start date possible (the date the articles are accepted by the secretary of state).

How long does it take for your articles to be approved (or rejected)? Most states process online filings within a few business days, with a number of states offering immediate responses. Mail-in processing times are generally longer.

What If Your Articles Are Rejected?

Articles can be rejected for two primary reasons: (1) the requested business name is not available, and (2) there's a defect in the articles.

Your Name Is Unavailable

As discussed in Chapter 2 and above, you can file articles without having first reserved your desired business name. If the name is unavailable, your articles will be rejected and you'll need to resubmit them with a new name. It's really no harder to resubmit your articles with a new name than it is to reserve the name ahead of time. Of course, whether you're reserving a name or filing articles without having reserved a name, you'll want to do a name search in advance to minimize the chance of being rejected.

Your Filing is Defective

This category covers significant filing errors, such as:

- not including "LLC" or a similar designation in the name
- using a disallowed address, such as a P.O. box, as the street address for the business
- not naming a registered agent, and
- failing to provide any other required information or required signatures on the form.

The secretary of state will send a notice of rejection indicating the reason(s) for the rejection, with information on resubmitting the articles.

If you discover a mistake in your articles as filed, and before you've gotten a rejection, you might be able to save them by filing a "Certificate of Correction." For instance, if you find a typo in the business address, an incorrectly stated purpose, or a defect in the execution of the document (such as a missing signature), you might be able to correct it by filing a certificate of correction (or similarly titled form).

States vary in terms of what errors can be fixed via a certificate of correction, but generally speaking, you cannot change the name of the LLC, or the name or address of the registered agent, via a certificate of correction. Those changes and others need to be made in a certificate of amendment (or similarly titled form), which we cover in Chapter 9. Check your secretary of state's website for guidance on certificates of correction and certificates of amendment.

Forming a Professional LLC

In most states, professionals who want to operate as an LLC must form a specially-designated LLC called a professional limited liability company (PLLC). The filing process for a PLLC is the same as for an LLC, except that you use a PLLC version of your state's articles. PLLC articles are the same as LLC articles except that the PLLC version:

- requires that your name include PLLC, P.L.L.C., or a similar abbreviation, and
- requires you to identify the professional services offered (instead of the statement of business purpose).

The PLLC filing fee and process are the same as for LLCs.

The professions eligible to form PLLCs are designated by the state, but generally include accounting, legal, and medical professions. Some states don't have PLLCs, but instead allow professionals to form professional corporations. If you're forming a professional services business, check with your secretary of state for options and requirements.

Registering a Foreign LLC

If you form your LLC in one state (State A) but do business (defined below) in another state (State B), you might be required to register in State B as a "foreign LLC" (an out-of-state LLC). "Doing business" in a state usually means that you meet at least one of the following criteria:

- you have a physical presence—such as offices, warehouses, or retail stores—in the state
- you have employees in the state providing services to clients in that state
- you have company-owned vehicles making deliveries or pickups in the state, or
- you have a certain amount of sales in the state (usually measured by the total dollar amount or number of sales).

If you qualify as doing business in a state and are required to register as a foreign LLC, you would file a foreign LLC registration form, not articles, in that state. The registration form is called a certificate of authority, an application for registration, or a similar name. The Virginia foreign LLC registration form is provided below. It's a very simple form. Items I and II ask for information about the LLC in its home state. Parts III and IV are for the LLC's registered agent in Virginia, which it must have.

Once an LLC registers as a foreign LLC in a state, it is normally subject to ongoing reporting requirements, including annual reporting and change of registered agent reporting. We cover ongoing LLC reporting requirements in Chapter 9.

When your LLC is doing business in a state and is required to register as a foreign LLC there, the consequences for failing to register can be significant. Those consequences include not being able to file a lawsuit in the state, as well financial penalties. If you're unsure whether your LLC is required to register in a given state, check the laws in the state and, if the situation is unclear, consult with a business attorney.

Virginia Foreign LLC Registration Form

| Form **LLC1052** (Rev. 07/21) State Corporation Commission | **Application for Certificate of Registration to Transact Business in Virginia as a Foreign Limited Liability Company** | |

I   The foreign limited liability company's name: _____

The designated name (if required): _____

The jurisdiction of formation: _____

The original date of formation: _____ The period of duration is ☐ perpetual **or** ☐ expires on: _____

(If applicable, mark box and provide additional information on an attachment. See Instructions for requirements.)
☐ The LLC was previously authorized or registered to transact business in Virginia as a foreign entity.

(If applicable, mark box and provide additional information on an attachment.)
☐ The LLC is a foreign **series** limited liability company. The name and jurisdiction of each foreign protected series established by the foreign series LLC is attached to the application. **(See Instructions for important information.)**

II   The LLC's principal office address, including the street and number (if any), is

_____
  (number/street)   (city or town)   (state)   (zip)

III   The name of the LLC's registered agent in VIRGINIA: _____

The registered agent is: **(Mark appropriate box.)**
(1) an <u>INDIVIDUAL</u> who is a resident of Virginia **and**
  ☐ a member or manager of the LLC.
  ☐ a member or manager of a limited liability company that is a member or manager of the LLC.
  ☐ an officer or director of a corporation that is a member or manager of the LLC.
  ☐ a general partner of a general or limited partnership that is a member or manager of the LLC.
  ☐ a trustee of a trust that is a member or manager of the LLC.
  ☐ a member of the Virginia State Bar.
                           OR
(2) ☐ a Virginia or foreign stock or nonstock corporation, limited liability company or registered limited liability partnership authorized to transact business in Virginia.

IV   A. The LLC's VIRGINIA registered office address, including the street and number, if any, which is identical to the business office of the registered agent is

_____, VA _____
  (number/street)   (city or town)   (zip)

B. The registered office is physically located in the ☐ county **or** ☐ city of _____

Affirmation Statements
The Clerk of the Commission is irrevocably appointed as the agent of the limited liability company for service of process if (i) the LLC fails to maintain a registered agent in Virginia, (ii) the Virginia registered agent's authority is revoked, (iii) the Virginia registered agent resigns, or (iv) the Virginia registered agent cannot be found or served with the exercise of reasonable diligence.
The LLC affirms that it is a "foreign limited liability company" as defined in the Code of Virginia.

Signature
The official signing this document has been delegated the right and power to manage the company's business affairs and affirms the above statements are true.
Signed in the name of the foreign limited liability company by:

_____   _____   _____
Signature   **Date**   **Tel. # (optional)**

_____   _____   _____
Printed Name   **Title**   **Email Address (optional)**

_____   _____
Business Tel. # (optional)   **Business Email Address (optional)**

                                      Required Fee: $100.00

Using Nolo's Formation Service for Your Articles and Operating Agreement

You can file articles on your own, on your secretary of state's website. You can also prepare your own operating agreement using one of the forms provided in this book or some other template. Of course, you can also pay an attorney to file your articles and draft your operating agreement.

You have a third, more modern option—and it's the best one. Use an online formation service, like Nolo's LLC formation service, to file your articles and create an operating agreement. Nolo's service is easy to use and costs a fraction of what a lawyer would charge. After you answer a series of questions, designed to elicit information that the program will plug into the articles and agreement, you'll be done. Nolo's tool works with the registration process in each state, and was designed by lawyers who understand the law and state filing requirements. You can think of a commercial formation service as assisted DIY.

The operating agreement you receive from Nolo's formation service is very similar to the operating agreements contained in Chapters 6 and 7. You can access Nolo's formation service at www.nolo.com.

Tax Steps: Getting an EIN and Electing a Tax Status

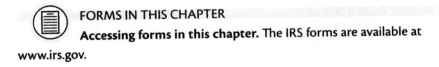

FORMS IN THIS CHAPTER

Accessing forms in this chapter. The IRS forms are available at www.irs.gov.

A s we noted at the beginning of the book, our coverage of LLC taxation is limited to the IRS forms you need to file or can elect to file upon forming your LLC. In this chapter, we focus on the following IRS forms:

- Form SS-4, *Application for Employer Identification Number*
- Form 8832, *Entity Classification Election* (to elect to be taxed as a corporation), and
- Form 2553, *Election by a Small Business Corporation* (to elect S Corporation status).

Obtaining and completing these forms is not hard. We'll explain their purpose and tell you what you need to know when you need to make choices on the forms.

Getting Your Federal Employer Identification Number (EIN)

If you don't plan to hire employees, you are probably wondering, does my new LLC still need an employer identification number (EIN) from the IRS? Yes, it does—not because it's an employer, but because, to the IRS, it's a partnership. Unless an LLC elects another tax status, it will be taxed as a partnership. In any event, it needs to have an EIN.

You apply for an EIN using Form SS-4, a blank version of which is included below. We recommend using the IRS's online application form, which includes the same information as the SS-4 paper form, is easy to use, and assigns your EIN immediately. The IRS online application is on IRS.gov (search for "EIN").

Application for Employer Identification Number

Form **SS-4** (Rev. December 2023) Department of the Treasury Internal Revenue Service	**Application for Employer Identification Number** (For use by employers, corporations, partnerships, trusts, estates, churches, government agencies, Indian tribal entities, certain individuals, and others.) See separate instructions for each line. Keep a copy for your records. Go to *www.irs.gov/FormSS4* for instructions and the latest information.	OMB No. 1545-0003 EIN

Type or print clearly.

1	Legal name of entity (or individual) for whom the EIN is being requested

2	Trade name of business (if different from name on line 1)	3	Executor, administrator, trustee, "care of" name

4a	Mailing address (room, apt., suite no. and street, or P.O. box)	5a	Street address (if different) (Don't enter a P.O. box.)

4b	City, state, and ZIP code (if foreign, see instructions)	5b	City, state, and ZIP code (if foreign, see instructions)

6	County and state where principal business is located

7a	Name of responsible party	7b	SSN, ITIN, or EIN

8a	Is this application for a limited liability company (LLC) (or a foreign equivalent)? . . . . ☐ Yes ☐ No	8b	If 8a is "Yes," enter the number of LLC members . . . .

8c If 8a is "Yes," was the LLC organized in the United States? . . . . ☐ Yes ☐ No

9a **Type of entity** (check only one box). **Caution:** If 8a is "Yes," see the instructions for the correct box to check.

☐ Sole proprietor (SSN) _____
☐ Partnership
☐ Corporation (enter form number to be filed) _____
☐ Personal service corporation
☐ Church or church-controlled organization
☐ Other nonprofit organization (specify) _____
☐ Other (specify)

☐ Estate (SSN of decedent) _____
☐ Plan administrator (TIN) _____
☐ Trust (TIN of grantor) _____
☐ Military/National Guard   ☐ State/local government
☐ Farmers' cooperative   ☐ Federal government
☐ REMIC   ☐ Indian tribal governments/enterprises
Group Exemption Number (GEN) if any _____

9b If a corporation, name the state or foreign country (if applicable) where incorporated

	State	Foreign country

10 **Reason for applying** (check only one box)
☐ Started new business (specify type) _____

☐ Hired employees (Check the box and see line 13.)
☐ Compliance with IRS withholding regulations
☐ Other (specify)

☐ Banking purpose (specify purpose) _____
☐ Changed type of organization (specify new type) _____
☐ Purchased going business
☐ Created a trust (specify type) _____
☐ Created a pension plan (specify type) _____

11	Date business started or acquired (month, day, year). See instructions.	12	Closing month of accounting year

13	Highest number of employees expected in the next 12 months (enter -0- if none). If no employees expected, skip line 14.	14	If you expect your employment tax liability to be $1,000 or less in a full calendar year **and** want to file Form 944 annually instead of Forms 941 quarterly, check here. (Your employment tax liability will generally be $1,000 or less if you expect to pay $5,000 or less, $6,536 or less if you're in a U.S. territory, in total wages.) If you don't check this box, you must file Form 941 for every quarter. ☐

Agricultural	Household	Other

15 First date wages or annuities were paid (month, day, year). **Note:** If applicant is a withholding agent, enter date income will first be paid to
nonresident alien (month, day, year) . . . .

16 Check **one** box that best describes the principal activity of your business.
☐ Construction ☐ Rental & leasing ☐ Transportation & warehousing
☐ Real estate ☐ Manufacturing ☐ Finance & insurance

☐ Health care & social assistance ☐ Wholesale—agent/broker
☐ Accommodation & food service ☐ Wholesale—other ☐ Retail
☐ Other (specify)

17 Indicate principal line of merchandise sold, specific construction work done, products produced, or services provided.

18 Has the applicant entity shown on line 1 ever applied for and received an EIN? ☐ Yes ☐ No
If "Yes," write previous EIN here

Third Party Designee	Complete this section **only** if you want to authorize the named individual to receive the entity's EIN and answer questions about the completion of this form.	
	Designee's name	Designee's telephone number (include area code)
	Address and ZIP code	Designee's fax number (include area code)

Under penalties of perjury, I declare that I have examined this application, and to the best of my knowledge and belief, it is true, correct, and complete.

Name and title (type or print clearly)

		Applicant's telephone number (include area code)
		Applicant's fax number (include area code)

Signature _____ Date _____

For Privacy Act and Paperwork Reduction Act Notice, see separate instructions.   Cat. No. 16055N   Form **SS-4** (Rev. 12-2023)

Whether you use Form SS-4 or the online application, be aware that an individual with a Social Security number needs to be the responsible party (SS-4 Lines 7a and 7b). Here are the instructions for Form SS-4:

> *Responsible party defined. The "responsible party" is the person who ultimately owns or controls the entity or who exercises ultimate effective control over the entity. The person identified as the responsible party should have a level of control over, or entitlement to, the funds or assets in the entity that, as a practical matter, enables the person, directly or indirectly, to control, manage, or direct the entity and the disposition of its funds and assets. Unless the applicant is a government entity, the responsible party must be an individual (that is, a natural person), not an entity.*

The responsible party identified on the SS-4 becomes the contact person for the LLC with the IRS, and will receive all future communications from the IRS. To change your LLC's responsible party (or the business address on file with the IRS), file Form 8822-B, *Change of Address or Responsible Party—Business.*

> **TIP**
>
> **If your LLC was previously a partnership with an EIN, you can use the partnership's EIN.** You don't need to apply for a new EIN.

Electing to Be Taxed as a Corporation

A multi-member LLC is taxed as a partnership by default. A partnership is a pass-through tax entity, meaning that the company does not pay income tax, but rather profits and losses are allocated to the partners and reported on the partners' individual tax returns. We cover partnership tax reporting in Chapter 9. Most LLCs stick with the default designation and are taxed as partnerships. However, you can elect to be taxed as a corporation (C corporation or S corporation). An S corporation is also a pass-through entity, but a C corporation is not. For this reason, few LLCs elect to be taxed as a C corporation.

If you decide on corporate status (usually S corporation status), you make the election on Form 8832, *Entity Classification Election*. You can download the form directly from IRS.gov (type "Form 8832" in any search box on the site).

If you want your LLC to be taxed as a corporation from the outset (the date the LLC was formed), file Form 8832 within 75 days of formation.

Electing S Corporation Taxation

Since S corporations and partnerships are pass-through tax entities, why choose to be an S corporation? Owners (shareholders) in an S corporation, unlike owners (members) in an LLC, can be employees of the company. As employees, they can be paid a salary, with income and FICA taxes withheld (we discuss FICA taxes in Chapter 10). LLC member-employees, on the other hand, must pay self-employment taxes of 15.3%, representing both the employer and employee portions of FICA taxes.

Also, health and accident insurance premiums paid on behalf of a shareholder-employee who owns more than 2% of the S corporation are deductible by the S corporation and reportable as wages on the shareholder-employee's Form W-2, subject to income tax withholding.

Form 8832 gives you C corporation tax status. If your goal is S corporation status, you need to make an additional election using Form 2553, *Election by a Small Business Corporation* (more commonly known as the "S Corp Election"). You can download the form directly from IRS.gov (type "Form 2553" in the search box).

TIP

We recommend working with a tax adviser on deciding your tax entity and completing Forms 8832 and 2553 if you decide on S corporation treatment. But if you're completing Form 8832 or Form 2553 on your own, carefully read the instructions provided with the forms. With Form 8832, the instructions are appended to the form. With Form 2553, the instructions are a separate document on the IRS website (Instructions for Form 2553).

PART

B

Operating Agreements

Chapter 5—Why You Need an Operating Agreement

Chapter 6—Member-Managed LLC Operating Agreement

Chapter 7—Manager-Managed LLC Operating Agreement

Why You Need an Operating Agreement

An operating agreement is an agreement among the members of an LLC, covering the rules that will govern ownership and management of the company. It's similar to a shareholder agreement in a corporation and a partnership agreement in a partnership.

But do you need one?

Except for a handful of states, as discussed in Chapter 3, you're not legally required to have an operating agreement for your multi-member LLC. In the states that require an operating agreement, you don't file the agreement with the state and it's unclear whether or how they enforce the statute. In all remaining states, an operating agreement is legally optional. Your LLC is formed when articles are filed, and the presence or lack of an operating agreement has no effect on your LLC's legal existence. If you have an operating agreement, you don't file it with the state.

But yes, you need one.

Think of it this way. You're not required to look both ways before crossing a busy street; you can take your chances and cross without looking. But the potential consequences of not checking for traffic more than justify taking the time to look. You're not required to look both ways, but you need to. Similarly, the potential consequences of not having an operating agreement, while they (hopefully) don't include a trip to the hospital or worse, more than justify the effort of creating one. You're not required to have an operating agreement, but you need one. To put it another way, not having an operating agreement for a multi-member LLC is a bad idea.

In this brief introduction to the operating agreement chapters contained in Chapters 6 and 7, we cover the major benefits of having an operating agreement.

The Agreement Confirms That Members Are on the Same Page

To create and finalize an operating agreement, you and your fellow members will need to think through and come to agreement on a number of ownership and management questions. The decisions you'll need to make include:

- whether the LLC will be member-managed or manager-managed (more on that in Chapter 1)
- what matters will be decided by the members (as owners), and what matters will be decided by managers (or members acting as managers)
- how ownership decisions will be made, including what decisions can be made by simple majority and what decisions require a super majority or a unanimous vote
- how management decisions will be made
- how manager compensation will be approved
- whether members can have financial interests or other involvements in competing or potentially competing businesses
- how profits and losses will be allocated among the members
- how distributions to members will be made
- how members can withdraw from the LLC
- how to remove a manager
- how to remove ("dissociate") a member
- how to approve new members
- what restrictions to place on transfers of members' interests
- what events can trigger dissolution and what happens upon dissolution, and
- whether to require mediation or arbitration in the event of an ownership dispute.

These items are only some of the provisions in a standard operating agreement. We take up each question and other operating agreement provisions in the chapters that follow. We listed them here to demonstrate the types of issues that creating an LLC will force the members of your LLC to consider. Chances are you've thought about some but not all of them before now. Also, you might find that members have different ideas or expectations as to how a given aspect of ownership or management should work. The operating agreement is your vehicle to consider the important rules governing ownership and management of your LLC and to make sure that you have consensus on those rules.

Without an Operating Agreement, State Law Governs Your LLC

Every state has LLC laws (often called a "Limited Liability Act" or something similar), which contain default rules governing an LLC—these apply if the owners have not agreed upon their own provisions in a written LLC operating agreement. These default rules are obviously one-size-fits-all, and they might not align with how you want to run your LLC. Here are some default rules under various states' LLC statutes.

- **Who manages?** In all states, an LLC is presumed to be member-managed unless manager-management is provided for in the articles or a written operating agreement. Some state articles forms don't include an item to designate the company as being manager-managed, so that choice would need to be expressed in a written operating agreement.
- **How is voting allocated?** Some states provide that in a member-managed LLC, each member has one vote on management and ownership matters, even when members don't own equal interests

in the company. In other states, the default is that voting is done according to percentage membership interests.

> EXAMPLE 1: Returning to 4C Candles LLC (introduced in Chapters 1 and 2), Constance owns 40% of 4C Candles, while Carmen, Chris, and Carly each own 20%. If the company is in a state where the default rule is equal voting rights, a majority would require three of the four members. In such a state, if the owners want proportionate voting, they would need to provide for it in a written operating agreement. If they did so, then a majority would consist of Constance plus one of the 20% owners, or the three 20% owners voting together.

If, on the other hand, the default rule in 4C Candles' state is that voting is done based on percentage interests, but the members want to have equal voting, they would need to provide for equal voting in their operating agreement.

- **Allocation of profits and losses.** In most states, absent an agreement to the contrary, profits and losses are allocated and distributions are made in proportion to ownership interests. If the members want a different allocation formula, they must provide it in a written operating agreement.

> EXAMPLE 2: Ownership in 4C Candles is 40/20/20/20, as in Example 1, and the company has no operating agreement. By default, Constance would be allocated 40% of the profits and the other three members would be allocated 20% each. If the members want a different formula, they would need to spell it out in a written operating agreement. (We discuss allocations and distributions in Chapter 6 on member-managed LLC operating agreements.)

The IRS Has Its Own Rules Regarding Profit and Loss Allocations and Distributions

The IRS has its own rules for allocating partnership profits, losses, and distributions (recall that multi-member LLCs are taxed as partnerships unless they elect corporate tax status). For the most part, the IRS will respect the allocation arrangements set forth in an operating agreement, but this rule has exceptions. We recommend consulting a tax adviser for most LLC tax matters, especially if you're going to be allocating profits and losses or making distributions that don't align with members' ownership percentages.

- **Required distributions?** Most state laws do not require LLCs to distribute profits (in the form of cash or other property). Frequently, members want a guarantee that the LLC will distribute enough cash to cover their income taxes attributable to LLC profits in each year. If the members want the LLC to distribute cash to cover taxes, this obligation would need to be stated in an operating agreement.

An operating agreement allows you to customize the rules governing the ownership and management of your LLC. By agreeing on these rules from the outset, you will avoid surprises down the road.

> EXAMPLE 3: 4C Candles LLC is member-managed and still has no operating agreement. The company has a chance to buy the warehouse building it's been renting. Constance (40% owner), Chris (20%), and Carly (20%) are in favor of the purchase, but Carmen (20%) is against it. Carmen, believing she'd be stopping the company from making a significant mistake, researches her rights as a member. She reads the default state law, which provides that decisions in the ordinary course of a member-managed LLC's business are made by majority vote. However, decisions outside the ordinary course of business (which she thinks includes buying a building) require a unanimous vote of the members. If Carmen is correct and the transaction would be outside the ordinary

course of business, the vote must be unanimous and she can block the transaction with her 20% vote. Constance, Chris, and Carly are a bit chagrined that their combined 80% isn't sufficient to overcome Carmen's objection.

Example 3 demonstrates the downside of flying without an operating agreement and relying on state law default rules: You might not know what the default rule is until you need it and, once you find it, you might not like what it says.

State Law Limitations on Operating Agreements

LLC laws limit what can be done in an operating agreement. Many of these limitations relate to legal rights and obligations among the members. For example, an operating agreement can't eliminate the fiduciary duties that the members owe to one another and the company. Nor can it eliminate the contractual obligation of good faith and fair dealing between members and between themselves and the company. It's unlikely that you'd come up with operating agreement provisions that run afoul of such restrictions, but if you want to be sure, check your state's LLC Act for the applicable rules.

On to the Operating Agreements

If you weren't already committed to having a written operating agreement, we hope the explanation above has convinced you to do so. In the next two chapters, we present and explain an operating agreement for a member-managed operating agreement (Chapter 6) and a manager-managed operating agreement (Chapter 7). Think of these agreements as "starter" agreements—the minimum of what you should have in place from Day One of your LLC.

Using Nolo's Formation Service for Your Articles and Operating Agreement

You can file articles on your own, on your secretary of state's website. You can also prepare your own operating agreement using one of the forms provided in this book or some other template. Of course, you can also pay an attorney to file your articles and draft your operating agreement.

You have a third, more modern option—and it's the best one. Use an online formation service, like Nolo's LLC formation service, to file your articles and create an operating agreement. Nolo's service is easy to use and costs a fraction of what a lawyer would charge. After you answer a series of questions, designed to elicit information that the program will plug into the articles and agreement, you'll be done. Nolo's tool works with the registration process in each state, and was designed by lawyers who understand the law and state filing requirements. You can think of a commercial formation service as assisted DIY.

The operating agreement you receive from Nolo's formation service is very similar to the operating agreements contained in Chapters 6 and 7.

You can access Nolo's formation service at www.nolo.com.

Member-Managed LLC Operating Agreement

This chapter contains an operating agreement, with explanations, for a member-managed LLC (remember, a member-managed LLC is managed by its owners, as opposed by a manager-managed LLC, where the members designate managers to run the company).

Sections of Your Operating Agreement

The sections in this chapter walk you through each provision, or clause, of the agreement. After a short explanation, you'll see the provision itself. The agreement in this chapter is for a fictional company in California (4C Candles LLC), so of course, some details in your agreement will be different.

You can create a customized version of this agreement for your LLC at www.nolo.com, either as a standalone document or as part of Nolo's LLC formation service.

FORMS

A sample Operating Agreement is shown below. You can find a complete version of the sample in Appendix B. A blank version is included in Appendix C and is downloadable from this book's companion page. See Appendix A for the link.

Your Agreement's Title

Your operating agreement should identify itself by using the name you used when filing for LLC status, followed by the name of the state in which you are incorporated.

Operating Agreement of 4C Candles LLC
A California Limited Liability Company

The Effective Date and Other Provisions

The body of the agreement begins with standard statements concerning the date that the agreement becomes effective, your business intentions, the name of your "registered agent," and so on.

- In Paragraph 1(a), you describe the "effective date." This date is the date that the members intend the agreement to be binding. It is not the date on which you filed your articles, nor need it be the date that everyone signs the agreement.

---

1. Preliminary Provisions
   a. Effective Date
   This operating agreement of 4C Candles, LLC (the "LLC"), effective as of June 5, 2023, is adopted by the members whose signatures appear at the end of this agreement.

The next clauses in "Preliminary Provisions" recite some basic facts about your LLC. By mentioning these facts here, you are "ratifying" them, which is a lawyerly way of saying that you approve the filing of articles and the information that was included in your articles. Specifically,

- Paragraphs 1(b) and 1(c) state that you formed the LLC on a certain date and that the LLC has a certain name (but you can, if you wish, do business under a fictitious business name if you follow the rules for so doing).
- Paragraph 1(d) affirms that you have named and given the address for a registered agent (we covered registered agents in Chapter 1).
- Paragraph 1(e) describes your business purpose, and simply states that you will operate as allowed under the state law that regulates LLCs.

- Paragraph 1(f), the final provision of the first paragraph, gives the LLC open-ended life, until the members voluntarily terminate it according to the terms of this agreement, or the LLC is terminated by law (for example, when the state terminates the LLC for failure to file annual reports).

b. Formation

This limited liability company (LLC) was formed by filing its articles of organization with the California Secretary of State. The legal existence of the LLC commenced on the date of such filing. A copy of this organizational document will be placed in the LLC's records book.

c. Name

The formal name of the LLC is as stated above. However, the LLC may do business under a different name by complying with California's fictitious or assumed business name statutes and procedures.

d. Registered Office and Registered Agent

The registered office and registered agent are as indicated in the articles of organization. The LLC may change its registered office and/or agent from time to time by filing a change of registered agent or office statement with the California Secretary of State.

e. Business Purpose

The purpose of the limited liability company is to engage in any lawful act or activity for which a limited liability company may be organized under the California Revised Uniform Limited Liability Company Act.

f. Duration of LLC

The duration of the LLC is perpetual. However, the LLC will terminate when a proposal to dissolve the LLC is adopted according to the terms of this agreement or when the LLC is otherwise terminated in accordance with law.

Member Duties and Rights

Your agreement's second provision explains members' duties and their status.

- Paragraph 2(a) acknowledges and reinforces the concept of limited liability, which was one of the main reasons you decided to form an LLC.
- Paragraph 2(b) covers reimbursing members' reasonable expenses, and
- Paragraph 2(c) concerns paying members for their services: member-managed LLCs can't compensate members who manage the LLC. That's because paying them would make them LLC employees, which is against the tax law (unless the LLC elected to be taxed as a corporation, which most don't). Members "get paid" for their work in the business through their shares of the profits.

---

2. Membership Provisions

a. Nonliability of Members

No member will be personally liable for the expenses, debts, obligations, or liabilities of the LLC or for claims made against it.

b. Reimbursement of Expenses

Members are entitled to reimbursement by the LLC for reasonable expenses incurred on behalf of the LLC, including expenses incurred in the formation, dissolution, and liquidation of the LLC.

c. Compensation

A member will not be paid for performing any duties associated with membership, including management of the LLC. Members may be paid, however, for services rendered in another capacity for the LLC, as allowed by law and as approved by a majority vote of the members.

Paying Members as Independent Contractors

Technically, a member can be compensated for providing services to the LLC if the member truly works as an independent contractor. (You can't just decide to call the worker an independent contractor—to qualify as a contractor, the worker and the work must meet specific legal requirements.) For example, Carly was a software developer before she cofounded 4C Candles LLC. 4C Candles needs to modify its inventory management software. They could hire a third-party programmer, but the members believe Carly would do a better job. The company pays Carly for her programming hours.

The rules around compensating members are tricky. If you're considering paying a member as an independent contractor, we recommend consulting your tax adviser.

Members' Business Activities, Calculating Ownership Interests, and Voting

Additional provisions in Paragraph 2 address members' outside business activities, how a member's ownership interest is calculated, and how voting works:

- Paragraph 2(d) addresses members' other business activities. LLCs vary in their approach to member involvement in other businesses, including competing businesses. Whether members should be allowed to engage in competing businesses depends on the circumstances of each LLC and the preferences of its owners. The members of 4C Candles decided to restrict member ownership or involvement only in competing businesses. If the other business doesn't compete with 4C Candles, no member consent is required.

- Paragraph 2(e) explains how to calculate a member's interest.
- Paragraph 2(f) explains that a member's vote is in proportion to their membership (percentage) interest, and that a simple majority is needed unless the operating agreement provides for a different vote (a super majority or a unanimous vote).

---

d. Other Business by Members

A member may engage in any business activity without the other members' consent, so long as the business activity does not directly compete with the LLC.

e. Members' Percentage interests

A member's membership interest is computed as a percentage of total membership interests, as shown on Exhibit A.

f. Membership Voting

Except as otherwise may be required by the articles of organization, other provisions of this operating agreement; or under the laws of this state, each member will vote in proportion to the member's percentage interest. Further, unless otherwise stated in another provision of this operating agreement, the phrase "majority of members" means a majority of percentage interests.

Let's look at the rule in Paragraph 2(f) a little more closely. Under this sample operating agreement, the following member actions require a unanimous vote, not just a simple majority:

- taking an action by unanimous written consent in lieu of a meeting—Paragraph 3(h)
- admitting a new member—Paragraph 3(i)
- changing the tax classification, tax year, or accounting method of the LLC—Paragraph 3(a) & (b)

- requiring additional capital contributions—Paragraph 5(d)
- allowing capital withdrawals—Paragraph 5(f), and
- voluntarily dissolving the LLC—Paragraph 7(a)(ii).

We recommend that you, too, require unanimous votes for the matters listed above. Whether other matters should require a super majority (for example, 75%) or a unanimous vote, rather than a majority vote depends on the circumstances of the LLC and the preferences of the members. Discuss voting with your members and be sure that your operating agreement clearly identifies all member decisions and actions that require more than a majority vote.

Meetings and New Members

The operating agreement also covers important procedural details about meetings and new members.

- Under Paragraph 2(g), when members need to take a formal action, they can call a meeting and vote on it, or they can take the action by unanimous written consent. If a meeting is to result in enforceable company decisions, each member must be in attendance or have provided a written consent for the meeting to take place in their absence.

   A unanimous written consent allows the members to take an action without meeting. The consent must state the action being taken and it must be signed by all the members. We cover unanimous written consents and include a sample consent form in Chapter 11.

- Paragraph 2(h) works in tandem with Paragraph 6(b), below (restrictions on ownership transfers) to protect members from being stuck with a new member they don't want. Any member can block the admission of a new member.

g. Members' Meetings and Actions Taken by Written Consent

The LLC is not required to hold regular members' meetings. However, one or more members can call a meeting at any time. The member calling the meeting will provide notice of the business to be transacted at the meeting, but other business may be discussed and conducted at the meeting with the consent of all members present. A quorum consists of all members, unless members who cannot attend consent in writing for the meeting to take place in their absence. Except as otherwise provided in this agreement, a vote of the majority of members present at a meeting of the members is required to approve any action taken at the meeting.

Any action required or permitted by this agreement to be taken at a meeting of the members may be taken without a meeting, without prior notice, by unanimous written consent of the members.

h. Admission of New Members

Except as otherwise provided in this agreement, a person or entity will not be admitted into membership unless each member consents in writing to the admission of the new member.

Management Provisions

- Paragraph 3(a) states, again, that yours is a member-managed LLC. By law, when LLC members don't elect to be manager-managed and appoint managers, authority and responsibility for managing the LLC vests in all the members. In other words, the LLC is member-managed. Paragraph 3(a) confirms that 4C Candles is member-managed.

- Paragraph 3(b) provides for indemnification of the members by the company in the event that a member incurs a liability to a third party as a result of the member's activities in managing the LLC. Indemnification means that the company will reimburse the member for their financial loss. The indemnification clause here provides for reimbursement so long as the member was acting in accordance with their duties of care and loyalty.

EXAMPLE: A supplier sues 4C Candles LLC and its members, individually, for breach of contract. The company loses the suit, but the individual members are held to be not liable due to their limited liability protection. However, each of the members incurred legal costs in defending against the suit. The LLC is obligated to reimburse the members for their legal costs.

3. Management Provisions

a. Management by Members

This LLC will be managed exclusively by all of its members.

b. Indemnification of Members

A member will be indemnified by the LLC for any debt, obligation, or other liability, including reasonable attorneys' fees, incurred in the course of the member's activities or performance of duties on behalf of the LLC as long as the member complied with the duties of loyalty and care when incurring the debt, obligation, or other liability. This provision does not in any way limit the indemnification the member would be entitled to under applicable state law. The indemnification provided will inure to the benefit of successors and assigns of any such member.

Taxes and Accounting

Paragraph 4 covers taxes and related matters.

- Paragraph 4(a) states that the LLC will be classified and taxed, at least initially, as a partnership. We discuss LLC tax elections in Chapter 4.
- Paragraph 4(b) covers the LLC's accounting methods.
- Paragraph 4(c) states that the LLC's real and personal property must be owned by the LLC, not its individual members. This rule is very important: the LLC is a legal entity, apart from its owners. If the lines between the company and the members get blurred, such as by having LLC assets held in the name of a member, the members can lose limited liability. In other words, if a court were to determine that the business is not truly separate from its owners, the owners could be held personally liable for LLC debts—a consequence they sought to avoid by choosing an LLC in the first place. Paragraph 4(c) reminds owners not to blur the lines when it comes to property ownership and titling.
- Paragraph 4(d) recites how bank accounts will be set up and used.
- Paragraph 4(e) agrees that if asked by the IRS, the LLC will name a "tax partner"—the unlucky soul that the IRS will deal with in case they take an unwelcome interest in your LLC. We noted in Chapter 4 that the person named as the responsible party on an application for an employer identification number (EIN) becomes the contact person for the LLC with the IRS. If the LLC is required to separately name a tax matters partner, the members can name the member who acted as the responsible party on its EIN application or it can name another member.
- Paragraph 4(f) concerns tax returns and reports (we cover income tax reporting in Chapter 10). Paragraph 4(f) requires the LLC to share tax returns with members and provide the members with the information they need to complete their own returns, and to provide a balance sheet and income statement for the year.

4. **Taxes and Accounting**

a. **Tax Classification of LLC**

The LLC will be initially classified as a partnership for federal and, if applicable, state income tax purposes. The LLC may change its tax treatment with the consent of all members and by filing the necessary election with the IRS and, if applicable, the state tax department.

b. **Tax Year and Accounting Method**

The tax year of the LLC will end on the last day of the month of December. The LLC will use the accrual method of accounting.

The tax year and the accounting method of the LLC may each be changed with the consent of all members.

c. **Title to Assets**

All personal and real property of the LLC will be held in the name of the LLC, not in the name of any individual member.

d. **Bank Accounts**

All funds of the Company will be deposited in one or more separate bank accounts, using such banks or trust companies as the members may designate. Withdrawals from such bank accounts are to be made upon such signature or signatures as the members may designate. The funds of the LLC, however and wherever deposited or invested, will not be commingled with the personal funds of any member of the LLC.

e. **Tax Matters Partner**

If required under Internal Revenue Code provisions or regulations, the LLC will designate a member as its "tax matters partner" in accordance with Internal Revenue Code Section 6231(a)(7) and corresponding regulations, who will fulfill this role by being the spokesperson for the LLC in dealings with the IRS and performing such other duties as required under the Internal Revenue Code and Regulations.

f. **Annual Income Tax Returns and Reports**
Within 60 days after the end of each tax year of the LLC, a copy of
the LLC's state and federal income tax returns for the preceding
tax year will be mailed or otherwise provided to each member
of the LLC, together with any additional information and forms
necessary for each member to complete their individual state
and federal income tax returns. Along with the necessary tax information and forms, the LLC will also provide a financial report
that includes a balance sheet and profit and loss statement for
the year.

How Your LLC Is Funded and How It Handles Assets

The fifth paragraph of the operating agreement covers funding the LLC
and spending its assets.

- Paragraph 5(a) describes members' capital contributions—whatever
a member contributes in return for their percentage interest in the
company, including cash, other property, and services. The value of
each member's capital contribution and their percentage interests
are shown in Exhibit A.

> **EXAMPLE:** Carly contributes $10,000 in cash in exchange for a 20%
> interest in 4C Candles LLC. Chris contributes services in exchange for
> a similar 20% interest. Chris's services have a value of $10,000.

5. **Capital Provisions**
a. **Capital Contributions**
Members have made initial contributions of cash, property, or
services as specified in Exhibit A.

- Paragraph 5(b) reinforces the fact that your contributions to the LLC are an investment, not a loan. In exchange for your capital contributions, you receive equity (a percentage interest) in the LLC. As the value of the company grows, the value of your owner-ship share grows—that's how you earn a return on your investment. Paragraph 5(b) reinforces that your capital contribution is an equity investment, not a loan.

> **b. No Interest on Capital Contributions**
> No interest will be paid on capital contributions or on capital account balances.

- Paragraph 5(c) describes bookkeeping. Each member will have a capital account that tracks the member's equity in the LLC. Capital accounts are used for tax reporting purposes and come into play when distributing assets upon the liquidation of the company.

> **c. Capital Account Bookkeeping**
> A capital account will be set up and maintained on the books of the LLC for each member. It will reflect each member's capital contribution, increased by any additional contributions by the member and by the member's share of LLC profits, decreased by any distributions to the member and by the member's share of LLC losses, and adjusted as required in accordance with applicable provisions of the Internal Revenue Code and corre-sponding income tax regulations. Upon a valid transfer of a member's membership interest, the member's capital account will carry over to the new owner.

- Paragraph 5(d) gives the LLC the right to require members to invest more money, if your LLC needs additional capital in the future. Under Paragraph 5(d), members cannot be required to make additional capital contributions unless all members agree to require them.

> **d. Additional Contributions**
> The members may agree, from time to time, by unanimous vote, to require the payment of additional capital contributions by the members.

- Paragraph 5(e) describes how income, loss, and so on will be allocated to members. Most LLCs allocate profits and losses according to percentage interests, but you can use a different allocation formula. For example, let's say that one member of the LLC is in a better position than the others to take tax advantage of LLC losses. The allocation formula might allocate more of the losses to that member than they would receive according to their percentage interest. If you're thinking of allocating profits and losses other than by percentage interests, consult your tax adviser.

> **e. Allocations of Profits and Losses**
> The profits and losses of the LLC, and all items of its income, gain, loss, deduction, and credit will be allocated to members in accordance with the member's percentage interest.

- Paragraph 5(f) covers capital withdrawals. Capital invested in the company stays in the company unless all members agree that a member can withdraw it.

> **f. Capital Withdrawals**
> Members will not be allowed to withdraw any part of their capital contributions or to receive distributions, whether in property or cash, except as otherwise allowed by this agreement. A capital withdrawal requires the written consent of all members.

- Paragraph 5(g) covers cash distributions, and includes important safeguards. Members get money out of the LLC primarily through distributions of profits. To understand distributions, recall that your LLC is a pass-through tax entity. Profits and losses are allocated (passed through) to members, who then report the income or loss on their personal tax returns and pay any income tax owed. LLC profits are taxed when they're earned, not when they're distributed.

   Distributions are a matter of cash flow—the LLC's cash flow and each member's cash flow. Let's say that an LLC is profitable and generating cash. The profits can be left in the company and reinvested in the business, or they can be distributed to the owners, or both. Members make these decisions by majority vote.

> **g. Distributions of Cash**
> Cash from business operations, as well as cash from a sale or other disposition of LLC capital assets, may be allocated and distributed from time to time to members in accordance with each member's percentage interest in the LLC, as may be decided by a majority of members. However, the member(s) will direct distributions to be made each year in an amount sufficient to cover any member's tax liability that may arise based on the allocation of LLC income, gains, losses or deductions.

- Paragraph 5(h) concerns how the LLC distributes non-cash proceeds. "Proceeds" include any and all property received by the LLC through the sale of goods, services, or assets. Noncash proceeds arise when the LLC accepts property other than cash as payment for goods, services, or assets. Most LLCs don't deal in noncash proceeds, but Paragraph 5(h) applies if your LLC does.

> **h. Allocation of Noncash Proceeds**
> If proceeds consist of property other than cash, the members will decide the value of the property and allocate such value among the members in accordance with each member's percentage interest in the LLC.

- Paragraph 5(i) deals with distributions made when the LLC is liquidated or when a member's entire interest is being liquidated. When a member withdraws from the LLC and the company redeems the member's interest (as opposed to having the remaining members buy the departing member's interest), the redemption is called a liquidating distribution. Under either sort of liquidation (of the LLC or one member's interest), the capital account of a member receiving a distribution must be updated and distributions can be made only to the extent that the member's capital account shows a positive balance.

    Accounting for capital accounts is complicated, and any sort of liquidating distribution must be accounted for correctly (especially for tax purposes). We recommend working with an accounting or tax professional when liquidating a member's interest or the entire LLC.

i. **Allocation and Distribution of Liquidation Proceeds**

Regardless of any other provision in this agreement, if there is a distribution in liquidation of the LLC, or when a member's interest is liquidated, all items of income and loss will be allocated to a member's capital account, and all appropriate credits and deductions will then be made to the capital account before any final distribution is made. A final distribution will be made to members only to the extent of, and in proportion to, any positive balance in a member's capital account.

Membership Withdrawals and Transfers

Paragraph 6 of your operating agreement addresses members' withdrawals and transfers of interests. As members' life circumstances change, involving retirement or divorce, for example, members might want or need to change their relationship with the LLC.

- Paragraph 6(a) addresses withdrawals. You can't force a member to remain a member, but you can provide for an orderly exit process. Paragraph 6(a) is a simple buyout clause that leaves most of the terms up for negotiation at the time of a member's withdrawal. It includes a mechanism for valuing the departing member's interest (a formal appraisal) if the parties can't agree on a price. Once the price has been determined, the departing and remaining members will need to agree on a payment schedule, which sometimes involves installments paid over a number of years. The departing member usually wants payment as soon as possible, while the remaining members must consider the LLC's ability to pay. In the end, the parties need to agree on a schedule that both sides are confident can be met.

In terms of the notice requirement for withdrawal, the notice period gives the departing and remaining members time to negotiate the terms of the buyout. 4C Candles settled on three months' notice, but your notice period could be shorter or longer. In Chapter 8, we discuss buyout (buy-sell) agreements.

---

6. Membership Withdrawal and Transfer Provisions

a. Withdrawal of Members

A member may withdraw from the LLC by giving written notice to all other members at least three months before the date the withdrawal is to be effective. In the event of such withdrawal, the LLC will pay the departing member the fair value of their LLC interest, less any amounts owed by the member to the LLC. The departing and remaining members will agree at the time of departure on the fair value of the departing member's interest and the schedule of payments to be made by the LLC to the departing member, who will receive payment for their interest within a reasonable time after departure from the LLC. If the departing and remaining members cannot agree on the value of departing member's interest, they will select an appraiser, who will determine the current value of the departing member's interest. This appraised amount will be fair value of the departing member's interest and will form the basis of the amount to be paid to the departing member.

- Paragraph 6(b) addresses restrictions on transferring membership in the LLC. It recognizes that LLC member interests are made up of two sets of rights: economic rights and governance rights.

  Economic rights include the right to receive distributions, and these rights can be transferred *without* the consent of the other members.

  Governance rights include voting rights, management rights, and information rights (the right to receive information about the company and its operations). Governance rights cannot be transferred without the consent of the other members.

EXAMPLE: Carly owns a 20% interest in 4C Candles LLC. The company is doing well and the value of Carly's interest has appreciated considerably. She'd like to cash out and her cousin Clayton, who's an experienced entrepreneur, is interested in buying her full 20% stake. Another LLC member, Constance, knows Clayton and has had some unpleasant business dealings with him in the past. Constance does not want to work with Clayton and will not consent to admit him as a member. Carly can sell her economic rights in the LLC to Clayton, but she can't sell her governance rights.

b. Restrictions on the Transfer of Membership

Notwithstanding any other provision of this agreement, a member will not transfer their membership in the LLC unless all of the nontransferring members first agree in writing to approve the admission of the transferee into the LLC. Further, no member may encumber a part or all of their membership in the LLC by mortgage, pledge, granting of a security interest, lien, or otherwise, unless the encumbrance has first been approved in writing by all other members of the LLC.

Notwithstanding the above provision, any member will be allowed to assign an economic interest in their membership to another person without the approval of the other members. Any assignment of economic interest will not include a transfer of the member's voting or management rights, and the assignee will not become a member except as provided elsewhere in this agreement.

Dissolving the LLC

Despite your best intentions and plans, or perhaps according to plan, your LLC might need to come to an end. Paragraph 7(a) spells out the circumstances that would trigger the dissolution of the LLC and places the manager(s) in charge of winding up and liquidating the company. The triggering events for a dissolution are the expiration of the LLC's term if a dissolution date was specified in the company's articles, a vote by all the members to dissolve, or a court-ordered dissolution.

When some members want to dissolve the LLC and others want to continue it, the company continues to exist (for lack of a unanimous vote to dissolve). The two sides would need to overcome the stalemate, probably via a buyout of the members who favor dissolution. If the members simply can't resolve the disagreement themselves and it becomes impractical to continue to operate the company, the member(s) seeking to terminate the LLC can go to court seeking an order from a judge (a decree) to dissolve the LLC.

---

7. Dissolution Provisions

    a. Events That Trigger Dissolution of the LLC

        The following events will trigger a dissolution of the LLC:

          i. Expiration of LLC Term. The expiration of the term of existence of the LLC, if such term is specified in the articles of organization or this operating agreement, will cause the dissolution of the LLC.

          ii. Written Agreement or Consent to Dissolve. The written agreement of all members to dissolve the LLC will cause a dissolution of the LLC.

          iii. Entry of Decree. The entry of a decree of dissolution of the LLC under state law will cause a dissolution of the LLC.

        If the LLC is to dissolve according to any of the above provisions, the members will wind up the affairs of the LLC, and take other actions appropriate to complete a dissolution of the LLC in accordance with applicable provisions of state law.

- Paragraph 7(b) covers what happens when a member dies, becomes incapacitated, declares bankruptcy, and so on. In some states, the default rule is that, absent a contrary provision in an operating agreement, the death of a member triggers the dissolution of the LLC unless the remaining members vote to continue it. In other states, the LLC doesn't automatically terminate upon the death of a member (so the surviving members don't have to vote to continue it). Paragraph 7(b) states that this LLC will continue after the death or other dissociation of a member.

> **b. Dissociation of a Member**
> The dissociation of a member, which means the death, incapacity, bankruptcy, retirement, resignation, or expulsion of a member, or any other event that terminates the continued membership of a member, will not cause a dissolution of the LLC. The LLC will continue its existence and business following such dissociation of a member.

General Provisions

We've nearly reached the end of your LLC's operating agreement! Now it's just a matter of slogging through the final provisions, which you can think of as a kind of playbook—"if any of these things happen, here's what we will do." People (and lawyers) are apt to snooze through these provisions, but we urge you to pay a little attention. There's a reason they appear in almost every operating agreement.

- Paragraph 8(a) concerns officers and others with titles. Unlike corporations, LLCs are not required to have officers. But LLCs can have officers, and Paragraph 6(a) authorizes their designation.

8. General Provisions

a. Officers

The LLC may designate one or more officers, such as a President, Vice President, Secretary, and Treasurer. Persons who fill these positions need not be members of the LLC. Such positions may be compensated or noncompensated according to the nature and extent of the services rendered as a part of the duties of each office.

- Paragraph 8(b) contains basic legal and financial record-keeping requirements.

b. Records

The LLC will keep at its principal business address a copy of all proceedings of membership meetings and resolutions, as well as books of account of financial transactions. A list of the names and addresses of the current membership also will be maintained at this address, with notations on any transfers of members' interests to nonmembers or persons being admitted into membership.

The LLC's articles of organization, a signed copy of this operating agreement, the LLC's tax returns for the preceding three tax years, and written records of votes taken at member meetings or by unanimous consent, will be kept at its principal business address.

Any member may inspect any and all records maintained by the LLC upon reasonable notice.

- Paragraph 8(c) deals with the authority of members and officers to form and run the company. Some operating agreements spell out the "powers" of the members and officers (and managers in a manager-managed LLC)—specific actions they may or may not take on behalf of the company. For example, officers might be authorized to obtain financing for the company, but not to pledge company assets as part of any loans (member approval would be required). Or they might be authorized to enter into contracts under a certain dollar amount (member approval would be required for larger contracts).

The clause as presented here doesn't lay out specific powers, but rather gives members and officers a blanket authorization to do whatever is necessary to finish forming the company ("perfect the organization") and to run the business ("carry out its business operations").

> **c. All Necessary Acts**
>
> The members and officers (if any) of the LLC are authorized to perform all acts necessary to perfect the organization of the LLC and to carry out its business operations expeditiously and efficiently as authorized by this agreement and by law.

- Paragraph 8(d) is the lawyer's best friend: If a court deems any part of the agreement to be invalid, the remaining clauses will still be enforceable.

> **d. Severability**
>
> If any provision of this agreement is determined by a court or arbitrator to be invalid, unenforceable, or otherwise ineffective, that provision will be severed from the rest of this agreement, and the remaining provisions will remain in effect and enforceable.

- Paragraph 8(e) sets some ground rules if the members have a dispute concerning ownership. In the event of an ownership dispute, the warring parties can go to court, or they can choose alternative means of resolving the dispute: mediation, arbitration, or mediation followed by arbitration. Mediation involves working with a neutral third party to reach a mutual settlement of differences. Mediators don't issue rulings, but rather try to bring the two sides together end the dispute. Mediation is the required first step under Paragraph 8(e).

Arbitration is generally considered to be simpler and more efficient than litigation (although it doesn't always work out that way). Paragraph 8(e) mandates arbitration when the parties are unable to resolve the dispute in mediation. Binding arbitration means that the parties agree to accept the arbitrator's ruling and not pursue additional legal avenues.

> **e. Mediation and Arbitration of Disputes Among Members**
>
> In any dispute over the provisions of this operating agreement and in other disputes among the members, if the members cannot resolve the dispute to their mutual satisfaction, the matter will be submitted to mediation. The terms and procedure for mediation will be arranged by the parties to the dispute.
>
> If good-faith mediation of a dispute proves impossible or if an agreed-upon mediation outcome cannot be obtained by the members who are parties to the dispute, the dispute will be submitted to binding arbitration in accordance with the rules of the American Arbitration Association. Any party may commence arbitration of the dispute by sending a written request for arbitration to all other parties to the dispute. The request will state the nature of the dispute to be resolved by arbitration, and, if all parties to the dispute agree to arbitration, arbitration will be commenced as soon as practical after such parties receive a copy of the written request.
>
> All parties will initially share the cost of arbitration, but the prevailing party or parties may be awarded attorneys' fees, costs, and other expenses of arbitration at the discretion of the arbitrator. All arbitration decisions will be final, binding, and conclusive on all the parties to arbitration, and legal judgment may be entered based upon such decision in accordance with applicable law in any court having jurisdiction to do so.

Paragraph 8(f) contains two clauses: the "entire agreement" clause and the "amendments must be written and mutual" clause. Together, they work to draw strict boundaries around the agreement. The agreement between the members is defined by what's contained within the four corners of this document, and the terms can only be changed by a written, unanimous amendment.

The entire agreement clause means that this agreement is the final word (for now) on the matters it addresses. Each member should read the agreement carefully to make sure that they understand and consent to its terms. If there are any conflicts between the language of the agreement and what a member understood the arrangement to be, you should obviously resolve those conflicts before signing the agreement. Members should also consider whether anything is missing from the agreement.

The amendment clause, by requiring that any amendment must be in writing and be agreed to by all the members, avoids any confusion about whether the agreement has been changed verbally. The agreement can't be amended verbally.

> **f. Entire Agreement and Amendment**
> This operating agreement represents the entire agreement among the members, and replaces and supersedes all prior written and oral agreements among them. This agreement will not be amended, modified, or replaced except by written agreement of all members.

> ⓘ **TIP**
>
> **You should retitle your operating agreement each time you amend it.** For example, the first time 4C Candles amends this operating agreement, they should title the document "First Amended Operating Agreement." The second time they amend the agreement would be the "Second Amended Operating Agreement," and so on.

Signing Your Operating Agreement

The members sign and adopt this agreement as the operating agreement of the LLC and agree to abide by its terms.

Members

Date: _____

Signature: _____

Name of member: Carly Abelson

Date: _____

Signature: _____

Name of member: Carmen Becerra

Date: _____

Signature: _____

Name of member: Constance Li

Date: _____

Signature: _____

Name of member: Chris Williams

Listing Members' Interests: Exhibit A

Earlier in the agreement, Paragraph 5(a) addressed how to compute a member's membership interest—it is computed as a percentage of total membership interests. Paragraph 2(e) referred to Exhibit A, which is where you list the members' names, their initial contributions, and their corresponding membership interests. You also list the officers, if any.

Exhibit A
Members, Initial Contributions; Interests; Other Information

Members

Member Name	Initial Contribution	Interest
Carly Abelson	$10,000	20%
Carmen Becerra	$10,000	20%
Constance Li	$20,000	40%
Chris Williams	$10,000	20%

Officers

None.

Manager-Managed LLC Operating Agreement

T his chapter contains an operating agreement, with explanations, for a manager-managed LLC (remember, in a manager-managed LLC, the members designate managers to run the company, as opposed to a member-managed LLC, where the company is run by all the members).

Sections of Your Operating Agreement

The sections in this chapter walk you through each paragraph of the agreement. After a short explanation, you'll see the provision itself. The agreement in this chapter is for a fictional company in California, so of course, some details in your agreement will be different.

You can create a customized version of this agreement for your LLC at www.nolo.com, either as a standalone document or as part of Nolo's LLC formation service.

FORMS

A sample Operating Agreement is shown below. You can find a complete version of the sample in Appendix B. A blank version is included in Appendix C and is downloadable from this book's companion page. See Appendix A for the link.

Your Agreement's Title

Your operating agreement should identify itself by using the name you used when filing for LLC status, followed by the name of the state in which you are incorporated.

> **Operating Agreement of 4C Candles LLC**
> **A California Limited Liability Company**

The Effective Date and Other Provisions

The body of the agreement begins with standard statements concerning the date that the agreement becomes effective, your business intentions, the name of your "registered agent," and so on.

- In Paragraph 1(a), you describe the "effective date." This date is the date that the members intend the agreement to be binding. It is not the date on which you filed your articles, nor need it be the date that everyone signs the agreement.

> **1. Preliminary Provisions**
>   **a. Effective Date**
>   This operating agreement of 4C Candles, LLC (the "LLC"), effective as of June 5, 2023, is adopted by the members whose signatures appear at the end of this agreement.

The next paragraphs in "Preliminary Provisions" recite some basic facts about your LLC. By mentioning these facts here, you are "ratifying" them, which is a lawyerly way of saying that you approve the filing of articles and the information that was included in your articles. Specifically,

- Paragraphs 1(b) and 1(c) state that you formed the LLC on a certain date and that the LLC has a certain name (but you can, if you wish, do business under a fictitious business name if you follow the rules for so doing).
- Paragraph 1(d) affirms that you have named and given the address for a registered agent (we covered registered agents in Chapter 1).
- Paragraph 1(e) describes your business purpose, and simply states that you will operate as allowed under the state law that regulates LLCs.

- Paragraph 1(f), the final provision of the first paragraph, gives the LLC open-ended life, until the members terminate it according to the terms of this agreement, or the LLC is terminated by law (for example, when the state terminates the LLC for failure to file annual reports).

---

b. Formation

This limited liability company (LLC) was formed by filing its articles of organization with the California Secretary of State. The legal existence of the LLC commenced on the date of such filing. A copy of this organizational document will be placed in the LLC's records book.

c. Name

The formal name of the LLC is as stated above. However, the LLC may do business under a different name by complying with California's fictitious or assumed business name statutes and procedures.

d. Registered Office and Registered Agent

The registered office and registered agent are as indicated in the articles of organization. The LLC may change its registered office and/or agent from time to time by filing a change of registered agent or office statement with the California Secretary of State.

e. Business Purpose

The purpose of the limited liability company is to engage in any lawful act or activity for which a limited liability company may be organized under the California Revised Uniform Limited Liability Company Act.

f. Duration of LLC

The duration of the LLC is perpetual. However, the LLC will terminate when a proposal to dissolve the LLC is adopted according to the terms of this agreement or when the LLC is otherwise terminated in accordance with law.

Member Duties and Rights

Your agreement's second set of provisions explains members' duties and their status.

- All state LLC statutes provide limited liability statutes for members. Paragraph 2(a) acknowledges and reinforces the concept of limited liability for LLC owners, which was one of the main reasons you decided to form an LLC.
- Paragraph 2(b) covers reimbursing members' reasonable expenses.
- Paragraph 2(c) concerns paying members for their services: member-managed LLCs can't compensate members who manage the LLC. That's because paying them would make them LLC employees, which is against the tax law (unless the LLC elected to be taxed as a corporation, which most don't). Members "get paid" for their work in the business through their shares of the profits.

---

2. Membership Provisions

a. Nonliability of Members

No member will be personally liable for the expenses, debts, obligations, or liabilities of the LLC or for claims made against it.

b. Reimbursement of Expenses

Members are entitled to reimbursement by the LLC for reasonable expenses incurred on behalf of the LLC, including expenses incurred in the formation, dissolution, and liquidation of the LLC.

c. Compensation

A member will not be paid for performing any duties associated with membership, including management of the LLC. Members may be paid, however, for services rendered in any other capacity for the LLC, as allowed by law and as approved by a majority vote of the managers.

Paying Members as Independent Contractors

Technically, a member can be compensated for providing services to the LLC if the member truly works as an independent contractor. (You can't just decide to call the worker an independent contractor—to qualify as a contractor, the worker and the work must meet specific legal requirements.) For example, Carly was a software developer before she cofounded 4C Candles LLC. 4C Candles needs to modify its inventory management software. They could hire a third-party programmer, but the members believe Carly would do a better job. The company pays Carly for her programming hours.

The rules around compensating members are tricky. If you're considering paying a member as an independent contractor, we recommend consulting your tax adviser.

Members' Business Activities, Calculating Ownership Interests, and Voting

Additional provisions in Paragraph 2 address members' outside business activities, how a member's ownership interest is calculated, and how voting works:

- Paragraph 2(d) addresses members' other business activities. LLCs vary in their approach to member involvement in other businesses, including competing businesses. Whether members should be allowed to engage in competing businesses depends on the circumstances of each LLC and the preferences of its owners. The members of 4C Candles decided to restrict member ownership or involvement only in competing businesses. If the other business doesn't compete with 4C Candles, no member consent is required.
- Managers, however, owe fiduciary duties to the LLC and the members. A manager can't participate in a competing business (at least not without the consent of the members, which the members might be unlikely to give).

- Paragraph 2(e) explains how to calculate a member's interest.
- Paragraph 2(f) concerns voting. In a manager-managed LLC, the managers run the LLC and make most LLC decisions. Members still need to decide certain matters, including the appointment and removal of managers, whether to make distributions (unless that decision is left to the managers, as it is in this operating agreement), or to dissolve the LLC. For matters to be voted on by members, the operating agreement should be clear about voting requirements. Paragraph 2(g) specifies that voting is by percentage interest and that a simple majority is needed unless the operating agreement provides for a different vote (a super majority or a unanimous vote).

---

d. **Other Business by Members**

A member may engage in any business activity without the other members' consent, so long as the business activity does not directly compete with the LLC.

e. **Members' Percentage interests**

A member's membership interest is computed as a percentage of total membership interests, as shown on Exhibit A.

f. **Membership Voting**

Except as otherwise may be required by the articles of organization, other provisions of this operating agreement; or under the laws of this state, each member will vote on any matter provided for in this agreement and any matter submitted to the membership for their approval by the managers in proportion to the member's percentage interest. Further, unless otherwise stated in another provision of this operating agreement, the phrase "majority of members" means a majority of percentage interests.

Let's look at the rule in Paragraph 2(f) a little more closely. Under this operating agreement, the following member actions require a unanimous vote of the members:

- taking an action by unanimous written consent in lieu of a meeting—Paragraph 3(h)
- admitting a new member—Paragraph 3(i)
- changing the tax classification, tax year, or accounting method of the LLC—Paragraphs 4(a) and 4(b)
- requiring additional capital contributions—Paragraph 5(d)
- allowing capital withdrawals—Paragraph 5(f), and
- voluntarily dissolving the LLC—Paragraph 7(a)(ii).

We recommend that you, too, require unanimous votes for the matters listed above. Whether other matters should require a super majority (for example, 75%) or a unanimous vote, rather than a majority vote depends on the circumstances of the LLC and the preferences of the members. Discuss voting with your members and be sure that your operating agreement clearly identifies all member decisions and actions that require more than a majority vote.

Meetings and New Members

The operating agreement also covers important procedural details about meetings and new members.

- Under Paragraph 2(g), when members need to take a formal action, they can call a meeting and vote on it, or they can take the action by unanimous written consent. If a meeting is to result in enforceable company decisions, each member must be in attendance or have provided a written consent for the meeting to take place in their absence.

A unanimous written consent allows the members to take an action without meeting. The consent must state the action being taken and it must be signed by all the members. We cover unanimous written consents and include a sample consent form in Chapter 11.

- Paragraph 2(h) works in tandem with Paragraph 6(b), below (restrictions on ownership transfers) to protect members from being stuck with a new member they don't want. Any member can block the admission of a new member.

> **g. Members' Meetings and Actions Taken by Written Consent**
>
> The LLC is not required to hold regular members' meetings. However, one or more members can call a meeting at any time. The member calling the meeting will provide notice of the business to be transacted at the meeting, but other business may be discussed and conducted at the meeting with the consent of all members present. A quorum consists of all members, unless members who cannot attend consent in writing for the meeting to take place in their absence. Except as otherwise provided in this agreement, a vote of the majority of members present at a meeting of the members is required to approve any action taken at the meeting.
>
> Any action required or permitted by this agreement to be taken at a meeting of the members may be taken without a meeting, without prior notice, by unanimous written consent of the members.
>
> **h. Admission of New Members**
>
> Except as otherwise provided in this agreement, a person or entity will not be admitted into membership unless each member consents in writing to the admission of the new member.

Management Provisions

- Paragraph 3(a) confirms the decision to be manager-managed. Rather than listing the managers here in Paragraph 3(a), we list them on Exhibit A. That way, when managers change, you can simply amend Exhibit A rather than having to amend the body of the agreement.

> **3. Management Provisions**
> **a. Management by Manager(s)**
> The LLC will be managed by one or more managers. The current managers are listed in Exhibit A.

- Paragraph 3(b) states the basic proposition that a manager is not personally liable for the debts of the LLC. A manager can be held personally liable in rare instances, such as when the manager mixes their personal assets with business assets and causes the loss of limited liability (piercing of the LLC veil). A manager could also be held liable if they mislead the creditor into believing that the creditor is dealing with the manager personally, not with the LLC. Otherwise, managers have limited liability.

> **b. Nonliability of Manager(s)**
> No manager of the LLC will be personally liable for the expenses, debts, obligations, or liabilities of the LLC, or for claims made against it.

- Paragraph 3(c) confirms that the LLC is manager-managed (the managers make all management decisions), and provides that management decisions will be made by majority vote.

c. **Authority and Votes of Manager(s)**

Except as otherwise set forth in this agreement, the articles of organization, or under the laws of this state, all management decisions relating to the LLC's business will be made by its manager(s). If there is more than one manager, management decisions will be approved by a majority vote of the managers, with each manager entitled to cast one vote for or against any matter submitted to the managers for a decision.

- Paragraph 3(d) sets the rules for appointing and removing managers. Managers are appointed and removed by majority vote of the members. A manager will also stop being a manager if they become disabled, die, retire from the business, or withdraw from management.

    Some LLCs set the number of managers in the operating agreement. This operating agreement does not, and instead leaves the number managers up to the members, who can increase or decrease the number by majority vote.

d. **Appointment, Removal, and Term of Manager(s)**

The members will have the exclusive right to set the number of managers and to appoint the manager(s), who will be responsible for the day-to-day management of the business of the LLC. The manager(s) will be appointed by a majority of members.

A manager may be removed at any time by a vote of the majority of the members. In addition, each manager will cease to serve upon any of the following events:

- the manager becomes disabled, dies, retires, or otherwise withdraws from management, or
- the manager's term expires, if a term has been designated in other provisions of this agreement.

Upon the occurrence of any of these events, a new manager may be appointed to replace the departing manager by a majority vote of the members.

Paragraph 3(e) places express dues on managers to act in good faith and in the best interests of the company in their management decisions. Some operating agreements specify that managers are expected to devote all or substantially all of their working time to the business. But in some LLCs, the manager role is part-time by design, so "all or substantially all" language wouldn't work. In this operating agreement, the time commitment is simply whatever the business needs—the manager is expected to understand those needs and spend whatever time is necessary to meet them.

> e. **Manager Commitment to LLC**
> Each manager will conduct the affairs of the LLC in good faith and in the best interests of the LLC. Each manager will devote time to the LLC as the business requires.

Compensating Managers, Indemnification, and Managers' Meetings

- Under Paragraph 3(f), managers are not automatically owed any payment for being a manager, but the members can vote to compensate them. As discussed in Paragraph 2(c) above, members can't be employees of the LLC unless the LLC is being taxed as a corporation. This rule applies to managers who are members—they can't be paid a salary for their work managing the company. A manager who is not a member can be compensated for their time (as an employee or independent contractor, depending on the circumstances).

> f. **Compensation of Manager(s)**
> No manager is entitled to any fee for managing the operations of the LLC unless such compensation is approved by a majority vote of the members.

- Paragraph 3(g) covers a scenario in which a manager is sued by a third party for something the manager did in their capacity as a manager and ends up with a money judgment for damages against them. In such a circumstance, so long as the manager exercised due care in the matter over which they were sued (in other words, didn't cause the third party's injury through their own negligence), the manager is not liable to the third party.

> **g. Indemnification of Manager(s)**
>
> A manager will be indemnified by the LLC for any debt, obligation, or other liability, including reasonable attorneys' fees, incurred in the course of the manager's activities or performance of duties on behalf of the LLC as long as the manager complied with the duties of loyalty and care when incurring the debt, obligation, or other liability. This provision does not in any way limit the indemnification the manager would be entitled to under applicable state law. The indemnification provided will inure to the benefit of successors and assigns of any such manager.

- Paragraph 3(h) concerns meetings. It doesn't require managers to hold meetings, but rather provides rules for calling and conducting meetings. It also provides that managers can take an action if all of them sign a written consent, rather than holding a meeting and taking a vote. We cover unanimous written consents and provide a sample consent form in Chapter 11.

h. Management Meetings and Actions Taken by Written Consents
Meetings of the managers will be held on five (5) days' notice or on such shorter notice as may be mutually agreeable to the managers, on the call of any one or more managers. Members will be provided with a written notice of the time and place of each meeting, along with a description of the purpose of the meeting. The presence of a majority of managers constitutes a quorum. Except as otherwise provided in this agreement, the vote of a majority of the managers present at any managers' meeting is required to approve any action taken at the meeting.

Any action required or permitted by this agreement to be taken at a meeting of the managers may be taken without a meeting, without prior notice, by unanimous written consent of the managers.

Taxes and Accounting

Paragraph 4 covers taxes and related matters.
- Paragraph 4(a) states that the LLC will be classified and taxed, at least initially, as a partnership. We discuss tax elections in Chapter 4.
- Paragraph 4(b) covers the LLC's accounting methods. We discuss LLC tax elections in Chapter 4.
- Paragraph 4(c) states that the LLC's real and personal property must be owned by the LLC, not its individual members. This rule is very important: the LLC is a legal entity, apart from its owners. If the lines between the company and the members get blurred, such as by having LLC assets held in the name of a member, the members can lose limited liability. In other words, if a court were to determine that the business is not truly separate from its owners, the owners could be held personally liable for LLC debts—a consequence they sought to avoid by choosing an LLC in the first place. Paragraph 4(c) reminds owners not to blur the lines when it comes to property ownership and titling.

- Paragraph 4(d) recites how bank accounts will be set up and used.
- Paragraph 4(e) says that if asked by the IRS, the LLC will name a "tax partner"—the unlucky soul that the IRS will deal with in case they take an unwelcome interest in your LLC. We noted in Chapter 4 that the person named as the responsible party on an application for an employer identification number (EIN) becomes the contact person for the LLC with the IRS. If the LLC is required to separately name a tax matters partner, the members can name the member who acted as the responsible party on its EIN application or it can name another member.
- Paragraph 4(f) concerns tax returns and reports (we cover income tax reporting in Chapter 10). Paragraph 4(f) requires the LLC to share tax returns with members and provide the members with the information they need to complete their own returns, and to provide a balance sheet and income statement for the year.

---

4. Tax and Financial Provisions

a. Tax Classification of LLC

The LLC will be initially classified as a partnership for federal and, if applicable, state income tax purposes. The LLC may change its tax treatment with the consent of all members and by filing the necessary election with the IRS and, if applicable, the state tax department.

b. Tax Year and Accounting Method

The tax year of the LLC will end on the last day of the month of December. The LLC will use the accrual method of accounting.

The tax year and the accounting method of the LLC may each be changed with the consent of all members.

c. Title to Assets

All personal and real property of the LLC will be held in the name of the LLC, not in the name of any individual member.

d. Bank Accounts

All funds of the Company will be deposited in one or more separate bank accounts, using such banks or trust companies as the managers may designate. Withdrawals from such bank accounts are to be made upon such signature or signatures as the managers may designate. The funds of the LLC, however and wherever deposited or invested, will not be commingled with the personal funds of any member of the LLC.

e. Tax Matters Partner

If required under Internal Revenue Code provisions or regulations, the LLC will designate a member as its "tax matters partner" in accordance with Internal Revenue Code Section 6231(a)(7) and corresponding regulations, who will fulfill this role by being the spokesperson for the LLC in dealings with the IRS and performing such other duties as required under the Internal Revenue Code and Regulations.

f. Annual Income Tax Returns and Reports

Within 60 days after the end of each tax year of the LLC, a copy of the LLC's state and federal income tax returns for the preceding tax year will be mailed or otherwise provided to each member of the LLC, together with any additional information and forms necessary for each member to complete their individual state and federal income tax returns. Along with the necessary tax information and forms, the LLC will also provide a financial report that includes a balance sheet and profit and loss statement for the year.

How Your LLC Is Funded and How It Handles Assets

The fifth paragraph of the operating agreement covers funding the LLC and spending its assets.

- Paragraph 5(a) describes members' capital contributions—whatever a member contributes in return for their percentage interest in the company, including cash, other property, and services. The value of each member's capital contribution and their percentage interests are shown in Exhibit A.

> **EXAMPLE:** Carly contributes $10,000 in cash in exchange for a 20% interest in 4C Candles LLC. Chris contributes services in exchange for a similar 20% interest. Chris's services have a value of $10,000.

> **5. Capital Provisions**
>   **a. Capital Contributions**
>   Members have made initial contributions of cash, property, or services as specified in Exhibit A.

- Paragraph 5(b) reinforces your intentions that your contributions to the LLC are an investment, not a loan. In exchange for your capital contributions, you receive equity (a percentage interest) in the LLC. As the value of the company grows, the value of your ownership share grows—that's how you earn a return on your investment. Paragraph 5(b) reinforces that your capital contribution is an equity investment, not a loan.

> **b. No Interest on Capital Contributions**
>   No interest will be paid on capital contributions or on capital account balances.

- Paragraph 5(c) describes bookkeeping. Each member will have a capital account that tracks the member's equity in the LLC. Capital accounts are used for tax reporting purposes and come into play when distributing assets upon the liquidation of the company.

> **c. Capital Account Bookkeeping**
> A capital account will be set up and maintained on the books of the LLC for each member. It will reflect each member's capital contribution, increased by any additional contributions by the member and by the member's share of LLC profits, decreased by any distributions to the member and by the member's share of LLC losses, and adjusted as required in accordance with applicable provisions of the Internal Revenue Code and corresponding income tax regulations. Upon a valid transfer of a member's membership interest, the member's capital account will carry over to the new owner.

- Paragraph 5(d) gives the LLC the right to require members to invest more money, if your LLC needs additional capital in the future. Under Paragraph 5(d), members cannot be required to make additional capital contributions unless all members agree to require them.

> **d. Additional Contributions**
> The members may agree, from time to time, by unanimous vote, to require the payment of additional capital contributions by the members.

- Paragraph 5(e) describes how income, loss, and so on will be allocated to members. Most LLCs allocate profits and losses according to percentage interests, but you can use a different allocation formula. For example, let's say that one member of the LLC is in a better position than the others to take tax advantage of LLC losses. The allocation formula might allocate more of the losses to that member than they would receive according to their percentage interest. If you're thinking of allocating profits and losses other than by percentage interests, consult your tax adviser.

> **e. Allocations of Profits and Losses**
> The profits and losses of the LLC, and all items of its income, gain, loss, deduction, and credit will be allocated to members in accordance with the member's percentage interest.

Paragraph 5(f) covers capital withdrawals. Capital invested in the company stays in the company unless all members agree that a member can withdraw it.

> **f. Capital Withdrawals**
> Members will not be allowed to withdraw any part of their capital contributions or to receive distributions, whether in property or cash, except as otherwise allowed by this agreement. A capital withdrawal requires the written consent of all members.

- Paragraph 5(g) covers cash distributions, and includes important safeguards. Members get money out of the LLC primarily through distributions of profits. To understand distributions, recall that your LLC is a pass-through tax entity. Profits and losses are allocated (passed through) to members, who then report the income or loss on their personal tax returns and pay any income tax owed. LLC profits are taxed when they're earned, not when they're distributed.

Distributions are a matter of cash flow—the LLC's cash flow and each member's cash flow. Let's say that an LLC is profitable and generating cash. The profits can be left in the company and reinvested in the business, or they can be distributed to the owners, or both. Managers make these decisions by majority vote.

> **g. Distributions of Cash**
> Cash from business operations, as well as cash from a sale or other disposition of LLC capital assets, may be allocated and distributed from time to time to members in accordance with each member's percentage interest in the LLC, as may be decided by a majority of managers. However, the managers will direct distributions to be made each year in an amount sufficient to cover any member's tax liability that may arise based on the allocation of LLC income, gains, losses, or deductions.

• Paragraph 5(h) concerns how the LLC distributes non-cash proceeds. "Proceeds" include any and all property received by the LLC through the sale of goods, services, or assets. Noncash proceeds arise when the LLC accepts property other than cash as payment for goods, services, or assets. Most LLCs don't deal in noncash proceeds, but Paragraph 5(h) applies if your LLC does.

> **h. Allocation of Noncash Proceeds**
> If proceeds consist of property other than cash, the members will decide the value of the property and allocate such value among the members in accordance with each member's percentage interest in the LLC.

- Paragraph 5(i) deals with distributions made when the LLC is liquidated or when a member's entire interest is being liquidated. When a member withdraws from the LLC and the company redeems the member's interest (as opposed to having the remaining members buy the departing member's interest), the redemption is called a liquidating distribution. Under either sort of liquidation (of the LLC or one member's interest), the capital account of a member receiving a distribution must be updated and distributions can be made only to the extent that the member's capital account shows a positive balance.

  Accounting for capital accounts is complicated and any sort of liquidating distribution must be accounted for correctly (especially for tax purposes). We recommend working with an accounting or tax professional when liquidating a member's interest or the entire LLC.

---

  i. Allocation and Distribution of Liquidation Proceeds
  Regardless of any other provision in this agreement, if there is a distribution in liquidation of the LLC, or when a member's interest is liquidated, all items of income and loss will be allocated to a member's capital account, and all appropriate credits and deductions will then be made to the capital account before any final distribution is made. A final distribution will be made to members only to the extent of, and in proportion to, any positive balance in a member's capital account.

Membership Withdrawals and Transfers

Paragraph 6 of your operating agreement addresses members' withdrawals and transfers of interests. As members' life circumstances change, involving retirement or divorce, for example, members might want or need to change their relationship with the LLC.

- Paragraph 6(a) addresses withdrawals. You can't force a member to remain a member, but you can provide for an orderly exit process. Paragraph 6(a) is a simple buyout clause that leaves most of the terms up for negotiation at the time of a member's withdrawal. It includes a mechanism for valuing the departing member's interest (a formal appraisal) if the parties can't agree on a price. Once the price has been determined, the departing and remaining members will need to agree on a payment schedule, which sometimes involves installments paid over a number of years. The departing member usually wants payment as soon as possible, while the remaining members must consider the LLC's ability to pay. In the end, the parties need to agree on a schedule that both sides are confident can be met.

  In terms of the notice requirement for withdrawal, the notice period gives the departing and remaining members time to negotiate the terms of the buyout. 4C Candles settled on three months' notice, but your notice period could be shorter or longer. In Chapter 8, we discuss buyout (buy-sell) agreements.

---

6. Membership Withdrawal and Transfer Provisions

a. Withdrawal of Members

A member may withdraw from the LLC by giving written notice to all other members at least three months before the date the withdrawal is to be effective. In the event of such withdrawal, the LLC will pay the departing member the fair value of their LLC interest, less any amounts owed by the member to the LLC. The departing and remaining members will agree at the time of departure on the fair value of the departing member's interest and the schedule of payments to be made by the LLC to the departing member, who will receive payment for their interest within a reasonable time after departure from the LLC. If the departing and remaining members cannot agree on the value of departing member's interest, they will select an appraiser, who will determine the current value of the departing member's interest. This appraised amount will be fair value of the departing member's interest and will form the basis of the amount to be paid to the departing member.

- Paragraph 6(b) addresses restrictions on transferring membership in the LLC. It recognizes that LLC member interests are made up of two sets of rights: economic rights and governance rights.

   Economic rights include the right to receive distributions, and these rights can be transferred *without* the consent of the other members.

   Governance rights include voting rights, management rights, and information rights (the right to receive information about the company and its operations). Governance rights cannot be transferred without the consent of the other members.

   > **EXAMPLE:** Carly owns a 20% interest in 4C Candles LLC. The company is doing well and the value of Carly's interest has appreciated considerably. She'd like to cash out and her cousin Clayton, who's an experienced entrepreneur, is interested in buying her full 20% stake. Another LLC member, Constance, knows Clayton and has had some unpleasant business dealings with him in the past. Constance does not want to work with Clayton and will not consent to admit him as a member. Carly can sell her economic rights in the LLC to Clayton, but she can't sell her governance rights.

   b. Restrictions on the Transfer of Membership

   Notwithstanding any other provision of this agreement, a member will not transfer their membership in the LLC unless all of the nontransferring members first agree in writing to approve the admission of the transferee into the LLC. Further, no member may encumber a part or all of their membership in the LLC by mortgage, pledge, granting of a security interest, lien, or otherwise, unless the encumbrance has first been approved in writing by all other members of the LLC.

   Notwithstanding the above provision, any member will be allowed to assign an economic interest in their membership to another person without the approval of the other members. Any assignment of economic interest will not include a transfer of the member's voting or management rights, and the assignee will not become a member except as provided elsewhere in this agreement.

Dissolving the LLC

Despite your best intentions and plans, or perhaps according to plan, your LLC might need to come to an end. Paragraph 7(a) spells out the circumstances that would trigger the dissolution of the LLC and places the manager(s) in charge of winding up and liquidating the company. The triggering events for a dissolution are the expiration of the LLC's term if a dissolution date was specified in the company's articles, a vote by all the members to dissolve, or a court-ordered dissolution.

When some members want to dissolve the LLC and others want to continue it, the company continues to exist (for lack of a unanimous vote to dissolve). The two sides would need to overcome the stalemate, probably via a buyout of the members who favor dissolution). If the members simply can't resolve the disagreement themselves and it becomes impractical to continue to operate the company, the member(s) seeking to terminate the LLC can go to court seeking an order from a judge (a decree) to dissolve the LLC.

---

7. **Dissolution Provisions**

   a. **Events That Trigger Dissolution of the LLC**

   The following events will trigger a dissolution of the LLC:

   i. **Expiration of LLC Term.** The expiration of the term of existence of the LLC, if such term is specified in the articles of organization or this operating agreement, will cause the dissolution of the LLC.

   ii. **Written Agreement or Consent to Dissolve.** The written agreement of all members to dissolve the LLC will cause a dissolution of the LLC.

   iii. **Entry of Decree.** The entry of a decree of dissolution of the LLC under state law will cause a dissolution of the LLC.

   If the LLC is to dissolve according to any of the above provisions, the manager(s) will wind up the affairs of the LLC, and take other actions appropriate to complete a dissolution of the LLC in accordance with applicable provisions of state law.

- Paragraph 7(b) covers what happens when a member dies, becomes incapacitated, declares bankruptcy, and so on. In some states, the default rule is that, absent a contrary provision in an operating agreement, the death of a member triggers the dissolution of the LLC unless the remaining members vote to continue it. In other states, the LLC doesn't automatically terminate upon the death of a member (so the surviving members don't have to vote to continue it). Paragraph 7(b) states that this LLC will continue after the death or other dissociation of a member.

> **b. Dissociation of a Member**
> The dissociation of a member, which means the death, incapacity, bankruptcy, retirement, resignation, or expulsion of a member, or any other event that terminates the continued membership of a member, will not cause a dissolution of the LLC. The LLC will continue its existence and business following such dissociation of a member.

General Provisions

We've nearly reached the end of your LLC's operating agreement! Now it's just a matter of slogging through the final provisions, which you can think of as a kind of playbook—"if any of these things happen, here's what we will do." People (and lawyers) are apt to snooze through these provisions, but we urge you to pay a little attention. There's a reason they appear in almost every operating agreement.

- Paragraph 8(a) concerns officers and others with titles. Unlike corporations, LLCs are not required to have officers. But LLCs can have officers, and Paragraph 8(a) authorizes their designation.

8. General Provisions

a. Officers

The LLC may designate one or more officers, such as a President, Vice President, Secretary, and Treasurer. Persons who fill these positions need not be members of the LLC. Such positions may be compensated or noncompensated according to the nature and extent of the services rendered as a part of the duties of each office.

- Paragraph 8(b) contains basic legal and financial record-keeping requirements.

b. Records

The LLC will keep at its principal business address a copy of all proceedings of membership meetings and resolutions, as well as books of account of financial transactions. A list of the names and addresses of the current membership also will be maintained at this address, with notations on any transfers of members' interests to nonmembers or persons being admitted into membership.

The LLC's articles of organization, a signed copy of this operating agreement, the LLC's tax returns for the preceding three tax years, and written records of votes taken at member and manager meetings or by unanimous consent, will be kept at its principal business address.

Any member may inspect any and all records maintained by the LLC upon reasonable notice.

- Paragraph 8(c) deals with the authority of members and officers to form and run the company. Some operating agreements spell out the "powers" of the members and officers (and managers in a manager-managed LLC)—specific actions they may or may not take on behalf of the company. For example, officers might be authorized to obtain financing for the company, but not to pledge company assets as part of any loans (member approval would be required). Or they might be authorized to enter into contracts under a certain dollar amount (member approval would be required for larger contracts).

The clause as presented here doesn't lay out specific powers, but rather gives members and officers a blanket authorization to do whatever is necessary to finish forming the company ("perfect the organization") and to run the business ("carry out its business operations").

---

c. All Necessary Acts

The members, managers, and officers (if any) of the LLC are authorized to perform all acts necessary to perfect the organization of the LLC and to carry out its business operations expeditiously and efficiently.

- Paragraph 8(d) is the lawyer's best friend: If a court deems any part of the agreement to be invalid, the remaining clauses will still be enforceable.

---

d. Severability

If any provision of this agreement is determined by a court or arbitrator to be invalid, unenforceable, or otherwise ineffective, that provision will be severed from the rest of this agreement, and the remaining provisions will remain in effect and enforceable.

- Paragraph 8(e) sets some ground rules if the members have a dispute concerning ownership. In the event of an ownership dispute, the warring parties can go to court, or they can choose alternative means of resolving the dispute: mediation, arbitration, or mediation followed by arbitration. Mediation involves working with a neutral third party to reach a mutual settlement of differences. Mediators don't issue rulings, but rather try to bring the two sides together end the dispute. Mediation is the required first step under Paragraph 8(e).

Arbitration is generally considered to be simpler and more efficient than litigation (although it doesn't always work out that way). Paragraph 8(e) mandates arbitration when the parties are unable to resolve the dispute in mediation. Binding arbitration means that the parties agree to accept the arbitrator's ruling and not pursue additional legal avenues.

---

e. Mediation and Arbitration of Disputes Among Members

In any dispute over the provisions of this operating agreement and in other disputes among the members, if the members cannot resolve the dispute to their mutual satisfaction, the matter will be submitted to mediation. The terms and procedure for mediation will be arranged by the parties to the dispute.

If good-faith mediation of a dispute proves impossible or if an agreed-upon mediation outcome cannot be obtained by the members who are parties to the dispute, the dispute will be submitted to binding arbitration in accordance with the rules of the American Arbitration Association. Any party may commence arbitration of the dispute by sending a written request for arbitration to all other parties to the dispute. The request will state the nature of the dispute to be resolved by arbitration, and, if all parties to the dispute agree to arbitration, arbitration will be commenced as soon as practical after such parties receive a copy of the written request.

All parties will initially share the cost of arbitration, but the prevailing party or parties may be awarded attorneys' fees, costs, and other expenses of arbitration at the discretion of the arbitrator. All arbitration decisions will be final, binding, and conclusive on all the parties to arbitration, and legal judgment may be entered based upon such decision in accordance with applicable law in any court having jurisdiction to do so.

- Paragraph 8(f) contains two clauses: the "entire agreement" clause and the "amendments must be written and mutual" clause. Together, they work to draw strict boundaries around the agreement—the agreement between the members is defined by what's contained within the four corners of this document, and the terms can only be changed by a written, unanimous amendment.

  The entire agreement clause means that this agreement is the final word (for now) on the matters it addresses. Each member should read the agreement carefully to make sure that they understand and consent to its terms. If there are any conflicts between the language of the agreement and what a member understood the arrangement to be, you should obviously resolve those conflicts before signing the agreement. Members should also consider whether anything is missing from the agreement.

  The amendment clause, by requiring that any amendment must be in writing and be agreed to by all the members, avoids any confusion about whether the agreement has been changed verbally. The agreement can't be amended verbally.

> **f. Entire Agreement and Amendment**
>
> This operating agreement represents the entire agreement among the members, and replaces and supersedes all prior written and oral agreements among the members. This agreement will not be amended, modified, or replaced except by written agreement of all members.

Signing Your Operating Agreement

Your next task, in Paragraph 9, is to have all members and managers sign the agreement. Their signatures reflect their agreement to abide by its terms. A person who is both member and manager will sign twice, once in each capacity.

9. Signatures

The members and managers of the LLC sign and adopt this agreement as the operating agreement of the LLC and agree to abide by its terms. The members sign and adopt this agreement as the operating agreement of the LLC and agree to abide by its terms.

Members

Date: _____

Signature: _____

Name of member: Carly Abelson

Date: _____

Signature: _____

Name of member: Carmen Becerra

Date: _____

Signature: _____

Name of member: Constance Li

Date: _____

Signature: _____

Name of member: Chris Williams

Managers

Date: _____

Signature: _____

Name of member: Carly Abelson

Date: _____

Signature: _____

Name of member: Carmen Becerra

Date: _____

Signature: _____

Name of member: Constance Li

Listing Members' Interests: Exhibit A

Earlier in the agreement, Paragraph 5(a) addressed how to compute a member's membership interest—it is computed as a percentage of total membership interests. Paragraph 2(e) referred to Exhibit A, which is where you list the members' names, their initial contributions, and their corresponding membership interests. You also list the managers (and the officers, if any).

Exhibit A
Members, Managers; Initial Contributions; Interests; Other Information

Members

Member Name	Initial Contribution	Interest
Carly Abelson	$10,000	20%
Carmen Becerra	$10,000	20%
Constance Li	$20,000	40%
Chris Williams	$10,000	20%

Managers
Carly Abelson
Carmen Becerra
Constance Li

Officers
None.

PART

C

Buyout Agreements and Ownership Transfers

Chapter 8—Buyout Agreements and Ownership Transfers

Buyout Agreements and Ownership Transfers

L imited liability company members usually want to have control over who they're in business with, so they place restrictions on the transfer of ownership interests. The operating agreements presented in the previous chapters contain basic restrictions on ownership transfers that allow the transfer of economic interests, but require the consent of the other members to admit the transferee as a member. (An economic interest is a right to share in profits and losses, and to receive distributions, but not a right to participate in ownership decisions.) The operating agreements also provide for a mandatory buyout in the event that a member wants to withdraw from the LLC, with most terms of the buyout to be negotiated by the departing member and the remaining members.

The buyout and transfer provisions of the operating agreements in Chapters 6 and 7 represent the minimum of what should be in place for your LLC. But these provisions don't address other ownership transfer scenarios, such as when a member dies, gets divorced, files for bankruptcy, or wants to sell their ownership stake to a third party. To provide rules for these scenarios, we recommend having a separate buyout agreement, also known as a buy-sell agreement, like the one presented below. Alternatively, you can add enhanced buyout provisions to your operating agreement. You might find that separate operating and buyout agreements are easier to follow and administer than an expanded operating agreement.

When a buyout is triggered by the provisions of the buyout agreement, you'll use two additional agreements to accomplish the buyout: a member interest purchase agreement and an assignment of LLC interest. This chapter contains samples of a buyout agreement, a purchase agreement, and an assignment. We walk you through each provision, or clause, of each agreement. After a short explanation, you'll see the provision itself.

Creating a Buyout Agreement

The essence of a buyout agreement is that upon a triggering event (explained below), a party has the right to purchase a member's interest in order to prevent that interest from being transferred. For example, when a member wants to sell their interest to a third party, the LLC, or the other members, or both, have a right to step in and match the third-party offer (a right of first refusal). When a member dies, the company, or the other members, or both, have an option to buy the deceased member's interest rather than to have it pass to their heirs. The buyout agreement identifies the triggering events, the rights that are triggered, and the terms for arriving at and closing a deal on a buyout.

> **FORMS**
>
> **A sample buyout agreement is shown below.** A complete sample version is included in Appendix B. A blank version is included in Appendix C and is downloadable from this book's companion page. See Appendix A for the link.

Deciding on the Parties to a Buyout Agreement

The first big question you'll face in structuring your buyout agreement is who holds purchase rights: the company, the other members, or both? If the LLC holds purchase rights, the LLC is a party to the agreement. In the sample 4C Candles LLC buyout agreement presented below, the company and the other members hold purchase rights. The company has first rights, and the individual members' purchase rights kick in only if the company doesn't exercise its rights. Because the LLC is a potential purchaser under the agreement, it is a party to the agreement.

Redemption vs. Cross-Purchase: Purchase by the LLC or by the Members

When an LLC buys all or part of a member's interest, we say that the interest has been redeemed or liquidated. After a redemption, the remaining members own 100% of the LLC in the same proportions that existed prior to the liquidation.

> **EXAMPLE:** Eric, Fiona, and Grace are equal one-third owners of an LLC. Eric dies and the LLC purchases Eric's interest from his estate. Upon the redemption of Eric's interest, Fiona and Grace together own 100% of the LLC, each with 50%. Their ownership interests were equal before the redemptions, and their interests remain equal after. Let's say that the ownership interests prior to the redemption had instead been 40% for Eric, 40% for Fiona, and 20% for Grace. After the redemption of Eric's interest, Fiona would own two-thirds (67%) of the LLC, and Grace would own one-third (33%), maintaining the 2:1 ratio of Fiona's and Grace's interests.

When an individual member buys another member's interest, it's called a cross-purchase. The purchaser simply adds the purchased percentage interest to their preexisting total. In the equal one-third example above, if Fiona and Grace, as the surviving members, purchase Eric's interest instead of having the LLC do so, they still wind up as 50/50 owners. Each had 30% of the company and each adds their half of Eric's Interest (20% each), bringing them up to 50%.

Tax Considerations for Structuring Buyouts

As the examples above show, the remaining members after a buyout will end up with the same percentage interests whether the buyout is made by the company or by the other members. If the end result is the same, why give purchase rights to the company and the individual members, as 4C Candles does in its buyout agreement? Why not one or the other?

The main reasons to include purchase rights for both the LLC and the individual members are tax-related. Under some circumstances, a redemption by an LLC can be taxed differently than a cross-purchase by the other members, and one approach might be more advantageous than the other. By having the company and members hold purchase rights, the parties will have the flexibility to structure the buyout to minimize tax consequences. If a redemption would be better tax-wise, the members can vote to have the company exercise its purchase right. If a cross-purchase would be more tax-effective, the members can vote to have the company decline its right of first refusal or option and then purchase the right in question individually.

You might want to have purchase rights only for your LLC or only for your members, or you might have both but prioritize them differently (with the members having the first option). The downloadable Buyout Agreement on this book's companion page on Nolo.com can be adapted to fit your needs.

Paragraphs in Your Buyout Agreement

Having settled on the parties to the agreement, we can take up the various provisions of the agreement.

Restrictions on Transfers

Paragraph 1(a) establishes the overall boundaries of the Agreement: No transfers of Interests are allowed except those provided for under the Agreement. If a transfer is not specifically included below, it can't be made and any attempt to make it will be invalid.

Sample Buyout Agreement
4C Candles LLC

This Buyout Agreement ("Agreement") is made as of March 1, 2024 (the "Effective Date"), by and among Carly Abelson, Carmen Becerra, Constance Li, and Chris Williams (collectively "Members" and each a "Member"), and 4C Candles LLC (the "LLC") (each individually a "party" and collectively the "parties").

The Members own all of the ownership interests of the LLC ("Interests") and are parties to the Operating Agreement of the LLC. The Members seek to place certain controls on the transfer of Interests. The LLC is interested in facilitating the implementation of those controls. The parties therefore agree as follows:

1. Restrictions on Transfers and Permitted Transfers

a. While this Agreement is in effect, Members will not, except as provided below, have any right to transfer, encumber, or otherwise dispose of their Interests. Transfers made in violation of this Agreement will be invalid and will not be recognized on the books of the LLC.

b. Provided that the transferee duly executes and delivers to the LLC a written agreement to be bound as a Member by the provisions of this Buyout Agreement and the Operating Agreement of the LLC, the following transfers are permitted and may be made without complying with the provisions of paras. 2 and 3 below:

  i. Transfers of an Interest to a revocable trust of which the Member is the grantor and primary beneficiary

  ii. Transfers of the Interest of a deceased Member to the executor, administrator, or other legal representative of the estate of the deceased Member; or

  iii. Transfers to the other Members of the LLC provided that such transfers must be in the same proportion that the Interest of each such other Member bears to the total of all Interests.

Paragraph 1(b), above, allows specific transfers without triggering a purchase option or right of first refusal, and without requiring the consent of the other members. The allowed transfers are to a grantor trust, the estate of a deceased member, and to other members. Paragraphs 2 (Death of a Member) and 3 (Lifetime Transfers), which are referenced below, provide for purchase options by the LLC in the event of certain voluntary and involuntary transfers.

To be allowable under Paragraph 1(b)(iii), the transfer must be to all the other members in proportion to their Interests. In other words, the transfer must maintain the proportionate interests of the transferee members.

> **EXAMPLE:** Carmen owns 40% of 4C Candles LLC, Constance owns 30%, and Carly and Chris each own 15%. Carmen seeks to transfer half of her Interests (20%) to the other three Members. She can do so under Paragraph 1(b)(iii) by transferring 10% to Constance and 5% each to Carly and Chris. Post-transfer, Carmen will own 20% of the LLC, Constance will own 40%, and Carly and Chris will each own 20%. Constance will still own twice as much as Carly or Chris.

In the operating agreements presented in Chapters 6 and 7, no new member can be admitted to the LLC without the consent of all the members. If the members don't agree to allow a transferee to become a member, the transferee has received only an economic interest in the LLC. Paragraph 1(b) essentially preapproves a grantor trust or a legal representative of a deceased member's estate as a member, so long as the trust or estate agrees to be bound by the provisions of this Agreement and the Operating Agreement.

Additional Transfer Restrictions

The restrictions in Paragraph 2 apply to interests that transfer due to a member's death, and to transfers soon after the formation of the LLC.

2. Death of a Member

a. LLC Option to Purchase

Upon receipt of notice by the LLC that a legal representative of the estate of the deceased Member has been appointed, the LLC will have the right for ninety (90) days to agree to purchase all or part of the deceased Member's Interest for the price and on the terms provided in this Agreement. If the LLC elects not to exercise its purchase option, it will notify the surviving Members of this decision before the expiration of the 90-day option period.

When a member dies, the LLC has the right to purchase the deceased member's Interest from the estate, rather than having it go to the deceased member's heirs. A 90-day clock starts ticking when the LLC receives notice that an executor or other legal representative has been appointed for the estate (thereby making a purchase from the estate possible). If the LLC exercises the option in the 90-day window, it will then have 60 days to close on the purchase (per Paragraph 4 below).

b. Surviving Members' Option to Purchase

Upon receipt by the surviving Members of notice that the LLC is not exercising its purchase rights under Paragraph 2(a), the surviving Members, acting together, will have the right for thirty (30) days following such notice to agree to purchase all or a part of the deceased Member's Interest in the proportion that each surviving Member's Interest bears to the total Interests owned by all of the surviving Members, for the price and on the terms provided in this Agreement.

The 4C Candles buyout agreement is structured to give the LLC first purchase option or right of first refusal, with the surviving or remaining members' purchase rights kicking in only if the company doesn't exercise its rights. The price and payment terms of a purchase under Paragraph 2 are set out in Paragraphs 5 and 6 below.

3. Lifetime Transfers

a. Voluntary Transfers

i. Lock-in period. The Members agree that no voluntary transfers will be allowed in the first three (3) years of the existence of the LLC, beginning with the Effective Date of the First Operating Agreement of the LLC, without the prior consent of the other Member(s). During this lock-in period, any attempted voluntary transfer will be a violation of the Agreement and will be null and void.

Comment: A voluntary transfer is a sale of a member's interest to a third party (a nonmember). This lock-in clause prohibits voluntary transfers for the first three years of a LLC's existence. Some LLC owners skip the lock-in period, perhaps in the belief that no third party would ever be interested in buying a share of the LLC (and therefore a lock-in seems unnecessary). Others seek a permanent lock-in period—no member can ever sell to a third party without the consent of the other members. Whether to have a lock-in period and how long it should be depends on the circumstances of each LLC.

Once the lock-in period ends (or if the buyout agreement contains no lock-in period), a member may *negotiate* the sale of all or part of their interest to a third party. They can't *execute* the sale, though, unless the LLC declines to exercise the rights of first refusal provided below.

ii. Notification. After the lock-in period, when a Member intends to transfer any part of their Interest to a third party other than as provided in Paragraph 1(b), the Member will give written notice to the LLC of the proposed transfer, including the identity of the proposed transferee, the purchase price, and other terms of the deal.

The member wishing to make a voluntary transfer must notify the LLC of their intent, and the notice needs to identify the proposed transferee and the terms of the proposed transfer.

> iii. **LLC Right of First Refusal.** The LLC has a right to purchase the Interest proposed to be transferred for the same price and at the same terms as the proposed transfer to the third party. The LLC may exercise this right for sixty (60) days following receipt of the notice provided for in Paragraph 3(b)(ii).

Once notified of a proposed voluntary transfer, the LLC has 60 days to match the offer and purchase the interest in question. If the LLC exercises its right, it has 60 days to make the purchase (per Paragraph 4).

Most operating agreements provide that a third-party transferee can become a member only with the consent of the other members. If the operating agreement of this LLC contains such a provision, and if the other members don't consent, then the transferee will hold an economic interest in the LLC only. As explained above, an economic interest is a right to participate in profits and losses and to receive distributions, but not a right to participate in ownership decision.

> **EXAMPLE:** Carmen seeks to sell her 40% Interest in 4C Candles LLC to an investor friend, Denise. Carmen and Denise negotiate a price and other terms of a proposed purchase and sale. Carmen notifies the LLC of the proposed deal and the LLC declines to exercise its right of first refusal. Carmen sells her interest to Denise, but the other members don't consent to make Denise a voting member of the LLC. As a result, Denise owns a 40% economic interest (40% of the profits and losses), but has no voting rights.

Transfers that Happen by Operation of Law

Some LLC ownership transfers, known as "involuntary" transfers, happen by law, due to the application of relevant rules. Examples of involuntary transfers include a transfer of ownership to the bankruptcy estate of a bankrupt owner upon the filing of a bankruptcy petition; or a transfer by a court order, such as in a divorce decree.

Any involuntarily transferred interest is subject to an LLC purchase option. When an interest is transferred involuntarily, say by court order to the guardian of an incapacitated member, the LLC can purchase the interest from the guardian at a price determined under Paragraph 5 and under payment terms determined by Paragraph 6. If the LLC exercises the option, the transferee must sell.

> **B. Involuntary Transfers**
>> **i. Involuntary Transfers and Purchase Rights.** Any involuntary transfer made by operation of law or pursuant to a court order, other than by the death of a Member, including but not limited to transfers to a bankruptcy trustee, a creditor pursuant to a court judgment, a guardian or conservator of an incapacitated member, or a spouse or former spouse pursuant to a separation agreement or divorce decree, will be subject to the purchase rights described below.
>> **ii. LLC Purchase Option.** Upon being notified of an involuntary transfer, the LLC will have sixty (60) days to exercise a purchase option on the Interest in question for the price and on the terms provided in this Agreement.

Timing and Price

Your buyout agreement will include paragraphs describing the timing of any transfer, and its purchase price. Paragraph 4 sets the time limit to close on a purchase made by the LLC under Paragraphs 2 and 3. Paragraph 5 describes how the purchase price will be determined.

Closing

The closing of a purchase of a member's interest involves exchanging documents and funds to accomplish the transfer. Under Paragraph 4, the closing must take place within 60 days of the exercise of the purchase option by the LLC (or the other members if the company doesn't exercise its right). The mail closing document, the assignment of the member's interest to the company (or the other members), is covered later in the chapter.

> ### 4. Closing
> The closing for any purchase described in Paragraphs 2 or 3 will take place not more than sixty (60) days from the notification by the purchasing party or parties of the intent to exercise the purchase right.

Determining the Purchase Price

Determining the value of a member's interest can be the trickiest part of a buyout. LLCs are privately-owned, usually by no more than a handful of people, without a ready market for the purchase and sale of membership interests. Plus, there are countless methods for valuing an LLC and a member's stake in it. Valuation methods include:

- simple negotiation, meaning what the seller is looking for and the buyer is willing to pay
- a formula based on book value (assets minus liabilities as carried on the LLC's books), such as 100% or 150% of book value
- the fair market value of the LLC's assets, which might be similar to the book value of the assets but can differ, minus liabilities
- a multiple of profits, such as a 200% of the prior year's profits or 300% of the average of the prior three years' profits
- discounted cash flow, which involves projecting future cash flows and discounting them to present value
- market comparisons, meaning comparisons to similar companies that have been recently sold, and
- appraisal, with the appraiser using one or more of the methods described above.

As noted above, the simple buyout provisions of the operating agreements presented in the previous chapters provide for the price to be negotiated at the time of a transaction, with an independent appraiser to be brought in if the parties can't agree on a price. You might opt for a bit more certainty, or at least a bit more structure, by specifying a valuation formula to be used by the buyer and seller or by an appraiser.

> **EXAMPLE:** The 4C Candles LLC buyout agreement provides that the purchase price of a member's interest will be 200% of the average of the two prior years' profits, multiplied by the member's percentage interest. Carly dies owning a 20% interest in the LLC. Profits two years ago were $200,000 and profits last year were $300,000, for a two-year average of $250,000. The purchase price for a purchase of Carly's interest from the estate would be $100,000, calculated as follows:
>
> | | |
> |---|---|
> | Two-year average profits | $250,000 |
> | × 2 | $500,000 |
> | × 20% (Carly's interest) | $100,000 |

Does the result arrived at in the example mean that $500,000 is the market value of 4C Candles, the price that the members could get if the entire company was sold to a third party? Not necessarily. In fact, an outright sale of the LLC might fetch much more or much less than $500,000. The primary purpose of the profits-based formula is to provide certainty for the members in the event that a buyout is triggered. The formula is set, and all that's needed is to plug in the actual profit numbers.

Other valuation methods might be more subjective but still provide certainty as to how the purchase price will be determined. For example, let's say that the 4C Candles buyout agreement provides for the discounted cash flow method of valuation, which requires predicting future cash flows. As the noted philosopher Yogi Berra once remarked, "It's difficult to make predictions, especially about the future." But while the parties might argue about the cash flow projections themselves or the discount rate to be applied to arrive at the present value of those cash flows, at least they know in advance how the price will be determined.

Paragraph 5(a) of the 4C Candles agreement provides for the price to be negotiated at the time of the buyout. The blank form agreement that you can download from this book's companion page on Nolo.com includes an option for a valuation formula.

---

5. Purchase Price

a. **Purchase Price to Be Negotiated.** The purchase price for a purchase under Paragraph 2 or Paragraph 3(b) will be negotiated by the parties at the time of the purchase.

The purchase price will be determined as of the last day of the month immediately preceding (i) the date of death in the case of a purchase under Paragraph 2, or (ii) the effective date of the required notice in the case of a purchase under Paragraph 3(b).

A buyout agreement might provide for valuation by an independent appraiser, with or without specifying the methodology to be used by the appraiser. Paragraph 5(b) above provides for an independent appraisal if the parties aren't able to agree on a price (by predetermined formula or by negotiation). Alternatively, the parties could go straight to an independent appraisal, with no predetermined formula or negotiation (eliminating Paragraph 5(a)). However the appraisal comes to be, the agreement can specify the approach to be used by the appraiser, or not. Paragraph 5(a) above does not specify a valuation methodology. It does, however, require the parties to mutually select the appraiser, which at least implies mutual buy-in on the appraiser's approach.

Paragraph 5(b) also allows a party to hire a second appraiser, at their own expense, if they're dissatisfied with the first appraiser's number. The clause then provides for a simple averaging of the two valuations. Appraisal clauses can be more complicated, such as by allowing for or requiring a third appraisal when the first two appraisals are more than a certain limit apart. For example, the agreement could provide for a third appraisal, to be paid for by both parties, if the second appraisal comes in more than 30% higher or lower than the first appraisal.

> **b. Purchase Price Determined by Appraisal.** If the selling Members and the purchaser(s) (the LLC or the other Members) are unable to agree on a purchase price, the parties will mutually select a qualified business appraiser. The seller will pay one-half the cost of the appraisal and the purchaser(s) (the LLC or the other individual members) will pay the other half. If either party contests the valuation of the appraiser, that party can engage another qualified appraiser, at their own expense, to conduct a separate appraisal. In that event, the purchase price will be the average of the two valuations.

Some LLCs buy life insurance policies on the lives of their members so that funds (insurance proceeds) will be available for the purchase of a deceased member's interest. Paragraph 5(c) places an important limitation on the purchase price for a deceased member's interest—the existence of life insurance proceeds will not affect the purchase price in either direction. For example, let's say that a deceased member's interest is valued at $100,000, but life insurance proceeds are only $50,000. The purchase price is still $100,000. Similarly, if the LLC holds a $200,000 policy on the member, the purchase price is still $100,000. A shortfall in life insurance doesn't reduce the price, and an excess of life insurance doesn't increase the price. Life insurance proceeds do impact payment terms, though, as indicated in Paragraph 6(a).

> **c. Life Insurance Proceeds.** In the case of the death of a Member, the amount of any life insurance proceeds received by the LLC on account of such Member's death will not be considered in determining the purchase price to be paid for the deceased Member's Interest.

Discounting for Minority Interests

A minority discount pertains to the amount a buyer would pay for a non-controlling share of a business. The discount is a nod to the reality that, if you buy into a business as a minority owner, you have little control over its future, and thus, the price you pay should reflect that handicap. Minority discounts can come into play in buyout situations where the purchase price is intended to reflect the fair market value of the interest in question. Minority discounts can be especially useful for tax and estate planning purposes.

Let's say that an appraiser determines a value of $300,000 for an entire LLC, meaning what the members could expect to receive if they sold the company to a third party. Is a 20% interest in the LLC therefore worth $60,000? In other words, could a member expect to receive $60,000 if they sold their 20% interest to an independent buyer? Probably not. A buyer of 100% of an LLC has clear control of the LLC after the purchase. A buyer of as little as 51% would have control if membership voting is strictly by majority. But a 20% (or even 49%) owner doesn't have control. This lack of control can cause a minority interest to be discounted below its proportional value.

For example, suppose an independent appraisal results in a $500,000 valuation of 4C Candles LLC. This is theoretically what the entire LLC could be sold for. By straight proportions, Carly's 20% interest is worth $100,000. But an independent buyer might not pay $100,000 for a 20% stake, because they'd have little control over the LLC as a minority owner. Such a buyer might seek a minority discount of, say, 30%, meaning that they'd be willing to pay only $70,000 ($100,000 minus 30%) for a 20% stake in the LLC.

Consult your tax adviser or estate planner if you want to learn more about using minority discounts to value LLC interests.

Paying the Purchase Price

Paragraph 6(a) describes how the purchase price will be paid for a purchase of a deceased member's interest, and Paragraph 6(b) explains the payment for a purchase made in the event of an involuntary transfer. Payment terms for a purchase made in a voluntary transfer scenario don't need to be spelled out here. Under a right of first refusal, the purchaser (company or individual members) has a right to match the price and payment terms of the proposed voluntary transfer (see Paragraph 3 above). So, the purchase terms for the buyout are the terms of the proposed deal.

Using Promissory Notes to Purchase Member Interests

Many LLCs and their members aren't sufficiently capitalized to be able to pay cash in a buyout without hurting the business or the members' personal finances. Consequently, they need to use a promissory note to make the purchase, sometimes spreading the payout over several years. Paragraphs 6(a) and 6(b) provide for a 5-year note. Whether you would need to use promissory notes for member buyouts and how those notes should be structured depends on the ability of the LLC to generate profits and cash flows to pay off any notes, as well as the personal finances of the individual members.

Paragraph 6(c) allows the purchaser to prepay the note without penalty. Prepayments are typically made when the purchaser has extra cash and wants to avoid or reduce future interest charges on the note. Sometimes a note is paid off early because of acrimony between the purchaser and the selling member. Paying the note allows the parties to sever their relationship.

Under Paragraphs 6(a) and 6(b), the promissory note is secured by the interest being purchased. In other words, if the purchaser defaults on the note, the selling member can take back their membership interest (usually reduced by the proportion of the note that was paid before the default).

Under Paragraph 6(a), if the LLC or the other members have proceeds from an insurance policy on the deceased member's life, those proceeds must be applied toward the purchase price. Any unpaid purchase price after life insurance proceeds are applied becomes payable via a promissory note. Any excess of life insurance proceeds over the purchase price amount remains with the LLC (see Paragraph 7(c) below).

> **EXAMPLE:** The purchase price for a deceased member's interest is $150,000. Life insurance proceeds total $100,000. The deceased member's estate receives $100,000 at closing and is given a $50,000 note for the balance.

> **EXAMPLE:** The purchase price for a deceased member's interest is $150,000. Life insurance proceeds total $250,000. The deceased member's estate receives $150,000 and the company keeps the remaining $50,000 of insurance proceeds.

6. Payment of Purchase Price

a. **Payment for a Deceased Member's Interest.** In the event of a purchase following the death of a Member, the purchase price will be due and payable on the date of the closing but only to the extent that there are life insurance proceeds available to pay said purchase price. The balance of the purchase price, if any, will be paid by means of a promissory note ("Note") payable in sixty (60) consecutive equal monthly payments of principal, with interest at the applicable federal rate as provided under Section 1274 of the Code, determined as of the Closing Date. The Note will be secured by a pledge of the purchased Interest.

b. **Payment for a Purchase Made Pursuant to an Involuntary Transfer.** The purchase price will be paid with a promissory note ("Note") payable in sixty (60) consecutive equal monthly payments of principal, with interest at the applicable federal rate as provided under Section 1274 of the Code, determined as of the Closing Date. The Note will be secured by a pledge of the purchased Interest.

c. **Prepayment of Note.** The purchasing party will have the right at any time or times to prepay the Note in whole or in part without penalty, provided that any such prepayments will be applied first to any interest then due and the balance to principal.

Life Insurance

It seems fair to say that most LLCs don't take out life insurance policies on their members. Even if your LLC doesn't plan to purchase life insurance, we recommend including Paragraph 7 and other insurance-related provisions in your buyout agreement. These provisions don't require you to buy life insurance, but they'll come in handy if you ever do.

> **7. Life Insurance**
> a. **Purchase of Life Insurance.** The LLC may, but is not required to, purchase and be the owner and beneficiary of life insurance policies on the life of one or more of the Members.
> b. **Life Insurance Claims.** Upon the death of a Member, the LLC will promptly file a claim to collect any insurance death benefit in one lump sum on each policy covering the life of the deceased Member.

As explained under Paragraph 5(c) above, purchase price is determined without regard for the availability of life insurance proceeds. Paragraph 7(c) reiterates that if life insurance proceeds exceed the purchase price of the interest, the LLC keeps the excess proceeds.

> c. **Balance of Life Insurance Proceeds.** The LLC will retain the balance of any insurance proceeds in excess of the purchase price for the deceased Member's Interest.

When a member sells their interest in the LLC and ceases to be a member, the LLC no longer needs any life insurance policy it took out on the person. The withdrawing member might like to own the policy. Paragraph 7(d) acknowledges the possibility that the LLC could sell the policy to the member, without requiring it to do so.

> **d. Sale of Policy to a Withdrawing Member.** The LLC may, but is not required to, offer to sell a life insurance policy on a withdrawing Member to the applicable Member. The purchase price for any such policy will be its cash surrender value minus any outstanding indebtedness on the policy. If the applicable Member declines to purchase the policy, the policy will no longer be subject to this Agreement, and the LLC may retain or dispose of the policy.

Terminating the Agreement

When the LLC is dissolved, member interests are dissolved and a buyout agreement is no longer necessary (Paragraph 8(a)). If all members but one leave, the LLC becomes a single-member LLC, also with no need for a buyout agreement (Paragraph 8(b)). Finally, the members can decide at any time to do away with this agreement, although Paragraph 8(c) provides that they can only do so unanimously.

> **8. Termination**
>
> This Agreement will terminate and the Interests subject to this Agreement will be released from the terms of this Agreement on the occurrence of any of the following events:
>
>   **a.** The LLC is dissolved
>
>   **b.** A single Member becomes the sole owner of all the Interests in the LLC; or
>
>   **c.** All Members provide written consent to terminate this Agreement.

General Provisions

The buy-sell agreement ends with a series of commonly used provisions (sometimes called "boilerplate" provisions), covering issues like giving notice, amending the agreement, and so on.

The Notices clause (Paragraph 9(a)) and the Amendment and Revocation provisions (Paragraph 9(b)) are straightforward. Paragraph 9(c) makes it clear that the provisions of this agreement attach to the members' interests and follow those interests wherever they go. Thus, anyone in receipt of such an interest, however and in whatever capacity they receive the interest, is bound by this agreement.

---

9. General Provisions

a. **Notices.** Any and all notices, including exercises of rights, designations, consents, offers, acceptances or any other communications under this Agreement will be made in writing, by registered or certified mail, return receipt requested, express courier, or by secure email if the parties agree. Notices to the LLC will be addressed to its principal place of business or to an email address designated by the LLC. Notices to Members will be addressed to their personal residences or to an email address designated by the Member. The effective date of a mailed notice will be the date on which it is mailed. The effective date of an email notice will be the date on which it is sent.

b. **Amendment and Revocation.** This Agreement can be modified, amended, or revoked only by a writing signed by the LLC and all of the Members.

c. **Binding Effect.** This Agreement is binding upon the parties, their heirs, legal representatives, successors, and assigns. This Agreement will also be binding upon any person to whom any Interest is transferred in accordance with or in violation of the provisions of this Agreement.

Paragraph 9(d) provides for a particular kind of remedy in the event of a breach of this agreement—specific performance. Monetary damages (a financial payment to the non-breaching party) are the most common form of remedy in a lawsuit for breach of contract. Sometimes, though, money doesn't do the job and a court will order the breaching party to perform its obligations under the contract, known as specific performance. Breach of a buyout agreement can present such a situation.

For example, let's say that a member is seeking to sell their interest to a third party (a voluntary transfer) without having notified the LLC, thereby depriving the LLC of its right of first refusal. The other members find out about the proposed sale and the LLC goes to court not only to block the sale, but also to compel the selling member to allow the LLC to exercise its right of first refusal and buy the interest. Under Paragraph 9(d), the parties acknowledge that in such a circumstance, it might be necessary for the court to order the selling member to abide by the terms of the agreement and allow the company to exercise its right of first refusal.

> **d. Specific Performance.** The parties agree that they will be irrevocably damaged in the event that this Agreement is not specifically enforced. Accordingly, if the LLC or any person defaults on an obligation to give a notice, make an offer, sell an Interest, or close a sale as specified above, the LLC or any Member may bring an action to compel specific performance by the defaulting party.

The following paragraphs are commonly found at the end of contracts. Paragraph 9(e) will allow the agreement to continue to be enforceable in case a judge holds one or more of its provisions invalid; Paragraph 9(f) allows each party to sign a separate signature page (taken together, the pages constitute a set of full signatures); and Paragraph 9(g) notes that the agreement will be governed by the laws of the state chosen by the members (almost always their home state).

> **e. Severability.** If any term or provision of this Agreement is held to be invalid or unenforceable, the remainder of this Agreement will remain valid and be enforceable to the fullest extent permitted by law.
>
> **f. Counterparts.** This Agreement may be executed in any number of counterparts each of which, when duly executed, will constitute an original.
>
> **g. Governing Law.** This Agreement will be governed and interpreted according to the laws of California.

The signature section of the agreement provides that the members are signing for the company and for themselves as individual members.

On behalf of the LLC and themselves individually, the Members hereby execute this Agreement, which is effective as of the date first written above.

By: _____   By:_____
Name: Carly Abelson   Name: Carmen Becerra

By: _____   By: _____
Name: Constance Li   Name: Chris Williams

Forced Sale Clauses

Some LLC buyout agreements include a forced sale clause, also known as a shotgun clause. The shotgun in this case is used not for a shotgun wedding, but rather for a shotgun divorce. Forced sales are most easily understood in the context of a two-member LLC, although they can work with more members.

Here's how the situation might come up. Let's say that Sonja and Terry are equal co-owners of an LLC. The business is doing well, but the working relationship between the two members is a disaster. Their buyout agreement contains a forced sale clause, under which either member can offer to sell their interest to the other member at a certain price. The member receiving the offer (the offeree) can either (a) accept the offer and buy out the other member, or (b) sell their interest to the other member at the same price. Sonja invokes the forced sale clause and offers to sell her interest to Terry for $100,000. Terry can buy Sonja's interest for $100,000, or sell his interest to Sonja for $100,000. Either way, one member gets bought out and one remains. The membership dispute is resolved by blunt force.

Forced sales can lead to gamesmanship between the disputing members, as each seeks to either buy at the lowest possible price or sell at the highest possible price. In other words, forced sales can add even more friction to a difficult dynamic. Forced sale clauses can be tricky to draft and interpret, so if you want to include forced sale provisions in your operating agreement or buyout agreement, consider consulting a business attorney.

Next Step: A Purchase Agreement

Let's suppose that a buyout has been triggered under Paragraph 2 or Paragraph 3 of the buyout agreement. All the necessary notice and other legal requirements under the buyout agreement were met. The parties (the selling member and the purchaser) have agreed on the purchase price and other terms of the buyout. The next step is to put the deal in writing, in the form of a member interest purchase agreement.

The purchase agreement presented below is a basic form that can be used with a purchase by the company or individual members. When the individual members are purchasing the interests, each member would enter into a purchase agreement with the seller for their portion of the purchase. Whether the closing will be quick or several weeks off, it's good to have a binding purchase agreement that addresses all the major terms and issues.

This purchase agreement and the assignment agreement that follows are not designed for the sale of a membership interest to an outsider (a nonmember), whether the seller is the company or an individual member. Such a sale requires an additional agreement, called a joinder agreement, under which the outside purchaser is admitted as a member and agrees to be bound by the terms of the operating agreement and buyout agreement. We discuss sales to outsiders and joinder agreements later in the chapter.

Boxed sections of the purchase agreement are below, followed by a brief explanation.

Sample LLC Interest Purchase Agreement

This LLC Interest Purchase Agreement (this "Agreement") is entered into as of May 15, 2025 (the "Effective Date") between Carmen Becerra, with an address of 567 Spencer Lane, Hayward, CA 94540 ("Seller"), and 4C Candles LLC, with an address of 1234 Sequoia Ave., Pleasanton, CA 94588 ("Purchaser").

Seller presently owns 40% of the membership interests in 4C Candles LLC, a California limited liability company (the "Company").

Seller desires to sell and Purchaser desires to purchase all of Seller's membership interests in the Company. The parties therefore agree as follows:

Paragraph 1 can be used when purchasing all of the selling member's interest or part of it. If the transaction here were for a partial purchase of one-half of Carmen's interests, "all of Seller's membership interests" would be replaced with "50% of Seller's membership interests" in the Company, equal to 20% of all interests in the Company.

---

1. **Sale of Membership Interests.** Subject to the terms and conditions of this Agreement, Seller agrees to sell and Purchaser agrees to purchase all of Seller's membership interests in the Company (the "Membership Interests"), including all rights and privileges associated with the Membership Interests.

We would expect the members of an LLC to be familiar with transfer restrictions in the company's operating agreement and buyout agreement. They confirm this knowledge in Paragraph 2, and agree that the buyout transaction is being made in accordance with the operating and buyout agreements.

> **2. Transfer Restrictions.** The parties acknowledge that the Membership Interests are subject to the terms and restrictions of the Company's Operating Agreement and a Buyout Agreement between the members and the Company, and stipulate that the purchase being made under this Agreement does not violate any provision of the Operating Agreement, Buyout Agreement, or applicable law.

Paragraph 3 summarizes the price being paid and the form of payment (in this case, part in cash and part in a promissory note).

> **3. Consideration.** The purchase price to be paid by Purchaser for the Membership Interests is $200,000 (the "Purchase Price"), payable as follows: $50,000 upon closing and $150,000 in the form of a 5-year, 5% promissory note payable in annual installments beginning one year from closing.

Paragraph 4 is written to allow substantial flexibility as to the closing. It doesn't specify the closing date, but rather provides a deadline (an outside date) for the closing. The buyout agreement (Paragraph 4) provides that the closing must take place within 60 days after the purchaser provides notice to the seller of the purchaser's intent to exercise a purchase right. For example, if the company notified Carmen of its intent to purchase the interest in question on May 1, the buyout agreement sets the closing as not later than June 30 (60 days). The parties could, of course, agree to waive the 60-day deadline and schedule a closing later than June 30.

Paragraph 4 is also flexible as to the method and mechanics of the closing. The parties could gather, in-person or virtually, for a simultaneous closing. Or the closing could be accomplished with the parties in separate places, exchanging documents and funds electronically or by mail.

4. Closing. The closing of the transaction contemplated by this Agreement (the "Closing") will take place on a date (the "Closing Date") and at a place to be agreed by the parties, but not later than June 30, 2025 without the consent of both parties. The Closing may be conducted simultaneously (in-person or virtually), or by exchange of documents of documents and payments electronically or by overnight courier. The parties agree and acknowledge that no certificate or certificates are necessary to evidence the Transferred Membership Interest that is being transferred under this Agreement, and that the transfer will occur automatically upon the execution of an assignment by the Seller at the Closing.

Paragraph 5 is designed to protect the purchasing party from any third-party claim on the interest being purchased. Paragraphs 5(a) and 5(b) contain assurances from the seller that interest being purchased and sold is free and clear of any such third-party claims. These assurances come in the form of representations and warranties.

Representations are statements that, to the best of the representing party's knowledge, something is true. A warranty is a guarantee that something is true. A representation is breached when the representing party misrepresents the truth of something. A warranty is breached when the statement in question is not true at the time the agreement is entered into or ceases to be true thereafter, without regard for the representing party's knowledge. In Paragraphs 5(a) and 5(b), the seller is guaranteeing (warranting) that they own the interests, that they own them free and clear, and that no one else has the authority to sell the interests.

Paragraph 5 also includes an obligation on the seller to notify the purchaser if any representation ceases to be true between the date of the purchase agreement and the closing.

5. **Representations and Warranties of Seller; Indemnification and Release.** Seller hereby represents and warrants that the following statements are true and correct as of the date of this Agreement and will be true and correct as of the Closing Date. Seller will notify Purchaser promptly if Seller learns between the date of this Agreement and the Closing that any representation made here has ceased to be true.

   a. **Authority; Capacity.** Seller has full power, authority, and capacity to execute and deliver, and to perform its duties and obligations under this Agreement.

   b. **Title.** Seller is the lawful owner of, and has good and marketable title to, the Membership Interests, free of any and all liens, restrictions, or claims of any kind, except for restrictions contained in the Operating Agreement and Buyout Agreement of the Company.

The indemnification provision of Paragraph 5(c) means that the seller must reimburse the purchaser for any loss suffered to a third party due to a breach of a warranty by the seller. For example, let's say that the seller doesn't disclose a lien that a creditor has on the seller's interest, and that the purchaser, not knowing, goes through with the buyout. The lien creditor could sue the purchaser over the transaction and win a judgment against the purchaser. The loss is attributable to the seller's breach of warranty (they guaranteed the purchaser that there were no liens against the interest), so the seller must indemnify (reimburse) the purchaser for the loss.

Under the release provisions of Paragraph 5(c), the seller is releasing the purchaser from any liability that attaches to the interest being sold prior to the closing. In other words, if the liability attached before the interest was transferred, the seller, not the purchaser, is on the hook.

   c. **Indemnification and Release by Seller.** Seller agrees to indemnify and release Purchaser from and against any liabilities arising from or caused by a breach of any representation or warranty made by Seller in this Agreement, and any liability related to or involving the Membership Interests, including any tax liability, arising or incurred on or prior to the Closing Date.

Paragraph 6 is designed to protect the seller. Paragraph 6(a) assures the seller that the purchaser (the company or an individual member) has the authority to enter into the transaction, including that all necessary member consents have been obtained. It would not be unusual for the selling member to request a copy of a document showing the consent of the other members (the meeting minutes showing the vote to approve the buyout, or the written consent of the other members to the buyout if no vote was taken at a meeting).

> **6. Representations and Warranties of Purchaser; Indemnification by Purchaser.** Purchaser hereby represents and warrants to Seller that the following statements are true and correct as of the date of this Agreement and will be true and correct as of the Closing Date.
>
> a. **Authority; Capacity.** Purchaser has full power and authority to enter into this Agreement, including any necessary consents from the members of the company, and to perform its obligations under this Agreement.

The indemnification and release provisions of Paragraph 6(b) are the reverse images of Paragraph 5(b) above. Under Paragraph 6(b), the purchaser will reimburse the seller for any third party losses that result from the breach of a purchaser's warranty. For example, let's say that the company is the purchaser and didn't have the necessary unanimous consent of the other members to make the buyout. If a dissenting member sues the seller over the buyout and earns a judgment against the seller, the purchaser must indemnify the seller, because the loss was attributable to the breach of the purchaser's warranty that it had the authority to make the purchase.

The release under Paragraph 6(b) means that the purchaser, not the seller, is on the hook for any liabilities relating to the purchased interest that arise after the closing. The ownership interest is transferred to the purchaser at the closing, so it makes sense that the purchaser would take responsibility for liabilities that arise after the transfer.

b. Indemnification and Release by Purchaser. Purchaser agrees to indemnify and release Seller from and against any liabilities arising from or caused by a breach of any representation or warranty made by Purchaser in this Agreement, and any liability related to or involving the Membership Interests, including any tax liability, arising or incurred after the Closing Date.

Paragraphs 7-14 are standard (boilerplate) provisions that are common to most business agreements and that have been explained above and in other chapters. Please review those previous explanations if you're unsure about any of these provisions.

7. **Entire Agreement.** This Agreement constitutes the entire agreement and understanding between Purchaser and Seller with respect to the subject matter of this Agreement and supersedes all prior under-standings, agreements, or communications between the parties related to the subject matter of this Agreement.

8. **Binding Effect.** This Agreement is binding upon, and shall inure to the benefit of, Purchaser, Seller, and their respective heirs, legal represen-tatives, successors, and permitted assigns.

9. **Assignment.** Neither party will assign any of its rights under this Agreement without the prior written consent of the other party.

10. **Multiple Counterparts.** This Agreement may be executed in one or more counterparts, each of which shall be deemed an original but all of which together will constitute one instrument.

11. **Notices.** Any notices or communications required or permitted to be given by this Agreement must be given in writing, and be personally delivered or sent by certified mail, express shipment, or electronically with receipt confirmed. A notice is to be sent to the addresses of the receiving party as written above, or to an email address provided by the receiving party.

12. **Amendments.** This Agreement may be amended only by a writing signed by both parties.

13. Severability. If any provision of this Agreement is determined by a court or arbitrator to be invalid, unenforceable, or otherwise ineffective, that provision will be severed from the rest of the Agreement and the remaining provisions will continue to be effective and enforceable.

14. Governing Law. This Agreement is to be governed and interpreted according to the law of the state of [*name of state*].

So Agreed:

4C Candles LLC (Purchaser):   Carmen Becerra (Seller):

By: _____   By: _____

Name: Constance Li, for 4C Candles LLC   Name: Carmen Becerra

Title: Member/Manager

Closing: Assignment of the Interest

The closing on our buyout transaction is accomplished by the following simple assignment of the interest being sold and purchased. It references the purchase agreement and transfers the interest according to the terms of that agreement. The assignment affirms that the representations and warranties made in the purchase agreement are still true, and executes the releases agreed to in the purchase agreement. Specifically, the seller/assignor releases the purchaser/assignee from liabilities and claims incurred prior to the assignment, and the purchaser/assignee releases the seller/assignor from liabilities and claims arising after the assignment.

In the sample assignment below, if the LLC was not the purchaser/assignee, it would consent to the assignment by signing in the "Consent of LLC" of LLC. In the assignment below, the LLC is the purchaser/assignee, and so no separate consent is needed.

FORMS

A sample assignment of LLC interest is shown below. A complete sample version is included in Appendix B. A blank version is included in Appendix C and is downloadable from this book's companion page. See Appendix A for the link.

Sample Assignment of LLC Interest

THIS ASSIGNMENT OF LLC INTEREST ("Assignment") is made by Carmen Becerra ("Assignor") to 4C Candles LLC ("Assignee") as of June 20, 2025 (the "Effective Date").

1. **Assignment.** Pursuant to a Membership Interest Purchase Agreement between the parties, dated May 15, 2025 (the "Purchase Agreement"), and in return for the Purchase Price and other valuable consideration set forth in the Purchase Agreement, the receipt of which Assignor hereby acknowledges, the Assignor irrevocably and unconditionally assigns a 40% Membership Interest (the "Assigned Interest") in 4C Candles LLC, a limited liability company (the "LLC") to Assignee.

2. **Representations and Warranties.** The parties reaffirm the representations and warranties made in the Purchase Agreement.

3. **LLC Consent.** If the LLC is not the Assignee, the LLC approves the transfer of the Assigned Interest from Assignor to Assignee.

4. **Releases.** The Assignor releases the Assignee from all liabilities and claims arising from the Assigned Interest prior to the date of this Assignment. The Assignee releases the Assignor from all liabilities and claims arising from the Assigned Interest on or after the date of this Assignment. The Assignor and the LLC release each other from all liabilities and claims arising under the LLC and Assignor's ownership interest therein.

So Agreed:

Carmen Becerra (Assignor):

By: _____

Name: Carmen Becerra

4C Candles LLC (Assignee):

By: _____

Name: Constance Li, for 4C Candles LLC

Title: Member/Manager

Selling Outside the Company: Joinder Agreements

As mentioned at the beginning of the chapter, a sale of an LLC interest to an outsider (nonmembers), whether by a member or by the company, requires a joinder agreement. The joinder agreement can be integrated into the assignment or can exist as a separate document. The main purpose of the joinder agreement is twofold: For the other members to admit the outside purchaser/assignee as a member of the LLC, and for the new member to agree to be bound by the company's operating agreement and (if applicable) buyout agreement. The joinder agreement should be signed by all the members. The operating agreement and buyout agreement should be amended to add the new member and, if the selling member sold their entire interest, remove the selling member. The amended operating agreement and buyout agreement should be signed by all the members.

PART

D

Maintaining Your LLC:
Legal and Tax Compliance

Annual Reports and Other Legal Filings

FORMS IN THIS CHAPTER

Accessing state government forms in this chapter. State government forms used to illustrate particular legal and tax filings are available on your state's appropriate state agency website.

M ost states require some sort of annual or biannual report from LLCs, and they also charge a fee for you to maintain your LLC in good standing. Annual reporting takes many forms, as explored in the sections on annual reporting requirements below. States also require LLCs to amend their articles when the information contained in the articles changes. We explore a range of state LLC filings in this chapter, including:

- annual reports
- franchise tax filings
- articles of amendment
- articles of restatement
- change of registered agent, and
- articles of conversion (to convert an LLC to another entity or another entity to an LLC).

Beginning in 2024, the federal government, specifically the U.S. Department of the Treasury's Financial Crimes Enforcement Network (FinCEN), added another chore to your list. FinCEN imposed a new beneficial ownership interest (BOI) reporting requirement on small entities, including LLCs. We also take up BOI reporting in this chapter.

Annual Reports and Franchise Tax Reports

In order to maintain the good standing of your LLC, most states require you to file a periodic report with the secretary of state's office, or franchise tax board, or both. In some states, the report must be filed annually (an annual report), while in other states the report is filed every two years (a biennial report). The report might also be known as a renewal, statement of information, or other similar name. For simplicity's sake, we'll refer to all such regular filings as annual reports. Most states also charge an annual fee that you must pay with the annual report.

Some states, including Delaware and Texas, don't require an annual report, but instead require a franchise tax filing that doubles as an annual report. We discuss franchise taxes below. A handful of states, including Arizona, Missouri, New Mexico, Ohio, and South Carolina, don't require an annual report, an annual fee, or a franchise tax. Check your state's laws to determine your LLC's annual reporting and fee requirements.

Annual Reports

Annual reports, unless they're part of a franchise tax filing, tend to be informational and simple. They usually contain the same information as the articles that you filed to form the company (and might have amended since—see the discussion of article amendments below), including the names and address of the business, the registered agent, and managers. Annual reports are the state's way of making sure that the information on your LLC in its business database is up-to-date.

Most states that require an annual report also charge an annual fee to be paid with the annual report filing. An annual fee is a filing fee that you submit with your annual report. It can be less than, the same as, or more than the fee you paid when you filed your articles. The Massachusetts Annual Report form is included below. It is nearly identical to the Massachusetts Articles of Organization (not reproduced here), which is logical, since the purpose of the annual report is to confirm (and if necessary, update) the information in the articles. In Massachusetts' case, annual LLC reports are also a revenue source, at $500 per report.

Massachusetts Annual LLC Report

D   𝕿𝖍𝖊 𝕮𝖔𝖒𝖒𝖔𝖓𝖜𝖊𝖆𝖑𝖙𝖍 𝖔𝖋 𝕸𝖆𝖘𝖘𝖆𝖈𝖍𝖚𝖘𝖊𝖙𝖙𝖘

William Francis Galvin
Secretary of the Commonwealth
One Ashburton Place, Room 1717, Boston, Massachusetts 02108-1512

Limited Liability Company Annual Report
(General Laws Chapter 156C, Section 12)

Federal Identification No.: _____   Year: _____

(1a) The exact name of the limited liability company:

_____

(1b) The exact name of the limited liability company as amended:

_____

(2a) Location of its principal office:

_____

(2b) The street address of the office in the commonwealth at which its records will be maintained:

(3) The general character of the business:

_____

(4) Latest date of dissolution, if specified: _____

(5) The name and street address of the resident agent in the commonwealth:

(6) The name and business address of each manager, if any:

Massachusetts Annual LLC Report (page 2)

(7) The name and business address of the person(s) in addition to manager(s) authorized to execute documents filed with the Corporations Division, and at least one person shall be named if there are no managers:

(8) The name and business address of the person(s) authorized to execute, acknowledge, deliver and record any recordable instrument purporting to affect an interest in real property.

(9) Additional matters:

Signed by *(by at least one authorized signatory)*: _____

Franchise Taxes

Some states charge a franchise tax and require a franchise tax report, instead of or in addition to an annual report and annual fee. Franchise taxes are also known as privilege taxes—you're paying for the privilege of continuing to operate your business in the state (and maintain your limited liability). Some franchise taxes are flat fees, like an annual report fee, but others are variable and based on an accounting formula, such as a percentage of revenue, profits, or assets.

The Arkansas LLC Franchise Tax Report form is shown below as an example of a franchise tax report and payment that looks like an annual report with an annual fee—the information requested is the same information as can be found in the company's articles and the "tax" is a flat amount for all filers.

By contrast, a franchise tax filing in Texas includes a Franchise Tax Report for calculating the tax owed (below) and a Public Information Report (below). Filers who qualify can use an EZ form, or a "No Tax Due" form, but even those forms are more involved than a simple informational filing with a flat fee payment. Other states' franchise tax reports are more complicated than the Texas report. The Tennessee Franchise and Excise Tax return (not reproduced here) runs nine pages and includes multiple factors for calculating franchise and excise taxes.

If your state imposes a formula-based franchise tax, especially if the report/return itself is complicated, consider having an accountant prepare your franchise tax report.

Arkansas LLC Franchise Tax Report

John Thurston, Arkansas Secretary of State

Filing Number: _____

AMENDED LLC FRANCHISE TAX REPORT 2024

For the year ending 12/31/2023

Sign in <u>black</u> ink and mail to the address listed below.

1. Business Name and Address:

Name: _____

Address: _____

City, State, Zip: _____

2. Correct any of the below information, if needed:

Tax Contact Name: _____

Address: _____

Address 2: _____

City, State, Zip: _____

Phone # of Tax Contact: _____

E-mail Address: _____

**ALL INFORMATION IN SECTIONS 3-5
BELOW ARE REQUIRED**

3. Registered Agent Information:

Name: _____

Address: _____

Address 2: _____

City, State, Zip: _____

4. Principal Office Information (in Arkansas):

Address: _____

City, State, Zip: _____

5. Limited Liability Company Management is (Select One):

☐ MEMBER(S)   ☐ MANAGER(S)

Please provide current names:

Member/Manager: _____

Member/Manager: _____

Member/Manager: _____

Member/Manager: _____

Member/Manager: _____

Tax Preparer: _____

Federal Tax ID#: _____

Nature of Business: _____

ALL LIMITED LIABILITY COMPANIES PAY $150.00.

I declare, under the penalties of perjury, that the foregoing statements are true to the best of my knowledge and belief.

Executed this _____ day of _____, _____
                     (Day)   (Month)   (Year)

Print Name_____ Signature_____
         Must be printed in black ink by: Member/Manager or Tax Preparer (Listed In 5)   Must be signed in black ink by: Member/Manager or Tax Preparer (Listed In 5)

Phone: 501-682-3409 or Toll Free: 888-233-0325
Mail to: Business and Commercial Services Division • P.O. Box 8014 • Little Rock, Arkansas 72203-8014

Rev. 01/24

Texas Franchise Tax Report

Comptroller of Public Accounts FORM 05-158-A (Rev.9-16/9)

Texas Franchise Tax Report - Page 1

■ **Tcode** 13250 Annual

■ Taxpayer number		■ Report year	Due date	
		2 0 2 2	05/16/2022	

Taxpayer name	Secretary of State file number or Comptroller file number
Mailing address	

City	State	Country	ZIP code plus 4	Blacken circle if the address has changed ■ ○

Blacken circle if this is a combined report ■ ○   Blacken circle if Total Revenue is adjusted for Tiered Partnership Election, see instructions ■ ○

Is this entity a corporation, limited liability company, professional association, limited partnership or financial institution? ○ Yes ○ No

** If not twelve months, see instructions for annualized revenue

	m m d d y y		m m d d y y	SIC code	NAICS code
Accounting year begin date**		Accounting year end date ■			

REVENUE (Whole dollars only)

1.	**Gross receipts or sales**	1. ■		0 0
2.	**Dividends**	2. ■		0 0
3.	**Interest**	3. ■		0 0
4.	**Rents** (can be negative amount)	4. ■		0 0
5.	**Royalties**	5. ■		0 0
6.	**Gains/losses** (can be negative amount)	6. ■		0 0
7.	**Other income** (can be negative amount)	7. ■		0 0
8.	**Total gross revenue** (Add items 1 thru 7)	8. ■		0 0
9.	**Exclusions from gross revenue** (see instructions)	9. ■		0 0
10.	**TOTAL REVENUE** (item 8 minus item 9 if less than zero, enter 0)	10. ■		0 0

COST OF GOODS SOLD (Whole dollars only)

11.	Cost of goods sold	11. ■		0 0
12.	Indirect or administrative overhead costs (Limited to 4%)	12. ■		0 0
13.	Other (see instructions)	13. ■		0 0
14.	TOTAL COST OF GOODS SOLD (Add items 11 thru 13)	14. ■		0 0

COMPENSATION (Whole dollars only)

15.	Wages and cash compensation	15. ■		0 0
16.	Employee benefits	16. ■		0 0
17.	Other (see instructions)	17. ■		0 0
18.	TOTAL COMPENSATION (Add items 15 thru 17)	18. ■		0 0

Texas Comptroller Official Use Only

VE/DE	○
PM Date	

Texas Franchise Tax Report (page 2)

Comptroller of Public Accounts FORM 05-158-B (Rev.9-16/9)

Texas Franchise Tax Report - Page 2

■ Tcode 13251 Annual

■ Taxpayer number	■ Report year	Due date	Taxpayer name
	2 0 2 2	05/16/2022	

MARGIN *(Whole dollars only)*

19. **70% revenue** *(item 10 x .70)* 19. ■ ☐ 0 0

20. **Revenue less COGS** *(item 10 - item 14)* 20. ■ ☐ 0 0

21. **Revenue less compensation** *(item 10 - item 18)* 21. ■ ☐ 0 0

22. **Revenue less $1 million** *(item 10 - $1,000,000)* 22. ■ ☐ 0 0

23. **MARGIN** *(see instructions)* 23. ■ ☐ 0 0

APPORTIONMENT FACTOR

24. **Gross receipts in Texas** *(Whole dollars only)* 24. ■ ☐ 0 0

25. **Gross receipts everywhere** *(Whole dollars only)* 25. ■ ☐ 0 0

26. **APPORTIONMENT FACTOR** *(Divide item 24 by item 25, round to 4 decimal places)* 26. ■ ☐

TAXABLE MARGIN *(Whole dollars only)*

27. **Apportioned margin** *(Multiply item 23 by item 26)* 27. ■ ☐ 0 0

28. **Allowable deductions** *(see instructions)* 28. ■ ☐ 0 0

29. **TAXABLE MARGIN** *(item 27 minus item 28)* 29. ■ ☐ 0 0

TAX DUE

30. **Tax rate** *(see instructions for determining the appropriate tax rate)* 30. ■ ☐

31. **Tax due** *(Multiply item 29 by the tax rate in item 30) (Dollars and cents)* 31. ■ ☐

TAX ADJUSTMENTS *(Dollars and cents) (Do not include prior payments)*

32. **Tax credits** *(item 23 from Form 05-160)* 32. ■ ☐

33. **Tax due before discount** *(item 31 minus item 32)* 33. ■ ☐

34. **Discount** *(see instructions, applicable to report years 2008 and 2009)* 34. ■ ☐

TOTAL TAX DUE *(Dollars and cents)*

35. **TOTAL TAX DUE** *(item 33 minus item 34)* 35. ■ ☐

Do not include payment if item 35 is less than $1,000 or if annualized total revenue is less than the no tax due threshold (see instructions). If the entity makes a tiered partnership election, ANY amount in item 35 is due. Complete Form 05-170 if making a payment.

Print or type name	Area code and phone number ( ) -

I declare that the information in this document and any attachments is true and correct to the best of my knowledge and belief.

sign here ▶   Date

Mail original to:
Texas Comptroller of Public Accounts
P.O. Box 149348
Austin, TX 78714-9348

Instructions for each report year are online at www.comptroller.texas.gov/taxes/franchise/forms/. If you have any questions, call 1-800-252-1381.

Texas Comptroller Official Use Only

VE/DE	○
PM Date	

Page 2 of 2

Texas Franchise Tax Public Information Report

Comptroller of Public Accounts FORM 05-102 (Rev.9-15/33)

Texas Franchise Tax Public Information Report

To be filed by Corporations, Limited Liability Companies (LLC), Limited Partnerships (LP), Professional Associations (PA) and Financial Institutions

■ **Tcode** 13196 Franchise

■ Taxpayer number	■ Report year	
	2 0 2 2	**You have certain rights** under Chapter 552 and 559, Government Code, to review, request and correct information we have on file about you. Contact us at 1-800-252-1381.

Taxpayer name	
	■ ○ Blacken circle if the mailing address has changed.
Mailing address	Secretary of State (SOS) file number or Comptroller file number

City	State	ZIP code plus 4	

○ Blacken circle if there are currently no changes from previous year; if no information is displayed, complete the applicable information in Sections A, B and C.

Principal office

Principal place of business

You must report officer, director, member, general partner and manager information as of the date you complete this report.

Please sign below! **This report must be signed to satisfy franchise tax requirements.**

1000000000000

SECTION A Name, title and mailing address of each officer, director, member, general partner or manager.

Name	Title	Director		m m d d y y
		○ YES	Term expiration	
Mailing address	City		State	ZIP Code

Name	Title	Director		m m d d y y
		○ YES	Term expiration	
Mailing address	City		State	ZIP Code

Name	Title	Director		m m d d y y
		○ YES	Term expiration	
Mailing address	City		State	ZIP Code

SECTION B Enter information for each corporation, LLC, LP, PA or financial institution, if any, in which this entity owns an interest of 10 percent or more.

Name of owned (subsidiary) corporation, LLC, LP, PA or financial institution	State of formation	Texas SOS file number, if any	Percentage of ownership
Name of owned (subsidiary) corporation, LLC, LP, PA or financial institution	State of formation	Texas SOS file number, if any	Percentage of ownership

SECTION C Enter information for each corporation, LLC, LP, PA or financial institution, if any, that owns an interest of 10 percent or more in this entity.

Name of owned (parent) corporation, LLC, LP, PA or financial institution	State of formation	Texas SOS file number, if any	Percentage of ownership

Registered agent and registered office currently on file (see instructions if you need to make changes)

Agent: You must make a filing with the Secretary of State to change registered agent, registered office or general partner information.

Office:	City	State	ZIP Code

The information on this form is required by Section 171.203 of the Tax Code for each corporation, LLC, LP, PA or financial institution that files a Texas Franchise Tax Report. Use additional sheets for Sections A, B and C, if necessary. The information will be available for public inspection.

I declare that the information in this document and any attachments is true and correct to the best of my knowledge and belief, as of the date below, and that a copy of this report has been mailed to each person named in this report who is an officer, director, member, general partner or manager and who is not currently employed by this or a related corporation, LLC, LP, PA or financial institution.

sign here ▶	Title	Date	Area code and phone number ( ) -

Texas Comptroller Official Use Only

VE/DE ○	PIR IND ○

Deadlines for Filing and Consequences of Not Filing

The due dates for annual reports and franchise tax reports vary among states. Some states have a uniform date for all reports, such as May 1. In other states, the filing deadline is the anniversary date or month of the LLC's formation. Be sure you know the due date for your annual report or franchise tax report.

If you fail to file your annual report or franchise tax report on time, you might be able to take advantage of a grace period or a late filing with a penalty (if your state offers them). Eventually, though, failure to file the required report(s) or make the required payment(s) can result in the state administratively dissolving (terminating) your LLC, thereby ending your personal limited liability. If your LLC has a bank loan or insurance policy, the termination of your LLC could put you in default on the loan or cause you to lose insurance coverage.

Interim Filings: Amended Articles and Change in Registered Agent

When certain information about your LLC changes between annual reports, you need to update your LLC's record with the state when the information changes. If your state doesn't require annual reporting, you must still update the information when it changes. The types of changes that require immediate updating include a name or address change for the LLC, a change in the type of management (for example, from being member-managed to manager-managed), changes in the identities or business addresses of managers, or a change in the name or address of your registered agent. You update the information by filing amended articles (known as articles of amendment), or, in the case of a change in registered agent or the registered agent's address, a change in registered agent form.

Amending Articles

Articles of amendment forms tend to be simple and self-explanatory, although they vary by state. The articles of amendment for Florida and New Hampshire are included below to show two different approaches to the form. The Florida form offers spaces specifically for certain changes—LLC name or address (Section A), registered agent (Section B), and managers or authorized members (Section C)—along with a blank section for other changes (Section D). The New Hampshire form, which is called a certificate of amendment, includes just a blank space for the "text of each amendment."

When you file articles of amendment, they join your articles of organization, any previously filed annual reports, and any previous amendments in your record in the state's business database. For example, let's say you filed your articles of organization in May 2023 and your first annual report in May 2024. In September 2024, your LLC changes from being member-managed to manager-managed, which prompts you to file articles of amendment. Someone looking up your business record in October 2024 would see all three filings (articles of organization, annual report, and articles of amendment). Your original articles and all amendments remain in your record unless you consolidate them by filing a restatement of your articles. We discuss restated articles below.

Changing the Name or Address of Your Registered Agent

As discussed in Chapter 2, all states require business entities, including LLCs, to have a registered agent—a person or business that can be served with papers in a lawsuit or receive certain correspondence from the state. States are very strict about this requirement, to the point that any change in the identity or address or your registered agent must be reported to the state immediately. You can't wait until your next annual report to update registered agent information when that information changes.

Florida Articles of Amendment

**ARTICLES OF AMENDMENT
TO
ARTICLES OF ORGANIZATION
OF**

_____
(Name of the Limited Liability Company as it now appears on our records.)
(A Florida Limited Liability Company)

The Articles of Organization for this Limited Liability Company were filed on _____ and assigned

Florida document number _____.

This amendment is submitted to amend the following:

A. If amending name, enter the new name of the limited liability company here:

_____
The new name must be distinguishable and contain the words "Limited Liability Company," the designation "LLC" or the abbreviation "L.L.C."

Enter new principal offices address, if applicable:

(Principal office address MUST BE A STREET ADDRESS)

Enter new mailing address, if applicable:

(Mailing address MAY BE A POST OFFICE BOX)

B. If amending the registered agent and/or registered office address on our records, enter the name of the new registered agent and/or the new registered office address here:

Name of New Registered Agent: _____

New Registered Office Address: _____
                                                  Enter Florida street address

_____, **Florida** _____
                    City   _Zip Code_

New Registered Agent's Signature, if changing Registered Agent:

I hereby accept the appointment as registered agent and agree to act in this capacity. I further agree to comply with the provisions of all statutes relative to the proper and complete performance of my duties, and I am familiar with and accept the obligations of my position as registered agent as provided for in Chapter 605, F.S. Or, if this document is being filed to merely reflect a change in the registered office address, I hereby confirm that the limited liability company has been notified in writing of this change.

_____
If Changing Registered Agent, Signature of New Registered Agent

Florida Articles of Amendment (page 2)

C. If amending Authorized Person(s) authorized to manage, <u>enter the title, name, and address of each person being added or removed from our records</u>:

MGR = Manager
AMBR = Authorized Member

<u>Title</u>	<u>Name</u>	<u>Address</u>	<u>Type of Action</u>
_____	_____	_____	☐ Add
		_____	☐ Remove
		_____	☐ Change
_____	_____	_____	☐ Add
		_____	☐ Remove
		_____	☐ Change
_____	_____	_____	☐ Add
		_____	☐ Remove
		_____	☐ Change
_____	_____	_____	☐ Add
		_____	☐ Remove
		_____	☐ Change
_____	_____	_____	☐ Add
		_____	☐ Remove
		_____	☐ Change
_____	_____	_____	☐ Add
		_____	☐ Remove
		_____	☐ Change

Florida Articles of Amendment (page 3)

D. If amending any other information, enter change(s) here: *(Attach additional sheets, if necessary.)*

_____

_____

_____

_____

_____

_____

_____

_____

_____

_____

_____

_____

_____

_____

_____

_____

_____

_____

E. Effective date, if other than the date of filing: _____ **(optional)**
(If an effective date is listed, the date must be specific and cannot be prior to date of filing or more than 90 days after filing.) Pursuant to 605.0207 (3)(b)
Note: If the date inserted in this block does not meet the applicable statutory filing requirements, this date will not be listed as the document's effective date on the Department of State's records.

If the record specifies a delayed effective date, but not an effective time, at 12:01 a.m. on the earlier of: (b) The 90th day after the record is filed.

Dated _____ , _____ .

_____
Signature of a member or authorized representative of a member

_____
Typed or printed name of signee

Filing Fee: $25.00

New Hampshire Certificate of Amendment

State of New Hampshire

Filing fee: $35.00
Use black print or type.

Form LLC-3
RSA 304-C:34

LIMITED LIABILITY COMPANY CERTIFICATE OF AMENDMENT
TO THE CERTIFICATE OF FORMATION

PURSUANT TO THE PROVISIONS of Chapter 304-C, Section 34 of the New Hampshire Revised Statutes Annotated, the undersigned submits the following Certificate of Amendment:

FIRST: The name of the limited liability company is _____

_____.

SECOND: The text of each amendment is:

[If more space is needed, attach additional sheet(s).]

*Signature: _____

Print or type name: _____

*Title: _____
(Enter "manager" or "member")

Date signed: _____

* Signature and title of person signing for the limited liability company. <u>MUST BE SIGNED BY A **MANAGER OF THE LIMITED LIABILITY COMPANY. IF NO MANAGER, IT MUST BE SIGNED BY A MEMBER**</u>. (If the limited liability company is in the hands of a receiver, executor, or other court appointed fiduciary, trustee, or other fiduciary, it must be signed by that fiduciary.)

DISCLAIMER: All documents filed with the Corporation Division become public records and will be available for public inspection in either tangible or electronic form.

Mailing Address - Corporation Division, NH Dept. of State, 107 N Main St, Rm 204, Concord, NH 03301-4989
Physical Location - State House Annex, 3rd Floor, Rm 317, 25 Capitol St, Concord, NH

Form LLC-3 (9/2015)

Many states have a specific form for changing registered agent information. The Massachusetts Statement of Change of Resident Agent/ Resident Office form is included below. (Recall that the terms resident agent and registered agent are interchangeable.) The form calls for the address of the current resident, the new address, the name of the current resident agent, and then the name of the new resident agent (if applicable). So, true to its name, the form can be used when the current resident is being retained but their address has changed, or when a new resident agent is appointed.

Other states handle changes in registered agent information through articles of amendment (not a separate form). In California, a change in registered agent or the agent's address necessitates the filing of an interim Statement of Information (that's the name of California's biennial LLC report—not reproduced here). Check with your state to see how changes in registered agent information are reported.

Restating Articles

If your LLC has filed multiple amendments to its articles of organization, you might want to consolidate those amendments by restating your articles. When you restate your articles, you replace your original articles of organization and any subsequent amendments with new articles that incorporate all the amendments. The Oklahoma Restated Articles of Organization form is included below. The restated articles form is nearly identical to the Oklahoma Articles of Organization form (not reproduced here). Once restated articles have been filed, the original articles and any prior amendments are superseded and can be ignored by anyone viewing an LLC's business record.

Massachusetts Change of Resident Agent/Resident Office

DF 𝕿𝖍𝖊 𝕮𝖔𝖒𝖒𝖔𝖓𝖜𝖊𝖆𝖑𝖙𝖍 𝖔𝖋 𝕸𝖆𝖘𝖘𝖆𝖈𝖍𝖚𝖘𝖊𝖙𝖙𝖘

William Francis Galvin
Secretary of the Commonwealth
One Ashburton Place, Room 1717, Boston, Massachusetts 02108-1512

Limited Liability Company
Statement of Change of
Resident Agent/Resident Office
(General Laws Chapter 156C Section 5A and Section 51)

(1) Exact name of limited liability company:

_____

(2) Current resident agent office address:

(3) New resident agent office address:

Current resident agent: _____

Resident agent will *(check appropriate box)*:

☐ change to _____ .

                                           (name of new resident agent)

☐ remain the same.

This certificate is effective at the time and on the date approved by the Division.

Signed by *(signature of authorized person)*: _____ ,

on this _____ day of _____ , _____ .

Consent of resident agent:

I, _____

resident agent of the above limited liability company, consent to my appointment as resident agent pursuant to G.L. Chapter 156C Section 5A and Section 51.

Oklahoma Restated Articles of Organization

RESTATED
ARTICLES OF ORGANIZATION
(Oklahoma Limited Liability Company)

Filing Fee: $50.00

TO: OKLAHOMA SECRETARY OF STATE
421 N.W. 13th, Suite 210
Oklahoma City, Oklahoma 73103
(405) 522-2520

I hereby execute the following articles for the purpose of **restating** the articles of organization in their entirety for:

_____,

an Oklahoma limited liability company, pursuant to the provisions of Title 18, Section 2011:

1. Name of the limited liability company:

_____

(**Note:** The name **must** contain either the words **limited liability company** or **limited company** or the abbreviations **LLC, LC, L.L.C. or L.C.** The word **limited** may be abbreviated as **Ltd.** and the word **company** may be abbreviated as **Co.**)

2. Date of filing of its original articles of organization: _____

3. Street address of its principal place of business, wherever located:

_____

Street address	City	State	Zip Code

(P.O. BOXES ARE **NOT** ACCEPTABLE)

4. **E-MAIL** address of the primary contact for the registered business:

❖ Notice of the Annual Certificate will **ONLY** be sent to the limited liability company at its last known electronic mail address of record.

5. **NAME** and street address of the registered agent for service of process in the state of Oklahoma:

❖ The registered agent **shall** be the limited liability company itself, an individual resident of Oklahoma, **or** a domestic or qualified foreign corporation, limited liability company, or limited partnership.

Oklahoma
_____

Name	Street Address	City	State	Zip Code

(P.O. BOXES ARE **NOT** ACCEPTABLE)

6. Term of existence: _____

❖ You may state either **perpetual**, a set number of years, **or** a future effective expiration date. Perpetual means continuous.

The restated articles of organization must be signed by a manager of the limited liability company.

• Signature of Manager: _____ Dated: _____

• Printed Name: _____

(SOS FORM 0086-07/12)

Converting an LLC to a Corporation

It seems safe to say that most businesses that form as LLCs remain as LLCs through their lives. But sometimes, it makes sense to change the structure of a business from an LLC to a corporation. The main reasons for converting to a corporation relate to the ownership (equity) and management (governance) structure of the business, not its tax treatment. We discuss those reasons below, before transitioning to an exploration of the legal mechanics (including state forms) of converting an LLC to a corporation.

Why LLCs Become Corporations: Equity and Governance

The equity (ownership) structure of an LLC is based on percentage interests. The equity structure of a corporation is based on shares of stock in the corporation. LLC member interests work well in a partnership-like structure, where percentage interests can easily be used for decision-making and profit-allocation purposes, and where the owners are generally involved in managing the business. The corporate equity structure works better than the LLC equity structure when owners are seeking to raise capital for the business, or want to offer equity incentives to employees, or want a more formal ownership and management structure.

Equity Considerations

Outside investors, at least those who don't qualify as friends or family, want the corporate structure, which brings with it these features:
- ownership stated in shares, including the ability to have multiple classes of stock
- ownership (shareholders) separate from management oversight (directors) separate from day-to-day management (officers), and
- certain formalities, such as directors' and shareholders' meetings and other formal processes for making and documenting ownership and management decisions.

Outside investors (angel investors and venture capitalists) also want corporate taxation. They don't want profits and losses of the companies they invest in flowing through automatically to their personal tax returns.

In terms of offering equity to employees, it's possible to structure an equity incentive plan with LLC membership interests, but such plans are much more common among corporations. Corporations can grant equity through stock options or restricted corporate shares, and the tax implications of corporate equity incentives are more straightforward than the taxation of LLC interests received as compensation.

If a business knows from the outset that it's likely to seek outside investors or have an equity incentive plan, it should probably form as a corporation and skip the LLC stage. But if the business was formed as an LLC and wants now to become a corporation, for whatever reason, it can be converted to a corporation.

Governance Considerations

One of the attractions of LLCs is that they usually require less formality than corporations when it comes to the ownership and management. For example, corporations are generally required under state law to hold annual shareholders' and directors' meetings, while LLCs are not required to hold formal member or manager meetings. Also, even when a corporation is closely-held (owned by a few people), and even when every shareholder is also a director and officer, the three roles are distinct, with separate responsibilities and authority. Shareholders elect the directors, to whom they entrust the management of the company. The directors appoint the officers, who run the company on a day-to-day basis. The directors are responsible to the shareholders for the performance of the company and the value of their shares. The directors and officers are identified in the corporation's articles of incorporation, and the decision-making processes for the company are spelled out in the corporate bylaws.

LLCs can operate more informally. As mentioned, they are not required by law to hold ownership or management meetings. LLCs are generally not required by law to have an operating agreement, while corporations are required to have bylaws. The members of an LLC can decide on the rights and responsibilities of members and managers, within fewer state-imposed parameters.

The members of an LLC might on their own, or with a push from potential outside investors, opt for the more formal structure of a corporation.

Changing Tax Status Without Converting to a Corporation

LLCs don't normally convert to corporations for tax reasons. If operating as an LLC works for a business, but the business doesn't want to be taxed as a partnership, it can elect to be taxed as a C corporation or S corporation without giving up the LLC form. We explore tax elections in Chapter 4.

Of course, when an LLC that's taxed as a partnership is converted to a corporation, it's taxed as a corporation after the conversion.

Making the Conversion: Three Ways to Convert an LLC to a Corporation

Once you decide to convert your LLC to a corporation, you'll need to choose a legal method for making of making the conversion. States generally recognize three methods for converting an LLC to a corporation, although the specific options vary by state. In the sections below, we explain these methods: the "statutory conversion," a "statutory merger," and a "nonstatutory (formation/dissolution) conversion." After exploring the three methods for making the legal conversion, we discuss how the IRS treats one type of conversion.

> **RESOURCE**
>
> **You can find more information on conversion methods and IRS treatment,** including several state-specific articles that explain the conversion processes for individual states, at www.nolo.com (search for "LLCs and corporations").

Statutory Conversion

You might be wondering why states provide multiple methods for converting your LLC to a corporation. Can't you just form a corporation, transfer the assets of the LLC to the corporation, trade your LLC interests for shares in the corporation, and dissolve the LLC? Yes, you can convert that way under what's known as a formation/dissolution conversion (also called a nonstatutory conversion). We cover formation/dissolution conversions below. But while nonstatutory conversions are possible, there are two better methods for converting an LLC to a corporation: statutory conversions and statutory mergers.

In a statutory conversion, you file a conversion document with the state (articles of conversion, certificate of conversion, or similar title) that changes the LLC to a corporation. You don't need to dissolve the LLC, because it automatically ceases to exist upon conversion. Looking at it another way, the entity still exists, except now it's a corporation instead of an LLC. Either way, you don't need to dissolve and liquidate the LLC.

Each state that allows statutory conversions has its own forms and rules. However, generally speaking, here are the basic steps for a statutory conversion.

1. Prepare a plan of conversion. In Virginia, for example, a plan of conversion must include the following:
   - a statement of the limited liability company's intention to convert to a corporation
   - the terms and conditions of the conversion, including the conversion of LLC member interests into corporate shares, and
   - a copy of the articles of incorporation for the corporation the LLC is being converted to (Va. Code § 13.1-1083 (2024)).

2. Have the LLC members approve the plan.

3. File articles of conversion and, typically, articles of incorporation (to form the new corporation) with the secretary of state or another filing office.

Upon conversion, the members of the converted LLC become the shareholders of the new corporation, the assets and liabilities of the LLC become the assets and liabilities of the corporation, and, again, the LLC ceases to exist. These results are accomplished automatically, by operation of law, rather than requiring multiple steps and multiple agreements to transition the ownership interests and the assets and liabilities of the business from the LLC to the corporation.

Statutory conversion is usually the quickest and most inexpensive way to convert from an LLC to a corporation. In those states where it's available, this type of conversion will generally be your best option.

The Hawaii Articles of Conversion form is included below. It asks for information about the entity being converted (the "converting" or "original" entity) (Sections 1 and 2), the entity being converted to (the "converted" or "new" entity) (Sections 3 and 4), and the conversion plan (Sections 5 and 6). States vary in their use of the phrases "converting entity" and "converted entity," with some reversing the Hawaii designations. Kudos to Hawaii for also using "original" and "new" to describe the two entities, making it clear which entity information should go where. Other state conversion forms would benefit from such clarity.

Hawaii doesn't require that the plan of conversion be filed with the articles of conversion, but only that it is on file at the company's place of business. Hawaii does, however require information about the vote to approve the plan of conversion (Section 8), on top of the affirmation in Section 5 that the plan was approved. Most states don't request vote tallies.

Hawaii Articles of Conversion

Nonrefundable Filing Fee: $100.00
*Nonprofit: $50.00

FORM X-10
7/2017

STATE OF HAWAII
DEPARTMENT OF COMMERCE AND CONSUMER AFFAIRS
Business Registration Division
335 Merchant Street
Mailing Address: P.O. Box 40, Honolulu, Hawaii 96810
Phone No. (808) 586-2727

ARTICLES OF CONVERSION
(Section 414-272, 415A-16.6, 414D-208 425-193, 425E-1103, 428-902.6, Hawaii Revised Statutes)

PLEASE TYPE OR PRINT LEGIBLY IN BLACK INK

The undersigned, submitting these Articles of Conversion, certify as follows:

1. The converting (original) entity was (check one):

   ☐ Profit Corp. ☐ Professional Corp. ☐ Nonprofit Corp. ☐ General Partnership ☐ Limited Partnership

   ☐ LLC ☐ LLP (If LLP must also check General Partnership) ☐ LLLP

2. The name and state/country of incorporation/formation/organization or qualification of the converting entity was:

   _____   _____
   (Type/Print Entity Name)   (State or Country)

3. The converted (new) entity is (check one):

   ☐ Profit Corp. ☐ Professional Corp. ☐ Nonprofit Corp. ☐ General Partnership ☐ Limited Partnership

   ☐ LLC ☐ LLP (If LLP must also check General Partnership) ☐ LLLP

4. The name and state/country of incorporation/formation/organization or qualification of the converted entity is:

   _____   _____
   (Type/Print Entity Name)   (State or Country)

5. The Plan of Conversion has been approved in accordance to Section 414-271, 415A-16.5, 414D-202, 425-192, 425E-1102, 428-902.5, as applicable.

6. An executed Plan of Conversion is on file at the principal place of business of the converting entity whose address is:

   _____

7. A copy of the Plan of Conversion shall be furnished by the converting entity prior to the conversion or by the converted entity after the conversion on written request and without cost, to any shareholder, partner, member, or owner of the converting entity or the converted entity.

Hawaii Articles of Conversion (page 2)

FORM X-10
7/2017

8. Complete the applicable section. The Plan of Conversion was approved by the converting entity as follows:

A. By vote of the shareholders of the converting domestic profit/professional corporation:

Number of Shares Outstanding	Class/Series	Number of Shares Voting For Conversion	Number of Shares Voting Against Conversion

OR

B. By vote of the converting domestic limited liability company:

Total Number of Authorized Votes	Number of Votes For the Conversion	Number of Votes Against the Conversion

OR

C. ☐ The converting entity was a foreign profit corporation, a foreign limited liability company, a foreign limited partnership, a foreign limited liability limited partnership, a domestic or a foreign general partnership, or a domestic or foreign limited liability partnership. The approval of the Plan of Conversion was duly authorized and complied with the laws under which the converting entity was incorporated, formed, organized, or qualified.

OR

D. ☐ The converting entity was a domestic limited partnership or a domestic limited liability limited partnership and that a majority of the general partners have agreed to the conversion.

9. The conversion is effective on the date and time of filing the Articles of Conversion or at a later date and time, no more than 30 days after the filing, if so stated. Check one of the following statements:

☐ Conversion is effective on the date and time of filing the Articles of Conversion.

☐ Conversion is effective on _____, at _____. m. , Hawaiian Standard Time, which date is not later than 30 days after the filing of the Articles of Conversion.

I/we certify under the penalties of Section 414-20, 415A-25, 414D-12, 425-13, 425-172, 425E-208, and 428-1302, Hawaii Revised Statutes, as applicable, that I/we have read the above statements, I/we are authorized to sign this Articles of Conversion, and that the above statements are true and correct.

Signed this _____ day of _____, _____

_____   _____
(Type/Print Name & Title)   (Signature)

_____   _____
(Type/Print Name & Title)   (Signature)

SEE INSTRUCTIONS ON REVERSE SIDE. The articles must be signed by an officer, partner, or other duly authorized representative of the converting entity.

Statutory Merger

A statutory merger is more complicated than a statutory conversion. However, if your state doesn't allow for statutory conversions, you'll likely use this method. While details will vary from state to state, a statutory merger usually involves the following steps.

1. Form a new corporation, with the LLC members as its shareholders.
2. Have the LLC members/corporate shareholders vote to approve the merger on behalf of the LLC and the corporation.
3. Formally exchange LLC membership interests for shares in the corporation.
4. File a certificate of merger and other legally required documents with the secretary of state.

As with a statutory conversion, a statutory merger automatically transfers your LLC's assets and liabilities to the new corporation by operation of law. However, unlike statutory conversions, you have to create your new corporation as a separate business entity before that transfer can occur—a process that involves multiple steps and fees. Additionally, you'll need to formally exchange membership rights for corporate shares through a merger agreement.

Nonstatutory (Formation/Dissolution) Conversion

A nonstatutory conversion is generally the most complicated and expensive way to convert from an LLC to a corporation. The main steps are as follows.

1. Form a new corporation.
2. Formally transfer the LLC's assets and liabilities to the corporation.
3. Formally exchange LLC membership interests for corporation shares.
4. Dissolve the LLC.

Nonstatutory conversions have been largely replaced by the more efficient and less expensive statutory conversions and statutory mergers. However, if you need to go through a nonstatutory conversion, we recommend working with a business lawyer and your tax adviser.

We next discuss the tax implications of nonstatutory conversions.

Nonstatutory Conversions and the IRS

Nonstatutory conversions can be taxable, meaning that the owners of the LLC recognize income on built-in gains on LLC assets at the time of the conversion. However, certain nonstatutory conversions qualify as tax-free reorganizations. In Revenue Ruling 84-111, the IRS described the following three types of nontaxable LLC-to-corporation conversions.

- **"Assets-over" conversion.** The LLC transfers all of its assets and liabilities to the newly-formed corporation in exchange for all outstanding stock of the corporation. The LLC is terminated by distributing all of the corporation's stock to the LLC members. (This conversion is called "assets-over" because assets are transferred "over" to the new corporation.)

- **"Assets-up" conversion.** The LLC distributes all of its assets and liabilities to its members to terminate the LLC. Then the members transfer all the assets received from the LLC to the corporation in exchange for all outstanding stock of the corporation plus the corporation's assumption of all of those LLC liabilities that previously had been assumed by the LLC's members. (This method is called "assets-up" because, after LLC assets are transferred "down" to LLC members, they're ultimately transferred "up" to the new corporation.)

- **"Interests-over" conversion.** The LLC members transfer their LLC interests to the newly-formed corporation in exchange for all the outstanding stock of the corporation. The LLC is terminated with all of the LLC assets and liabilities becoming assets and liabilities of the corporation. (This conversion is called "interests-over" because LLC members transfer their "interests over" to the new corporation.)

Revenue Ruling 84-111 doesn't address how the IRS views statutory conversions or statutory mergers, but in a subsequent Revenue Ruling (Rev. Rul. 2004-59), the IRS treated statutory conversions and mergers as assets-over conversions.

The tax treatment of entity conversions, including LLC-to-corporation conversions, is complicated. We recommend consulting with a tax adviser before converting your LLC.

Federal Beneficial Ownership Information (BOI) Reporting

Businesses formed by a state filing, including LLCs and corporations, must submit a beneficial ownership information report (a BOI report) to the Financial Crimes Enforcement Network (FinCEN), a bureau of the U.S. Department of Treasury. The BOI report collects identifying information about your company and its owners. This reporting requirement was established under the Corporate Transparency Act (CTA) (31 U.S.C. § 5336), and it took effect on January 1, 2024. While there are many exemptions under the CTA, most registered businesses will need to file BOI reports.

Legal Fight Over the Constitutionality of the FinCEN Reporting Requirement

In March 2024, a federal district court ruled that the reporting requirements of the CTA are unconstitutional (*National Small Business United v. Yellen*, ___ F. Supp. 3d ___ (N.D. Ala. 2024)). The named plaintiff, National Small Business United, does business as the National Small Business Association (NSBA). Under this decision, which the federal government has appealed, companies that were NSBA members as of March 1, 2024 are exempt from the BOI reporting requirements. All other registered businesses, unless they are exempt under the CTA itself, must still file BOI reports.

When this book went to press, the broader impact of *National Small Business United* remained unclear. Depending on the outcome of the appeal, and whether other federal courts follow the lead of the Alabama district court, the BOI reporting requirements could be modified, eliminated, or left intact. Be sure to check on the status of the law before filing your report.

Information in a BOI Report

The BOI report form is reproduced below. It contains three sections (parts). The first section is for information about the reporting company, the second for information about the company applicant, and the third for information about beneficial owners of the company. We explore each section below, including the company applicant designation and what constitutes beneficial ownership.

Part I—Company Information

Part I is prefaced by an introductory question (Question 1) about the type of filing—initial or other. The BOI report is not an annual report: you file it once, according to the schedule outlined below, and then again only if you are correcting a prior report, updating a prior report, or are declaring that your company has become exempt from reporting. If you have filed a previous BOI report for your company, you would enter the company information in Items 1(e)-1(h).

Part I itself is very straightforward, except perhaps Question 3 on requesting a FinCEN Identifier (FinCEN ID). You are not required to have a FinCEN ID for your company or any individual, but having one can facilitate filing. If you haven't already obtained a FinCEN ID for your company but want one, check the box in Question 3.

Part II—Company Applicant Information

The second section of the BOI report is required only for companies formed on or after January 1, 2024. If your company was formed before this date, you can skip this section. Otherwise, here are some tips on how to fill it out.

The company applicant for a reporting company is the person who directly filed the document to create the reporting company with the state. The person who filed the articles of organization with the secretary of state's office would be considered the company applicant for an LLC.

If more than one person was involved in filing the company's formation documents, then the person who's primarily responsible for directing or controlling the filing would be considered the company applicant. (If your formation filing was done by an attorney or accountant, then that person would likely be considered the company applicant.)

When reporting individual information for company applicants (and for beneficial owners in Part III), you can either provide all the requested information for the individual or you can enter their individual FinCEN ID if they have one. Individuals can apply for a FinCEN ID at login.gov (you'll need to have or create a login.gov account).

If a company applicant doesn't have an individual FinCEN ID, you'll need to provide the following information about them:

- full legal name
- date of birth
- current address, and
- a form of identification (such as a driver's license or passport).

You must upload a copy of the form of identification you're using (such as a driver's license or passport) and specify the document number and what governing body issued the identification. For example, if your identifying document is your driver's license, then you'll need to upload a picture of your license and type in your license number and the state that issued your license.

Part III—Beneficial Owner Information

As with the previous section on company applicant, you can enter your FinCEN ID in place of completing this section of the application. But if you don't have a FinCEN ID to report for a beneficial owner, then you must answer all of the questions in this section of the BOI report.

To accurately complete this section, you need to determine who qualifies as a beneficial owner of a reporting company for the purpose of this report. A "beneficial owner" of a reporting company is someone who directly or indirectly either:

- owns or controls at least 25% of the company's interest (such as through stock, equity, or voting rights), or
- has substantial control over the company.

FinCEN describes several situations where an owner would be considered to have substantial control over a company. Typically, an owner has substantial control when the owner has any of the following status or powers:

- is a senior officer of the company
- can appoint or remove certain officers or a majority of directors, or
- has significant influence over big company decisions (like selling company property or entering into business contracts).

You'll provide the same information about each beneficial owner as you provided about the company applicant, including their names, dates of birth, addresses, and identification.

Deadline to File the BOI Report

The deadline to file your BOI report depends on when your company was formed:

- If you created your company before January 1, 2024, you have until January 1, 2025 to submit your BOI report.
- If you created your company in 2024, you have 90 days from when your company is registered to file your BOI report.
- If you created your company after 2024, you have 30 days from when your company is registered to file your BOI report.

If you miss the deadline or you fail to update your report when information changes, you might face civil and criminal penalties. These penalties can include hefty daily fines and a prison sentence of up to two years.

Create and file your BOI report on the FinCEN website (www.fincen. gov). The FinCEN site also includes information about BOI reporting, including an excellent FAQ page and FinCEN's "Small Entity Compliance Guide."

Most business owners will likely be able to navigate the reporting process themselves. But if you're not sure whether you qualify for one of the exemptions or whether you qualify as a beneficial owner, talk to a business attorney.

Beneficial Ownership Information Report

Beneficial Ownership Information Report

Version Number: 1.0

OMB No. 1506-0076

Release Date: 05-29-2024

Report Preparation & Submission Instructions:

Instructions	1. Complete the report in its entirety with all required information. Click **Instructions** for help.
Validate	2. Click **Validate** to ensure all entered data is properly formatted and that all required fields are completed.
Finalize	3. Click **Finalize** to lock the entries in the report and prepare it for submission. Click **Edit Report** to unlock and re-edit.
Save	4. Click **Save** to retain a local copy of the report (this can be done at any time during report preparation).
Print	5. (Optional) Click **Print** to print a hard copy of your completed report.
Ready To File	6. Select **Ready to File** (activated after the report is finalized and saved locally) to begin the submission process.

Filing Information

1. ▪ Type of filing:

    a. Initial report ☐

    b. Correct prior report ☐

    c. Update prior report ☐

    d. Newly exempt entity ☐

Reporting Company information associated with most recent report, if any:

    e. Legal name

    f. Tax Identification type

    g. Tax Identification number

    h. Country/Jurisdiction *(if foreign tax ID only)*

2. Date prepared *(auto-filled when form is finalized)*

Beneficial Ownership Information Report (page 2)

Part I. Reporting Company Information

3. Request to receive FinCEN Identifier (FinCEN ID) ☐

4. Foreign pooled investment vehicle ☐

Full legal name and alternate name(s):

5. ＊ Reporting Company legal name

6. Alternate name (e.g. trade name, DBA) ⊕ ⊖

Form of identification:

7. ＊ Tax Identification type ▾

8. ＊ Tax Identification number

9. Country/Jurisdiction *(if foreign tax ID only)*

Jurisdiction of formation or first registration:

10. ＊ a. Country/Jurisdiction of formation ▾

Domestic Reporting Company:

b. State of formation

c. Tribal jurisdiction of formation

d. Name of the other Tribe

Foreign Reporting Company:

e. State of first registration

f. Tribal jurisdiction of first registration

g. Name of the other Tribe

Current U.S. Address:

11. ＊ Address (number, street, and apt. or suite no.)

12. ＊ City

13. ＊ U.S. or U.S. Territory ▾

14. ＊ State ▾

15. ＊ ZIP Code

Beneficial Ownership Information Report (page 3)

Beneficial Ownership Information Report

| Home | Reporting Company | Company Applicant(s) | Beneficial Owner(s) |

16. Existing Reporting Company ☐ *(check if Reporting Company was created or registered before January 1, 2024)*

17. *(This item is reserved for future use)*

Part II. Company Applicant Information   1 of 1   ⊕ ⊖

Company Applicant FinCEN ID:

18. **FinCEN ID**

Full legal name and date of birth:

19. * Individual's last name

20. * First name

21. Middle name

22. Suffix

23. * Date of birth

Current address:

24. * Address type   ☐ a. Business address   ☐ b. Residential address

25. * Address (number, street, and apt. or suite no.)

26. * City

27. * Country/Jurisdiction   ▼

28. * State   ▼

29. * ZIP/Foreign postal code

Form of identification and issuing jurisdiction:

30. * Identifying document type   ▼

31. * Identifying document number

32. * Identifying document issuing jurisdiction:

    a. Country/Jurisdiction   ▼

    b. State   ▼

    c. Local/Tribal

    d. Other local/Tribal description

33. * Identifying document image | Add Attachment | | Remove Attachment |

Beneficial Ownership Information Report (page 4)

Beneficial Ownership Information Report

| Home | Reporting Company | Company Applicant(s) | Beneficial Owner(s) |

34. *(This item is reserved for future use)*

Part III. Beneficial Owner Information   1 of 1   ⊕ ⊖

35. Parent/Guardian information instead of minor child   ☐ *(check if the Beneficial Owner is a minor child and the parent/guardian information is provided instead)*

Beneficial Owner FinCEN ID:

36. FinCEN ID

Exempt entity:

37. Exempt entity   ☐

Full legal name and date of birth:

38. * Individual's last name or entity's legal name.

39. * First name

40. Middle name

41. Suffix

42. * Date of birth

Residential address:

43. * Address (number, street, and apt. or suite no.)

44. * City

45. * Country/Jurisdiction

46. * State

47. * ZIP/Foreign postal code

Form of identification and issuing jurisdiction:

48. * Identifying document type

49. * Identifying document number

50. * Identifying document issuing jurisdiction:

   a. Country/Jurisdiction

   b. State

   c. Local/Tribal

   d. Other local/Tribal description

51. * Identifying document image   [Add Attachment] [Remove Attachment]

CHAPTER

10

Tax Registrations and Filings

FORMS IN THIS CHAPTER

Accessing state government and IRS forms in this chapter.

State government forms used to illustrate particular legal and tax filings are available on your state's appropriate state agency website. The IRS forms are available at www.irs.gov.

n Chapter 4, we covered getting an EIN for your LLC (Form SS-4) and making an election to be taxed as a C corporation (Form 8832) or S corporation (Form 2553). If you didn't elect corporate taxation (and most LLCs don't), your LLC is a partnership for income tax purposes.

While your LLC/partnership is a pass-through entity, meaning that it doesn't pay income tax but instead passes profits and losses to members to be reported on their individual tax returns, it must file a partnership tax return. In this chapter, we review the federal partnership tax return (Form 1065, *U.S. Return of Partnership Income*), and the form used to pass LLC profits and losses to the members (Schedule K-1).

If you elected to have your LLC taxed as an S Corporation, you would file Form 1120-S (*U.S. Income Tax Return for an S Corporation*) instead of Form 1065. Our focus, at least where income tax reporting is concerned, is on Form 1065. Briefly, S corporations are also pass-through entities, and the basic mechanics of S corporation tax reporting are the same as partnership tax reporting—calculate the profit or loss of the business and pass the profit or loss to the owners (shareholders in the case of an S corporation).

Income taxes aside, your LLC could be subject to other federal and state taxes. If you sell goods or services, you might be subject to state sales and use tax. If you have employees, you must pay federal and state employment taxes. We cover registering for and paying these taxes in this chapter.

Our goal in this chapter is to acquaint you with the forms, not to provide detailed instructions on how to complete them. You can find great instructions for the forms at their sources, including the IRS and your state department of revenue and department of labor. With those instructions and the information presented here, you can complete many of these forms on your own. But even if you use a professional to file a registration or complete a return, you will find that this chapter will help you to be an informed client.

Federal Partnership Tax Return— Form 1065 and Schedule K-1

LLC income (profit and loss) is computed and reported on IRS Form 1065, *U.S. Return of Partnership Income.* The LLC itself doesn't owe tax on the income and doesn't retain any losses. The LLC passes the profit or loss, along with certain special items, to the members via Schedule K-1. Every partner receives a K-1, showing their share of partnership income, deductions, and other items.

Form 1065 and Schedule K-1 are included below. We recommend taking a minute to skim through the two forms before returning to this discussion.

Form 1065 is an informational return, meaning that it's not filed for the purpose of paying a tax. But being informational doesn't make it simple—partnership tax returns are complicated. Schedule K-1, while only a page long, is also complicated in that it requires understanding how information flows from Form 1065 to the K-1. Partnership tax accounting itself is complicated. Unless an LLC has that expertise within the company, it's generally a good idea to use a professional tax preparer for partnership returns. But by familiarizing yourself with Form 1065 and Schedule K-1, you'll be better able to understand your returns, whoever prepares them.

The Sequence of Pass-Through Taxation— From Form 1065 to Form 1040

We tend to use shorthand language to explain pass-through taxation: profits and losses flow from the business to the individual owners. As Form 1065 shows, the process is a bit more complicated than the shorthand indicates. First comes the calculation of ordinary (operating) income or loss on the first page, arrived at by adding up various items of income (Lines 1-8) and then deducting various expenses (Lines 9-22), to arrive at ordinary income (Line 23). The ordinary income or loss on Line 23 is carried to Schedule K (Line 1) on page 5 of the return, where it is combined with other items of income, other deductions, credits, and other adjustments. Schedule K is for the partnership as a whole.

The amounts from Schedule K are then allocated to the partners via an individual Schedule K-1 (known as "a K-1") for each partner, specifically in Part III of the K-1 (Partner's Share of Current Year Income, Deductions, Credits, and Other Items). Allocations are made according to the LLC's allocation formula, as provided for in the operating agreement or under state law in the absence of an operating agreement. The items from Part III of a partner's K-1 are incorporated into the partner's individual tax return (Form 1040).

The paper trail of LLC income thus looks like this:

- Form 1065 to Schedule K
- Schedule K to Schedule K-1, and
- Schedule K-1 to each owner's Form 1040.

Additional Form 1065 Information

Pages 1-6 of Form 1065 make up the core of the partnership tax return. Those pages include:

- page 1 (discussed above)
- Schedule B (other information)
- Schedule K (discussed above)
- Schedule L (balance sheet)
- Schedule M-1 (reconciliation of book income and tax income), and
- Schedule M-2 (partners' aggregate capital accounts).

Technically, only page 1, Schedule B, and Schedule K are required of all partnership returns. Schedules L, M-1, and M-2, along with item F on page 1, can be omitted if the partnership meets all of the four conditions set out in Line 4 of Schedule B:

- Total receipts were less than $250,000.
- Total assets were less than $1 million.

- K-1's are included with the return and have been furnished to the partners.
- The partnership doesn't need to file Schedule M-3 (Schedule M-3 is for partnerships with revenue over $35 million or assets over $10 million).

Item F on page 1 is for total partnership assets.

You will include other forms and schedules with your return only if they apply. For example, you'll include Schedule D, *Capital Gains and Losses*, only if your LLC has capital gains or losses to report. You'll include Form 8825, *Rental Real Estate Income and Expenses of a Partnership or an S Corporation*, only if your LLC owned rental property during the year.

Additional K-1 Information

Part II of the K-1 contains information about the partner, including the partner's percentage share of income, deductions, and partnership capital (Line J), the partner's dollar share of partnership liabilities (Line K1), and the partner's capital account balance. In order to fill in this information, your LLC needs to do accurate capital account tracking (one of the most difficult aspects of partnership tax accounting).

State Tax Registration and Filing

Like the IRS, states treat multi-member LLCs as pass-through entities, meaning that the company pays no state income tax. However, the company will likely be subject to other state tax registrations and filings. If you sell goods or services in a state that has a sales tax, you'll be collecting the tax from your customers (unless your LLC is exempt from doing so). If you have employees in a state with a personal income tax, you'll be withholding state income taxes (if applicable). You'll need to register with your state, usually the department of revenue or its equivalent, to obtain permits for sales tax and income tax withholding purposes.

IRS Form 1065: U.S. Return of Partnership Income

Form 1065

Department of the Treasury
Internal Revenue Service

U.S. Return of Partnership Income

For calendar year 2023, or tax year beginning _____ , 2023, ending _____ , 20 _____.

Go to *www.irs.gov/Form1065* for instructions and the latest information.

OMB No. 1545-0123

2023

A Principal business activity	Name of partnership	D Employer identification number
B Principal product or service	**Type or Print** — Number, street, and room or suite no. If a P.O. box, see instructions.	E Date business started
C Business code number	City or town, state or province, country, and ZIP or foreign postal code	F Total assets (see instructions) $

G Check applicable boxes: (1) ☐ Initial return (2) ☐ Final return (3) ☐ Name change (4) ☐ Address change (5) ☐ Amended return

H Check accounting method: (1) ☐ Cash (2) ☐ Accrual (3) ☐ Other (specify): _____

I Number of Schedules K-1. Attach one for each person who was a partner at any time during the tax year: _____

J Check if Schedules C and M-3 are attached . . . . ☐

K Check if partnership: (1) ☐ Aggregated activities for section 465 at-risk purposes (2) ☐ Grouped activities for section 469 passive activity purposes

Caution: Include **only** trade or business income and expenses on lines 1a through 23 below. See instructions for more information.

Income

1a	Gross receipts or sales		
b	Less returns and allowances	c Balance	1c
2	Cost of goods sold (attach Form 1125-A)		2
3	Gross profit. Subtract line 2 from line 1c		3
4	Ordinary income (loss) from other partnerships, estates, and trusts (attach statement)		4
5	Net farm profit (loss) (attach Schedule F (Form 1040))		5
6	Net gain (loss) from Form 4797, Part II, line 17 (attach Form 4797)		6
7	Other income (loss) (attach statement)		7
8	**Total income (loss).** Combine lines 3 through 7		8

Deductions (see instructions for limitations)

9	Salaries and wages (other than to partners) (less employment credits)		9
10	Guaranteed payments to partners		10
11	Repairs and maintenance		11
12	Bad debts		12
13	Rent		13
14	Taxes and licenses		14
15	Interest (see instructions)		15
16a	Depreciation (if required, attach Form 4562) 16a		
b	Less depreciation reported on Form 1125-A and elsewhere on return . 16b		16c
17	Depletion (**Do not deduct oil and gas depletion.**)		17
18	Retirement plans, etc.		18
19	Employee benefit programs		19
20	Energy efficient commercial buildings deduction (attach Form 7205)		20
21	Other deductions (attach statement)		21
22	**Total deductions.** Add the amounts shown in the far right column for lines 9 through 21 . . .		22
23	**Ordinary business income (loss).** Subtract line 22 from line 8		23

Tax and Payment

24	Interest due under the look-back method—completed long-term contracts (attach Form 8697) .		24
25	Interest due under the look-back method—income forecast method (attach Form 8866) . . .		25
26	BBA AAR imputed underpayment (see instructions)		26
27	Other taxes (see instructions)		27
28	**Total balance due.** Add lines 24 through 27		28
29	Elective payment election amount from Form 3800		29
30	Payment (see instructions)		30
31	**Amount owed.** If the sum of line 29 and line 30 is smaller than line 28, enter amount owed . .		31
32	**Overpayment.** If the sum of line 29 and line 30 is larger than line 28, enter overpayment . . .		32

Sign Here

Under penalties of perjury, I declare that I have examined this return, including accompanying schedules and statements, and to the best of my knowledge and belief, it is true, correct, and complete. Declaration of preparer (other than partner or limited liability company member) is based on all information of which preparer has any knowledge.

Signature of partner or limited liability company member _____ Date _____

May the IRS discuss this return with the preparer shown below? See instructions. ☐ Yes ☐ No

Paid Preparer Use Only

Print/Type preparer's name	Preparer's signature	Date	Check ☐ if self-employed	PTIN
Firm's name			Firm's EIN	
Firm's address			Phone no.	

For Paperwork Reduction Act Notice, see separate instructions.

Cat. No. 11390Z

Form **1065** (2023)

IRS Form 1065: U.S. Return of Partnership Income (page 2)

Form 1065 (2023)   Page **2**

Schedule B	Other Information		

		Yes	No
1	What type of entity is filing this return? Check the applicable box:		
a	☐ Domestic general partnership **b** ☐ Domestic limited partnership		
c	☐ Domestic limited liability company **d** ☐ Domestic limited liability partnership		
e	☐ Foreign partnership **f** ☐ Other: _____		
2	At the end of the tax year:		
a	Did any foreign or domestic corporation, partnership (including any entity treated as a partnership), trust, or tax-exempt organization, or any foreign government own, directly or indirectly, an interest of 50% or more in the profit, loss, or capital of the partnership? For rules of constructive ownership, see instructions. If "Yes," attach Schedule B-1, Information on Partners Owning 50% or More of the Partnership		
b	Did any individual or estate own, directly or indirectly, an interest of 50% or more in the profit, loss, or capital of the partnership? For rules of constructive ownership, see instructions. If "Yes," attach Schedule B-1, Information on Partners Owning 50% or More of the Partnership		
3	At the end of the tax year, did the partnership:		
a	Own directly 20% or more, or own, directly or indirectly, 50% or more of the total voting power of all classes of stock entitled to vote of any foreign or domestic corporation? For rules of constructive ownership, see instructions. If "Yes," complete (i) through (iv) below		

(i) Name of Corporation	(ii) Employer Identification Number (if any)	(iii) Country of Incorporation	(iv) Percentage Owned in Voting Stock

b	Own directly an interest of 20% or more, or own, directly or indirectly, an interest of 50% or more in the profit, loss, or capital in any foreign or domestic partnership (including an entity treated as a partnership) or in the beneficial interest of a trust? For rules of constructive ownership, see instructions. If "Yes," complete (i) through (v) below . .	

(i) Name of Entity	(ii) Employer Identification Number (if any)	(iii) Type of Entity	(iv) Country of Organization	(v) Maximum Percentage Owned in Profit, Loss, or Capital

		Yes	No
4	Does the partnership satisfy **all four** of the following conditions?		
a	The partnership's total receipts for the tax year were less than $250,000.		
b	The partnership's total assets at the end of the tax year were less than $1 million.		
c	Schedules K-1 are filed with the return and furnished to the partners on or before the due date (including extensions) for the partnership return.		
d	The partnership is not filing and is not required to file Schedule M-3		
	If "Yes," the partnership is not required to complete Schedules L, M-1, and M-2; item F on page 1 of Form 1065; or item L on Schedule K-1.		
5	Is this partnership a publicly traded partnership, as defined in section 469(k)(2)?		
6	During the tax year, did the partnership have any debt that was canceled, was forgiven, or had the terms modified so as to reduce the principal amount of the debt?		
7	Has this partnership filed, or is it required to file, Form 8918, Material Advisor Disclosure Statement, to provide information on any reportable transaction?		
8	At any time during calendar year 2023, did the partnership have an interest in or a signature or other authority over a financial account in a foreign country (such as a bank account, securities account, or other financial account)? See instructions for exceptions and filing requirements for FinCEN Form 114, Report of Foreign Bank and Financial Accounts (FBAR). If "Yes," enter the name of the foreign country _____		
9	At any time during the tax year, did the partnership receive a distribution from, or was it the grantor of, or transferor to, a foreign trust? If "Yes," the partnership may have to file Form 3520, Annual Return To Report Transactions With Foreign Trusts and Receipt of Certain Foreign Gifts. See instructions		
10a	Is the partnership making, or had it previously made (and not revoked), a section 754 election? If "Yes," enter the effective date of the election . . . . _____		
	See instructions for details regarding a section 754 election.		
b	For this tax year, did the partnership make an optional basis adjustment under section 743(b)? If "Yes," enter the total aggregate net positive amount $ _____ and the total aggregate net negative amount $ (_____) of such section 743(b) adjustments for all partners made in the tax year. The partnership must also attach a statement showing the computation and allocation of each basis adjustment. See instructions		

Form **1065** (2023)

IRS Form 1065: U.S. Return of Partnership Income (page 3)

Form 1065 (2023)   Page **3**

Schedule B	Other Information *(continued)*	Yes	No
c	For this tax year, did the partnership make an optional basis adjustment under section 734(b)? If "Yes," enter the total aggregate net positive amount $ _____ and the total aggregate net negative amount $ (_____) of such section 734(b) adjustments for all partnership property made in the tax year. The partnership must also attach a statement showing the computation and allocation of each basis adjustment. See instructions		
d	For this tax year, is the partnership required to adjust the basis of partnership property under section 743(b) or 734(b) because of a substantial built-in loss (as defined under section 743(d)) or substantial basis reduction (as defined under section 734(d))? If "Yes," enter the total aggregate amount of such section 743(b) adjustments and/or section 734(b) adjustments for all partners and/or partnership property made in the tax year $ _____ . The partnership must also attach a statement showing the computation and allocation of the basis adjustment. See instructions		
11	Check this box if, during the current or prior tax year, the partnership distributed any property received in a like-kind exchange or contributed such property to another entity (other than disregarded entities wholly owned by the partnership throughout the tax year) . . . . ☐		
12	At any time during the tax year, did the partnership distribute to any partner a tenancy-in-common or other undivided interest in partnership property?		
13	If the partnership is required to file Form 8858, Information Return of U.S. Persons With Respect to Foreign Disregarded Entities (FDEs) and Foreign Branches (FBs), enter the number of Forms 8858 attached. See instructions . . . . _____		
14	Does the partnership have any foreign partners? If "Yes," enter the number of Forms 8805, Foreign Partner's Information Statement of Section 1446 Withholding Tax, filed for this partnership . . . . . . _____		
15	Enter the number of Forms 8865, Return of U.S. Persons With Respect to Certain Foreign Partnerships, attached to this return . . . . _____		
16a	Did you make any payments in 2023 that would require you to file Form(s) 1099? See instructions		
b	If "Yes," did you or will you file required Form(s) 1099?		
17	Enter the number of Forms 5471, Information Return of U.S. Persons With Respect to Certain Foreign Corporations, attached to this return . . . . _____		
18	Enter the number of partners that are foreign governments under section 892 . . . . _____		
19	During the partnership's tax year, did the partnership make any payments that would require it to file Forms 1042 and 1042-S under chapter 3 (sections 1441 through 1464) or chapter 4 (sections 1471 through 1474)?		
20	Was the partnership a specified domestic entity required to file Form 8938 for the tax year? See the Instructions for Form 8938		
21	Is the partnership a section 721(c) partnership, as defined in Regulations section 1.721(c)-1(b)(14)?		
22	During the tax year, did the partnership pay or accrue any interest or royalty for which one or more partners are not allowed a deduction under section 267A? See instructions . . . . If "Yes," enter the total amount of the disallowed deductions . . . . $ _____		
23	Did the partnership have an election under section 163(j) for any real property trade or business or any farming business in effect during the tax year? See instructions		
24	Does the partnership satisfy one or more of the following? See instructions		
a	The partnership owns a pass-through entity with current, or prior year carryover, excess business interest expense.		
b	The partnership's aggregate average annual gross receipts (determined under section 448(c)) for the 3 tax years preceding the current tax year are more than $29 million and the partnership has business interest expense.		
c	The partnership is a tax shelter (see instructions) and the partnership has business interest expense. If "Yes" to any, complete and attach Form 8990.		
25	Is the partnership attaching Form 8996 to certify as a Qualified Opportunity Fund? . . . . If "Yes," enter the amount from Form 8996, line 15 . . . . $ _____		
26	Enter the number of foreign partners subject to section 864(c)(8) as a result of transferring all or a portion of an interest in the partnership or of receiving a distribution from the partnership . . . . _____ Complete Schedule K-3 (Form 1065), Part XIII, for each foreign partner subject to section 864(c)(8) on a transfer or distribution.		
27	At any time during the tax year, were there any transfers between the partnership and its partners subject to the disclosure requirements of Regulations section 1.707-8?		
28	Since December 22, 2017, did a foreign corporation directly or indirectly acquire substantially all of the properties constituting a trade or business of your partnership, and was the ownership percentage (by vote or value) for purposes of section 7874 greater than 50% (for example, the partners held more than 50% of the stock of the foreign corporation)? If "Yes," list the ownership percentage by vote and by value. See instructions. Percentage: By vote: _____ By value: _____		
29	Is the partnership required to file Form 7208 relating to the excise tax on repurchase of corporate stock (see instructions):		
a	Under the applicable foreign corporation rules?		

Form **1065** (2023)

IRS Form 1065: U.S. Return of Partnership Income (page 4)

Form 1065 (2023)		Page 4

Schedule B	**Other Information** *(continued)*	Yes	No
b	Under the covered surrogate foreign corporation rules?		
	If "Yes" to either (a) or (b), complete Form 7208, Excise Tax on Repurchase of Corporate Stock. See the Instructions for Form 7208.		
30	At any time during this tax year, did the partnership (a) receive (as a reward, award, or payment for property or services); or (b) sell, exchange, or otherwise dispose of a digital asset (or financial interest in a digital asset)? See instructions		
31	Is the partnership electing out of the centralized partnership audit regime under section 6221(b)? See instructions		
	If "Yes," the partnership must complete Schedule B-2 (Form 1065). Enter the total from Schedule B-2, Part III, line 3		
	If "No," complete Designation of Partnership Representative below.		

Designation of Partnership Representative (see instructions)
Enter below the information for the partnership representative (PR) for the tax year covered by this return.

Name of PR

U.S. address of PR	_____	U.S. phone number of PR

If the PR is an entity, name of the designated individual for the PR

U.S. address of designated individual	_____	U.S. phone number of designated individual

Form **1065** (2023)

IRS Form 1065: U.S. Return of Partnership Income (page 5)

Form 1065 (2023)   Page **5**

Schedule K — Partners' Distributive Share Items

			Total amount
Income (Loss)	**1**	Ordinary business income (loss) (page 1, line 23)	**1**
	2	Net rental real estate income (loss) (attach Form 8825)	**2**
	3a	Other gross rental income (loss) **3a**	
	b	Expenses from other rental activities (attach statement) **3b**	
	c	Other net rental income (loss). Subtract line 3b from line 3a	**3c**
	4	Guaranteed payments: **a** Services **4a** **b** Capital **4b**	
	c	Total. Add lines 4a and 4b	**4c**
	5	Interest income	**5**
	6	Dividends and dividend equivalents: **a** Ordinary dividends	**6a**
		b Qualified dividends **6b** **c** Dividend equivalents **6c**	
	7	Royalties	**7**
	8	Net short-term capital gain (loss) (attach Schedule D (Form 1065))	**8**
	9a	Net long-term capital gain (loss) (attach Schedule D (Form 1065))	**9a**
	b	Collectibles (28%) gain (loss) **9b**	
	c	Unrecaptured section 1250 gain (attach statement) **9c**	
	10	Net section 1231 gain (loss) (attach Form 4797)	**10**
	11	Other income (loss) (see instructions) Type: _____	**11**
Deductions	**12**	Section 179 deduction (attach Form 4562)	**12**
	13a	Cash contributions	**13a**
	b	Noncash contributions	**13b**
	c	Investment interest expense	**13c**
	d	Section 59(e)(2) expenditures: **(1)** Type:_____ **(2)** Amount:	**13d(2)**
	e	Other deductions (see instructions) Type:_____	**13e**
Self-Employ-ment	**14a**	Net earnings (loss) from self-employment	**14a**
	b	Gross farming or fishing income	**14b**
	c	Gross nonfarm income	**14c**
Credits	**15a**	Low-income housing credit (section 42(j)(5))	**15a**
	b	Low-income housing credit (other)	**15b**
	c	Qualified rehabilitation expenditures (rental real estate) (attach Form 3468, if applicable)	**15c**
	d	Other rental real estate credits (see instructions) Type: _____	**15d**
	e	Other rental credits (see instructions) Type: _____	**15e**
	f	Other credits (see instructions) Type: _____	**15f**
Inter-national	**16**	Attach Schedule K-2 (Form 1065), Partners' Distributive Share Items—International, and check this box to indicate that you are reporting items of international tax relevance ☐	
Alternative Minimum Tax (AMT) Items	**17a**	Post-1986 depreciation adjustment	**17a**
	b	Adjusted gain or loss	**17b**
	c	Depletion (other than oil and gas)	**17c**
	d	Oil, gas, and geothermal properties—gross income	**17d**
	e	Oil, gas, and geothermal properties—deductions	**17e**
	f	Other AMT items (attach statement)	**17f**
Other Information	**18a**	Tax-exempt interest income	**18a**
	b	Other tax-exempt income	**18b**
	c	Nondeductible expenses	**18c**
	19a	Distributions of cash and marketable securities	**19a**
	b	Distributions of other property	**19b**
	20a	Investment income	**20a**
	b	Investment expenses	**20b**
	c	Other items and amounts (attach statement)	
	21	Total foreign taxes paid or accrued	**21**

Form **1065** (2023)

IRS Form 1065: U.S. Return of Partnership Income (page 6)

Form 1065 (2023)   Page **6**

Analysis of Net Income (Loss) per Return

| 1 | Net income (loss). Combine Schedule K, lines 1 through 11. From the result, subtract the sum of Schedule K, lines 12 through 13e, and 21 . . . . | **1** | |

2	Analysis by partner type:	**(i)** Corporate	**(ii)** Individual (active)	**(iii)** Individual (passive)	**(iv)** Partnership	**(v)** Exempt Organization	**(vi)** Nominee/Other
a	General partners						
b	Limited partners						

Schedule L — Balance Sheets per Books

	Assets	Beginning of tax year (a)	(b)	End of tax year (c)	(d)
1	Cash				
2a	Trade notes and accounts receivable				
b	Less allowance for bad debts				
3	Inventories				
4	U.S. Government obligations				
5	Tax-exempt securities				
6	Other current assets (attach statement)				
7a	Loans to partners (or persons related to partners) .				
b	Mortgage and real estate loans				
8	Other investments (attach statement)				
9a	Buildings and other depreciable assets				
b	Less accumulated depreciation				
10a	Depletable assets				
b	Less accumulated depletion				
11	Land (net of any amortization)				
12a	Intangible assets (amortizable only)				
b	Less accumulated amortization				
13	Other assets (attach statement)				
14	Total assets				
	Liabilities and Capital				
15	Accounts payable				
16	Mortgages, notes, bonds payable in less than 1 year				
17	Other current liabilities (attach statement)				
18	All nonrecourse loans				
19a	Loans from partners (or persons related to partners) .				
b	Mortgages, notes, bonds payable in 1 year or more .				
20	Other liabilities (attach statement)				
21	Partners' capital accounts				
22	Total liabilities and capital				

Schedule M-1 — Reconciliation of Income (Loss) per Books With Analysis of Net Income (Loss) per Return

Note: The partnership may be required to file Schedule M-3. See instructions.

1	Net income (loss) per books		6	Income recorded on books this year not included on Schedule K, lines 1 through 11 (itemize):	
2	Income included on Schedule K, lines 1, 2, 3c, 5, 6a, 7, 8, 9a, 10, and 11, not recorded on books this year (itemize): _____		a	Tax-exempt interest $ _____	
3	Guaranteed payments (other than health insurance)		7	Deductions included on Schedule K, lines 1 through 13e, and 21, not charged against book income this year (itemize):	
4	Expenses recorded on books this year not included on Schedule K, lines 1 through 13e, and 21 (itemize):		a	Depreciation $ _____	
a	Depreciation $ _____		8	Add lines 6 and 7	
b	Travel and entertainment $ _____		9	Income (loss) (Analysis of Net Income (Loss), line 1). Subtract line 8 from line 5	
5	Add lines 1 through 4				

Schedule M-2 — Analysis of Partners' Capital Accounts

1	Balance at beginning of year . . .		6	Distributions: **a** Cash	
2	Capital contributed: **a** Cash . . .			**b** Property	
	b Property . .		7	Other decreases (itemize): _____	
3	Net income (loss) (see instructions) .				
4	Other increases (itemize): _____		8	Add lines 6 and 7	
5	Add lines 1 through 4		9	Balance at end of year. Subtract line 8 from line 5	

Form **1065** (2023)

Schedule K-1 (IRS Form 1065)

☐ Final K-1 ☐ Amended K-1	**651123** OMB No. 1545-0123

Schedule K-1 (Form 1065)
Department of the Treasury
Internal Revenue Service

20**23**

For calendar year 2023, or tax year

beginning ___ / ___ / 2023 ending ___ / ___ / ___

Partner's Share of Income, Deductions, Credits, etc.

See separate instructions.

Part I Information About the Partnership

A Partnership's employer identification number

B Partnership's name, address, city, state, and ZIP code

C IRS center where partnership filed return:

D ☐ Check if this is a publicly traded partnership (PTP)

Part II Information About the Partner

E Partner's SSN or TIN (Do not use TIN of a disregarded entity. See instructions.)

F Name, address, city, state, and ZIP code for partner entered in E. See instructions.

G ☐ General partner or LLC member-manager   ☐ Limited partner or other LLC member

H1 ☐ Domestic partner   ☐ Foreign partner
H2 ☐ If the partner is a disregarded entity (DE), enter the partner's:
TIN _____ Name _____

I1 What type of entity is this partner? _____
I2 If this partner is a retirement plan (IRA/SEP/Keogh/etc.), check here ☐

J Partner's share of profit, loss, and capital (see instructions):

	Beginning	Ending
Profit	%	%
Loss	%	%
Capital	%	%

Check if decrease is due to:
☐ Sale or ☐ Exchange of partnership interest. See instructions.

K1 Partner's share of liabilities:

	Beginning	Ending
Nonrecourse	$	$
Qualified nonrecourse financing	$	$
Recourse	$	$

K2 ☐ Check this box if item K1 includes liability amounts from lower-tier partnerships
K3 ☐ Check if any of the above liability is subject to guarantees or other payment obligations by the partner. See instructions.

L **Partner's Capital Account Analysis**

Beginning capital account	$
Capital contributed during the year	$
Current year net income (loss)	$
Other increase (decrease) (attach explanation)	$
Withdrawals and distributions	$ ( )
Ending capital account	$

M Did the partner contribute property with a built-in gain (loss)?
☐ Yes ☐ No If "Yes," attach statement. See instructions.

N **Partner's Share of Net Unrecognized Section 704(c) Gain or (Loss)**
Beginning . . . . $
Ending . . . . $

Part III Partner's Share of Current Year Income, Deductions, Credits, and Other Items

1	Ordinary business income (loss)	14	Self-employment earnings (loss)
2	Net rental real estate income (loss)		
3	Other net rental income (loss)	15	Credits
4a	Guaranteed payments for services		
4b	Guaranteed payments for capital	16	Schedule K-3 is attached if checked . . . . . . ☐
4c	Total guaranteed payments	17	Alternative minimum tax (AMT) items
5	Interest income		
6a	Ordinary dividends		
6b	Qualified dividends	18	Tax-exempt income and nondeductible expenses
6c	Dividend equivalents		
7	Royalties		
8	Net short-term capital gain (loss)		
9a	Net long-term capital gain (loss)	19	Distributions
9b	Collectibles (28%) gain (loss)		
9c	Unrecaptured section 1250 gain	20	Other information
10	Net section 1231 gain (loss)		
11	Other income (loss)		
12	Section 179 deduction	21	Foreign taxes paid or accrued
13	Other deductions		

22	☐	More than one activity for at-risk purposes*
23	☐	More than one activity for passive activity purposes*

*See attached statement for additional information.

For IRS Use Only

For Paperwork Reduction Act Notice, see the Instructions for Form 1065.   www.irs.gov/Form1065   Cat. No. 11394R   Schedule K-1 (Form 1065) 2023

State tax requirements, procedures, and forms vary from state to state. Check with your state's department of revenue or similar department for the requirements in your state. Many states provide a starter guide for new businesses, including state tax registrations and filings.

The Iowa Business Tax Permit Registration form is included below. It is a representative example of a state department of revenue registration. In Section 4, it includes options for accounts or permits for sales and use tax and income tax withholding. Some states have separate registrations for sales tax and income tax withholding.

What's a Use Tax?

A use tax is a tax on the use or consumption of tangible goods that were purchased out-of-state but would have been subject to sales tax if they had been purchased in-state. In other words, it's the sales tax the state missed out on because your company bought from outside the state. Some states allow goods purchased for resale to be exempt from use taxes.

Employment Taxes and Income Tax Withholding—Forms 940 and 941

As noted above, if you're an employer and your state has a personal income tax, you'll need to register with the state department of revenue to withhold state income taxes from your employees' paychecks. You'll also need to register with the state labor department or its equivalent for unemployment tax and wage reporting purposes. Once registered, you'll file monthly, quarterly, or annual withholding and unemployment tax reports, as required by your state.

Iowa Business Tax Permit Registration

Iowa Department of
REVENUE ———————————————— **Iowa Business Tax Permit Registration**

tax.iowa.gov

Read the instructions page before filling out the application. If any information is incomplete or illegible, the form will be returned.

Registration Contacts
A registration contact is the individual authorized to discuss the business's registration form during the registration process. Designating a registration contact does not authorize that person to act on behalf of your business for other matters before the Department. The Department will not disclose tax information to a registration contact unless additional disclosure authorization has been obtained.

Registration Contact 1:
Last name: _____ First name: _____
Phone: _____ Email: _____

Registration Contact 2:
Last name: _____ First name: _____
Phone: _____ Email: _____

SECTION 1: Type of Ownership – Individual
Do not fill out section 2 if completing this section or the form will be returned.

☐ Sole proprietor
☐ Single-member limited liability company

SECTION 2: Type of Ownership – Business
Do not fill out this section if section 1 has been completed or the form will be returned.

☐ Corporation   ☐ Limited liability company
☐ Partnership   ☐ Limited liability partnership
☐ Association   ☐ Estate or Trust
☐ Government   ☐ Other (describe): _____

SECTION 3: Ownership Information
If ownership information is incomplete or illegible, the form will be returned.

NAICS Code: See the North American Industry Classification System for more information. Provide a code or description of your business: _____

Identification Number: All ownerships must provide either a social security number (SSN), individual taxpayer identification number (ITIN), or federal employer identification number (FEIN). If you have applied but not yet received a FEIN, write "applied for". A FEIN is required for a withholding account.

☐ Social Security Number (SSN) or Individual Taxpayer Identification Number (ITIN): _____
☐ Federal Employer Identification Number (FEIN): _____

Legal Name of Entity: For individuals, first and last name are required. For businesses, a legal name is required and a doing business as (DBA) is optional.
Last name: _____ First name: _____
Legal name: _____
Doing business as name: _____

For Office Use Only:

2378005019999

78-005a (09/13/2023)

Iowa Business Tax Permit Registration (page 2)

Iowa Business Tax Permit Registration, page 2

Headquarters or Primary Address: If you do not have a headquarters address, enter the primary location.
Attention:_____
Address: _____
City:_____ State: _____ ZIP:_____

Headquarters or Primary Mailing Address: (Optional) Is there a different mailing address used for correspondences? If so, provide the address here.
Attention: _____
Mailing address: _____
City:_____ State: _____ ZIP:_____

Sales and Use Account Mailing Address: (Optional) Is there a separate mailing address related to the sales and use account? If so, provide the address here.
Attention:_____
Mailing address: _____
City:_____ State: _____ ZIP:_____

Income Tax Withholding Account Mailing Address: (Optional) Is there a separate mailing address related to the income tax withholding account? If so, provide the address here.
Attention:_____
Mailing address: _____
City:_____ State: _____ ZIP:_____

SECTION 4: Accounts or Permits Needed

☐ **Sales and Use Tax** (For retailers required to collect and remit sales tax pursuant to Iowa Code sections 423.14A or 423.29.)

Start date for collecting sales and use tax: _____ You are required to file returns every tax period from this date forward until the account is cancelled.

What is your projected sales tax that will be collected per year? If section is left blank, your filing frequency will be File & Pay Monthly. For more information about filing frequencies see tax.iowa.gov.

☐ Less than $1,200 tax per year – File & Pay Annually

☐ More than $1,200 tax per year – File & Pay Monthly

Do you have a physical presence in Iowa?.. ☐ Yes ☐ No

- If Yes, is it the same address as your headquarters address? If no, complete the business location information below. See Instructions for more information.

Location address:_____ City:_____ State: ___ ZIP:_____

Will you have gross sales of $100,000 or more? .... ☐ Yes ☐ No

Will you exclusively be a marketplace seller? .... ☐ Yes ☐ No
See Instructions for more information.

78-005b (09/13/2023)

2378005029999

Iowa Business Tax Permit Registration (page 3)

Iowa Business Tax Permit Registration, page 3

Activities at the sales location. Check if applicable and see Instructions for more information.

☐ Hotel and Motel: **Filed monthly only.**

☐ Automobile Rental: **Filed monthly only.**

☐ Household Hazardous Material Permit (HHM).

☐ Regular ($25 fee)

☐ Special ($125 fee or more)

Include a payment with your HHM application. Make check payable to Iowa Department of Revenue. When you pay by check, you authorize the Department of Revenue to convert your check to a one-time electronic banking transaction.

☐ **Income Tax Withholding** (For employers or payers that are required to deduct and withhold Iowa income tax pursuant to Iowa Code section 422.16(1))

Start date for withholding:_____ You are required to file returns every tax period from this date forward until the account is cancelled.

What is the projected income tax being withheld per year? If section is left blank, your filing frequency will be File & Pay Quarterly. For more information about filing frequencies see tax.iowa.gov.

☐ Less than $6,000 tax per year – File & Pay Quarterly

☐ $6,000 - $120,000 tax per year – File Quarterly/Pay Monthly

☐ More than $120,000 tax per year – File Quarterly/Pay Semimonthly

Withholding contact (Required to be completed if registering for a withholding permit/account.) See Instructions for more information.

Last name: _____ First name: _____

SSN or ITIN: _____

Mailing address: _____

City: _____ State:_____ ZIP: _____

Phone: _____ Email: _____

SECTION 5: Authorized Individuals (Required to be completed if your entity is listed in Section 2. Optional if your entity is listed in Section 1.) See Instructions for more information.

For more information or to add, alter, or revoke authorizations on file with the Department, see tax.iowa.gov.

Individual last name:_____ First name: _____

SSN or ITIN: _____ Phone: _____

Home address: _____

City:_____ State:_____ ZIP: _____ Email: _____

Does this person have the authority to receive confidential information about the entity and to act on behalf of the entity?

☐ Yes

☐ No (If no is selected, the Department will not disclose confidential tax information to this individual unless additional disclosure authorization has been obtained.)

78-005c (09/13/2023)

2378005039999

Iowa Business Tax Permit Registration (page 4)

Iowa Business Tax Permit Registration, page 4

Individual last name: _____   First name: _____

SSN or ITIN: _____   Phone: _____

Home address: _____

City: _____   State: _____   ZIP: _____   Email: _____

Does this person have the authority to receive confidential information about the entity and to act on behalf of the entity?

☐ Yes

☐ No (If no is selected, the Department will not disclose confidential tax information to this individual unless additional disclosure authorization has been obtained.)

SECTION 6: Signature

This form must be signed by the owner or an authorized individual listed in section 5 above.

I, the undersigned, declare under penalties of perjury or false certificate, that I have examined this registration form, and, to the best of my knowledge and belief, it is true, correct, and complete. I declare that I am authorized to act on behalf of the taxpayer, and will only act within my authority.

Signature must be signed by hand or via a digital signature with a digital certificate. Stamped or typed signatures are not accepted.

Signature: _____   Date: _____

Print name: _____   Phone: _____

Title: _____   Contact email: _____

The integrity and security of sending personal information via fax or email cannot be guaranteed. By submitting this form via fax or email, you agree to hold the Department harmless if a fax or an email results in third party access to the information

Submit this form by:

Fax: 515-281-3906   OR   **Mail to:** ATTN Registration Services
                                                              Iowa Department of Revenue
                                                              PO Box 10470
                                                              Des Moines IA 50306-0470

Questions or Assistance:
Additional information can be found:
- On the Department website (tax.iowa.gov)
- By emailing the Department (idr@iowa.gov)
- By calling Taxpayer Services at (515) 281-3114 or (800) 367-3388

78-005d (09/13/2023)

2378005049999

State unemployment taxes are known as SUTA (State Unemployment Tax Act) taxes or SUI (state unemployment insurance) taxes. States set their own SUTA rates and limitations. We don't review specific state unemployment tax or withholding returns, as the forms and filing procedures vary significantly by state.

All employers, though, file the same federal withholding and unemployment tax returns:

- Form 940, *Employer's Annual Federal Unemployment (FUTA) Tax Return*, and
- Form 941, *Employer's Quarterly Federal Tax Return*.

Forms 940 and 941 are included below. Your state's unemployment tax and wage reports might be formatted differently from the federal reports, but they should ask for much of the same information. Of course, if you have employees in multiple states, you'll need to file SUTA and withholding returns (as applicable) in each of those states.

Federal Form 940—FUTA Tax Return

You're required to pay FUTA taxes if you pay more than $1,500 of wages (in the aggregate, to all employees) during any calendar quarter, or if you have one or more employees working at least 20 weeks during the tax year. (The criteria are different for wages paid to household workers—such as housekeepers, babysitters, and gardeners whom you employ to work in or at your home—and agricultural workers.) FUTA taxes are paid by employers, not employees, so they're not withheld from employees' paychecks.

FUTA Tax Rate

The FUTA tax rate for 2024 is 6% of the first $7,000 of each employee's wages (FUTA wages), so up to $420 for the year. However, you might be able to claim a credit of up to 5.4% of FUTA wages for state unemployment (SUTA) taxes paid, reducing your federal rate to 0.6% (6% minus 5.4%). The SUTA credit is reduced if your state is a "credit reduction state." Credit reduction states are states that haven't repaid loans from the federal government taken to cover unemployment benefit obligations. For 2024, credit reduction states are California, Connecticut, Illinois, New York, and the U.S. Virgin Islands.

Paying FUTA Taxes

You will file Form 940 annually, but if your FUTA tax liability for a given quarter is more than $500, you are required to make a tax deposit in that quarter. FUTA deposits are made electronically. Quarterly FUTA deposits are due by the last day of the month following the quarter— April 30 for the first quarter, July 31 for the second quarter, October 31 for the third quarter, January 31 for the fourth quarter. Your Form 940 for 2024 is due January 31, 2025, but the deadline can be extended to February 10, 2025 if you made all of your quarterly deposits on time.

The first steps toward completing Form 940 are coming up with FUTA wages (Lines 3-7) and unadjusted FUTA tax (Line 8). Then, through a series of adjustments (Lines 9-11), you arrive at adjusted FUTA tax (Line 12). If your deposits (Line 13) were less than your adjusted tax, then you have a balance due (Line 14). If the underpayment is $500 or less, you can pay it with your return. If the underpayment is more than $500, you need to determine the correct tax for each quarter (what you should have deposited, not what you actually deposited). In addition to the tax due, the IRS will assess a penalty and interest on each quarterly underpayment.

Form 941—Payroll Tax Return

As an employer, you are required, for federal purposes, to withhold income taxes and the employee portion of Social Security and Medicare insurance taxes from employees' wages (FICA taxes). You are also required to remit those withholdings, along with the employer portion of FICA taxes, to the federal government according to very strict procedures and schedules. While you never want to tangle with the IRS, as an employer you especially don't want to get into a dispute over withholdings or FICA taxes.

Form 940: Employer's Annual Federal Unemployment (FUTA) Tax Return

Form **940 for 2023:** **Employer's Annual Federal Unemployment (FUTA) Tax Return**   850113

Department of the Treasury — Internal Revenue Service

OMB No. 1545-0028

Employer identification number (EIN) ☐☐ – ☐☐☐☐☐☐☐

Name *(not your trade name)*

Trade name *(if any)*

Address

Number   Street   Suite or room number

City   State   ZIP code

Foreign country name   Foreign province/county   Foreign postal code

Type of Return
(Check all that apply.)

☐ **a.** Amended
☐ **b.** Successor employer
☐ **c.** No payments to employees in 2023
☐ **d.** Final: Business closed or stopped paying wages

Go to *www.irs.gov/Form940* for instructions and the latest information.

Read the separate instructions before you complete this form. Please type or print within the boxes.

Part 1: **Tell us about your return. If any line does NOT apply, leave it blank. See instructions before completing Part 1.**

1a If you had to pay state unemployment tax in one state only, enter the state abbreviation . **1a** ☐☐

1b If you had to pay state unemployment tax in more than one state, you are a multi-state employer . . . . **1b** ☐ Check here. Complete Schedule A (Form 940).

2 If you paid wages in a state that is subject to **CREDIT REDUCTION** . . . . **2** ☐ Check here. Complete Schedule A (Form 940).

Part 2: **Determine your FUTA tax before adjustments. If any line does NOT apply, leave it blank.**

3 Total payments to all employees **3**

4 Payments exempt from FUTA tax **4**

Check all that apply: **4a** ☐ Fringe benefits   **4c** ☐ Retirement/Pension   **4e** ☐ Other
4b ☐ Group-term life insurance   **4d** ☐ Dependent care

5 Total of payments made to each employee in excess of $7,000 . . . . **5**

6 Subtotal (line 4 + line 5 = line 6) **6**

7 Total taxable FUTA wages (line 3 – line 6 = line 7). See instructions **7**

8 FUTA tax before adjustments (line 7 × 0.006 = line 8) **8**

Part 3: **Determine your adjustments. If any line does NOT apply, leave it blank.**

9 If ALL of the taxable FUTA wages you paid were excluded from state unemployment tax, multiply line 7 by 0.054 (line 7 × 0.054 = line 9). Go to line 12 . . . . **9**

10 If SOME of the taxable FUTA wages you paid were excluded from state unemployment tax, OR you paid ANY state unemployment tax late (after the due date for filing Form 940), complete the worksheet in the instructions. Enter the amount from line 7 of the worksheet . . **10**

11 If credit reduction applies, enter the total from Schedule A (Form 940) **11**

Part 4: **Determine your FUTA tax and balance due or overpayment. If any line does NOT apply, leave it blank.**

12 Total FUTA tax after adjustments (lines 8 + 9 + 10 + 11 = line 12) **12**

13 FUTA tax deposited for the year, including any overpayment applied from a prior year . **13**

14 Balance due. If line 12 is more than line 13, enter the excess on line 14.
• If line 14 is more than $500, you must deposit your tax.
• If line 14 is $500 or less, you may pay with this return. See instructions **14**

15 Overpayment. If line 13 is more than line 12, enter the excess on line 15 and check a box below **15**

You **MUST** complete both pages of this form and **SIGN** it.   Check one: ☐ Apply to next return. ☐ Send a refund.

For Privacy Act and Paperwork Reduction Act Notice, see the back of the Payment Voucher.   Cat. No. 11234O   Form **940** (2023)

Form 940: Employer's Annual Federal Unemployment (FUTA) Tax Return (page 2)

850212

Name *(not your trade name)*	Employer identification number (EIN)
	—

Part 5: Report your FUTA tax liability by quarter only if line 12 is more than $500. If not, go to Part 6.

16 Report the amount of your FUTA tax liability for each quarter; do NOT enter the amount you deposited. If you had no liability for a quarter, leave the line blank.

16a **1st quarter** (January 1 – March 31) . . . . 16a [.]

16b **2nd quarter** (April 1 – June 30) . . . . 16b [.]

16c **3rd quarter** (July 1 – September 30) . . . . 16c [.]

16d **4th quarter** (October 1 – December 31) . . . . 16d [.]

17 **Total tax liability for the year** (lines 16a + 16b + 16c + 16d = line 17) 17 [.] **Total must equal line 12.**

Part 6: May we speak with your third-party designee?

Do you want to allow an employee, a paid tax preparer, or another person to discuss this return with the IRS? See the instructions for details.

☐ **Yes.** Designee's name and phone number

Select a 5-digit personal identification number (PIN) to use when talking to the IRS. ☐ ☐ ☐ ☐ ☐

☐ **No.**

Part 7: Sign here. You MUST complete both pages of this form and SIGN it.

Under penalties of perjury, I declare that I have examined this return, including accompanying schedules and statements, and to the best of my knowledge and belief, it is true, correct, and complete, and that no part of any payment made to a state unemployment fund claimed as a credit was, or is to be, deducted from the payments made to employees. Declaration of preparer (other than taxpayer) is based on all information of which preparer has any knowledge.

Sign your name here

Print your name here

Print your title here

Date   /   /

Best daytime phone

Paid Preparer Use Only   Check if you are self-employed ☐

Preparer's name		PTIN	
Preparer's signature		Date	/ /
Firm's name (or yours if self-employed)		EIN	
Address		Phone	
City	State	ZIP code	

Form 940: Employer's Annual Federal Unemployment (FUTA) Tax Return (page 3)

Form 940-V, Payment Voucher

Purpose of Form

Complete Form 940-V if you're making a payment with Form 940. We will use the completed voucher to credit your payment more promptly and accurately, and to improve our service to you.

Making Payments With Form 940

To avoid a penalty, make your payment with your 2023 Form 940 **only if** your FUTA tax for the fourth quarter (plus any undeposited amounts from earlier quarters) is $500 or less. If your total FUTA tax after adjustments (Form 940, line 12) is more than $500, you must make deposits by electronic funds transfer. See *When Must You Deposit Your FUTA Tax?* in the Instructions for Form 940. Also see sections 11 and 14 of Pub. 15 for more information about deposits.

 Use Form 940-V when making any payment with Form 940. However, if you pay an amount with Form 940 that should've been deposited, you may be subject to a penalty. See Deposit Penalties *in section 11 of Pub. 15.*

Specific Instructions

Box 1—Employer identification number (EIN). If you don't have an EIN, you may apply for one online by visiting the IRS website at *www.irs.gov/EIN*. You may also apply for an EIN by faxing or mailing Form SS-4 to the IRS. If you haven't received your EIN by the due date of Form 940, write "Applied For" and the date you applied in this entry space.

Box 2—Amount paid. Enter the amount paid with Form 940.

Box 3—Name and address. Enter your name and address as shown on Form 940.

• Enclose your check or money order made payable to "United States Treasury." Be sure to enter your EIN, "Form 940," and "2023" on your check or money order. Don't send cash. Don't staple Form 940-V or your payment to Form 940 (or to each other).

• Detach Form 940-V and send it with your payment and Form 940 to the address provided in the Instructions for Form 940.

Note: You must also complete the entity information above Part 1 on Form 940.

Detach Here and Mail With Your Payment and Form 940.

Form **940-V**		**Payment Voucher**	OMB No. 1545-0028
Department of the Treasury Internal Revenue Service		Don't staple or attach this voucher to your payment.	**2023**
1 Enter your employer identification number (EIN).	**2** Enter the amount of your payment. Make your check or money order payable to "**United States Treasury.**"		Dollars Cents
—	**3** Enter your business name (individual name if sole proprietor).		
	Enter your address.		
	Enter your city, state, and ZIP code; or your city, foreign country name, foreign province/county, and foreign postal code.		

On Form 941, you report the amount of federal income tax actually withheld (Line 3) and you calculate your FICA taxes (Line 5). Withholdings and FICA taxes are combined on Line 6 as total (unadjusted) taxes. After adjustments and credits, you enter your total taxes on Line 12.

Most employers are required to deposit employee income tax withheld, along with the employee and employer contributions to FICA taxes, with the government monthly or semiweekly. Some small employers with less than $2,500 in total (Line 12) taxes are not required to make deposits and can instead pay the taxes quarterly, with Form 941. Look carefully into the rules around deposits to be sure that you're remitting taxes on time, whether it be monthly, semiweekly, or quarterly. All deposits are made electronically.

Payroll Processing and Tax Returns— Handle In-House or Outsource?

You might be debating whether to handle payroll, and any related tax filings, in-house or instead through a payroll service. If you have just a handful of employees, you might encounter payroll services that either aren't all that interested in your business, or are simply too expensive. If you have payroll expertise on staff, you can take advantage of some very good DIY payroll software programs, such as *QuickBooks Payroll*, for payroll processing. Some programs automatically generate Form 941.

As good as some of the DIY solutions are, be sure that you have the knowledge and technology to do payroll and payroll tax reporting properly and efficiently. Obviously, your employees need timely and accurate paychecks. The company needs to stay compliant with the requirements outlined above. If you have any doubt about DIY payroll, we recommend trying to find a payroll service that is interested in your business and that you can afford.

Form 941: Employer's Quarterly Federal Tax Return

Form 941 for 2024: Employer's QUARTERLY Federal Tax Return
(Rev. March 2024)
Department of the Treasury — Internal Revenue Service

950124

OMB No. 1545-0029

Employer identification number (EIN) ☐☐ – ☐☐☐☐☐☐☐

Name (not your trade name)

Trade name (if any)

Address

Number   Street   Suite or room number

City   State   ZIP code

Foreign country name   Foreign province/county   Foreign postal code

Report for this Quarter of 2024
(Check one.)

☐ **1:** January, February, March

☐ **2:** April, May, June

☐ **3:** July, August, September

☐ **4:** October, November, December

Go to *www.irs.gov/Form941* for instructions and the latest information.

Read the separate instructions before you complete Form 941. Type or print within the boxes.

Part 1: Answer these questions for this quarter. Employers in American Samoa, Guam, the Commonwealth of the Northern Mariana Islands, the U.S. Virgin Islands, and Puerto Rico can skip lines 2 and 3, unless you have employees who are subject to U.S. income tax withholding.

1 Number of employees who received wages, tips, or other compensation for the pay period including: *Mar. 12* (Quarter 1), *June 12* (Quarter 2), *Sept. 12* (Quarter 3), or *Dec. 12* (Quarter 4)   **1** ☐

2 Wages, tips, and other compensation . . . .   **2** ☐

3 Federal income tax withheld from wages, tips, and other compensation . . . . .   **3** ☐

4 If no wages, tips, and other compensation are subject to social security or Medicare tax   ☐ Check here and go to line 6.

	Column 1		Column 2
5a Taxable social security wages . .	☐	× 0.124 =	☐
5b Taxable social security tips . . .	☐	× 0.124 =	☐
5c Taxable Medicare wages & tips . .	☐	× 0.029 =	☐
5d Taxable wages & tips subject to Additional Medicare Tax withholding	☐	× 0.009 =	☐

5e Total social security and Medicare taxes. Add Column 2 from lines 5a, 5b, 5c, and 5d . . . .   **5e** ☐

5f Section 3121(q) Notice and Demand—Tax due on unreported tips (see instructions) . .   **5f** ☐

6 Total taxes before adjustments. Add lines 3, 5e, and 5f . . . .   **6** ☐

7 Current quarter's adjustment for fractions of cents . . . .   **7** ☐

8 Current quarter's adjustment for sick pay . . . .   **8** ☐

9 Current quarter's adjustments for tips and group-term life insurance . . . . . .   **9** ☐

10 Total taxes after adjustments. Combine lines 6 through 9 . . . .   **10** ☐

11 Qualified small business payroll tax credit for increasing research activities. Attach Form 8974   **11** ☐

12 Total taxes after adjustments and nonrefundable credits. Subtract line 11 from line 10 . .   **12** ☐

13 Total deposits for this quarter, including overpayment applied from a prior quarter and overpayments applied from Form 941-X, 941-X (PR), or 944-X filed in the current quarter   **13** ☐

14 Balance due. If line 12 is more than line 13, enter the difference and see instructions . . .   **14** ☐

15 Overpayment. If line 13 is more than line 12, enter the difference   ☐ Check one: ☐ Apply to next return. ☐ Send a refund.

You MUST complete both pages of Form 941 and SIGN it.

For Privacy Act and Paperwork Reduction Act Notice, see separate instructions.   Cat. No. 17001Z   Form **941** (Rev. 3-2024)

Form 941: Employer's Quarterly Federal Tax Return (page 2)

950224

Name *(not your trade name)*	Employer identification number (EIN)
	—

Part 2: Tell us about your deposit schedule and tax liability for this quarter.

If you're unsure about whether you're a monthly schedule depositor or a semiweekly schedule depositor, see section 11 of Pub. 15.

16 Check one: ☐ Line 12 on this return is less than $2,500 or line 12 on the return for the prior quarter was less than $2,500, and you didn't incur a $100,000 next-day deposit obligation during the current quarter. If line 12 for the prior quarter was less than $2,500 but line 12 on this return is $100,000 or more, you must provide a record of your federal tax liability. If you're a monthly schedule depositor, complete the deposit schedule below; if you're a semiweekly schedule depositor, attach Schedule B (Form 941). Go to Part 3.

☐ You were a monthly schedule depositor for the entire quarter. Enter your tax liability for each month and total liability for the quarter, then go to Part 3.

Tax liability: Month 1 [.]

Month 2 [.]

Month 3 [.]

Total liability for quarter [.]   Total must equal line 12.

☐ You were a semiweekly schedule depositor for any part of this quarter. Complete Schedule B (Form 941), Report of Tax Liability for Semiweekly Schedule Depositors, and attach it to Form 941. Go to Part 3.

Part 3: Tell us about your business. If a question does NOT apply to your business, leave it blank.

17 If your business has closed or you stopped paying wages . . . . ☐ Check here and

enter the final date you paid wages [/ /] ; also attach a statement to your return. See instructions.

18 If you're a seasonal employer and you don't have to file a return for every quarter of the year . . . ☐ Check here.

Part 4: May we speak with your third-party designee?

Do you want to allow an employee, a paid tax preparer, or another person to discuss this return with the IRS? See the instructions for details.

☐ Yes. Designee's name and phone number [ ] [ ]

Select a 5-digit personal identification number (PIN) to use when talking to the IRS. ☐ ☐ ☐ ☐ ☐

☐ No.

Part 5: Sign here. You MUST complete both pages of Form 941 and SIGN it.

Under penalties of perjury, I declare that I have examined this return, including accompanying schedules and statements, and to the best of my knowledge and belief, it is true, correct, and complete. Declaration of preparer (other than taxpayer) is based on all information of which preparer has any knowledge.

Sign your name here		Print your name here [ ]
		Print your title here [ ]
Date [/ /]		Best daytime phone [ ]

Paid Preparer Use Only Check if you're self-employed . . . ☐

Preparer's name	[ ]	PTIN	[ ]
Preparer's signature	[ ]	Date	[/ /]
Firm's name (or yours if self-employed)	[ ]	EIN	[ ]
Address	[ ]	Phone	[ ]
City	[ ] State [ ]	ZIP code	[ ]

Form **941** (Rev. 3-2024)

Form 941: Employer's Quarterly Federal Tax Return (page 3)

Form 941-V, Payment Voucher

Purpose of Form

Complete Form 941-V if you're making a payment with Form 941. We will use the completed voucher to credit your payment more promptly and accurately, and to improve our service to you.

Making Payments With Form 941

To avoid a penalty, make your payment with Form 941 **only if:**

• Your total taxes after adjustments and nonrefundable credits (Form 941, line 12) for either the current quarter or the preceding quarter are less than $2,500, you didn't incur a $100,000 next-day deposit obligation during the current quarter, and you're paying in full with a timely filed return; or

• You're a monthly schedule depositor making a payment in accordance with the Accuracy of Deposits Rule. See section 11 of Pub. 15 for details. In this case, the amount of your payment may be $2,500 or more.

Otherwise, you must make deposits by electronic funds transfer. See section 11 of Pub. 15 for deposit instructions. Don't use Form 941-V to make federal tax deposits.

⚠️ *Use Form 941-V when making any payment with Form 941. However, if you pay an amount with Form 941 that should've been deposited, you may be subject to a penalty. See Deposit Penalties in section 11 of Pub. 15.*

Specific Instructions

Box 1—Employer identification number (EIN). If you don't have an EIN, you may apply for one online by going to *www.irs.gov/EIN*. You may also apply for an EIN by faxing or mailing Form SS-4 to the IRS. If you haven't received your EIN by the due date of Form 941, write "Applied For" and the date you applied in this entry space.

Box 2—Amount paid. Enter the amount paid with Form 941.

Box 3—Tax period. Darken the circle identifying the quarter for which the payment is made. Darken only one circle.

Box 4—Name and address. Enter your name and address as shown on Form 941.

• Enclose your check or money order made payable to "United States Treasury." Be sure to enter your EIN, "Form 941," and the tax period ("1st Quarter 2024," "2nd Quarter 2024," "3rd Quarter 2024," or "4th Quarter 2024") on your check or money order. Don't send cash. Don't staple Form 941-V or your payment to Form 941 (or to each other).

• Detach Form 941-V and send it with your payment and Form 941 to the address in the Instructions for Form 941.

Note: You must also complete the entity information above Part 1 on Form 941.

Detach Here and Mail With Your Payment and Form 941.

- -

Form **941-V**		**Payment Voucher**		OMB No. 1545-0029
Department of the Treasury Internal Revenue Service		Don't staple this voucher or your payment to Form 941.		20**24**

1 Enter your employer identification number (EIN).	2 **Enter the amount of your payment.** Make your check or money order payable to "United States Treasury."		Dollars	Cents
−				

3 Tax Period			4 Enter your business name (individual name if sole proprietor).
○ 1st Quarter	○ 3rd Quarter		Enter your address.
○ 2nd Quarter	○ 4th Quarter		Enter your city, state, and ZIP code; or your city, foreign country name, foreign province/county, and foreign postal code.

Good Governance:
Making and Documenting Decisions

One of the attractive features of LLCs is that they're less formal when it comes to structure and governance. Unlike corporations, LLC's don't have a board of directors and they aren't required to hold annual meetings. In practice, closely-held corporations in which the shareholders are the directors and the officers tend to run pretty informally. And while LLCs aren't required to hold annual meetings, they should, even if only to reappoint the managers (in a manager-managed LLC).

In fact, LLCs can be a little too informal when it comes to ownership and management decision-making and documentation. This is especially true in member-managed LLCs, where every owner is involved in management decisions. Why hold formal meetings and votes when all the principals participate in important decisions in the normal course of business? Even in manager-managed LLCs, which normally have at least one owner who isn't involved in management, the need for formal votes might not be apparent.

However, it's important to formalize and document important management and ownership decisions. First, you want to comply with your operating agreement, which includes provisions for member and manager voting. Second, you want to keep a record of important decisions and how they were made. We discuss both reasons below.

The Importance of the Record

Memories degrade over time. Memories also diverge over time. If a dispute arises among members, or your limited liability is being challenged by a third party, and the dispute involves past events, you don't want to have to rely on people's memories to reconstruct the events in question. You want a paper trail. Written consents and meeting minutes are the paper trail for the important ownership and management decisions in your LLC.

Complying With Your Operating Agreement

The operating agreements presented in Chapter 6 (member-managed LLC) and Chapter 7 (manager-managed LLC) call for certain actions to be taken by a vote of the members or managers. For example, in both agreements, members must vote to admit a new member and distributions require a vote of the members. The operating agreement itself, of course, can be modified only with the written agreement of all members. If your operating agreement doesn't follow our template, it still no doubt contains provisions requiring that certain actions be taken by a vote of the members or managers.

At a minimum, you should hold formal votes, either as votes taken at a meeting or by unanimous written consent in lieu of a meeting, as called for in your operating agreement. It's good practice to vote on and document all major ownership and management decisions, including those not specified in your operating agreement, but you should at least formalize the decisions called for in the agreement.

Following the Operating Agreement Indicates Adherence to the LLC Structure

Observing the decision-making rules spelled out in your operating agreement—voting on things that are called for in the operating agreement and applying the correct voting standard (majority, supermajority, or unanimous)—is evidence that the business is separate from its individual members. You respect the ownership and management structures and the decision-making process laid out in the operating agreement. This basic internal compliance, while not enough on its own, can be part of your defense against an attempt to pierce your limited liability veil.

Following the Operating Agreement Helps Avoid Confusion

Of course, the operating agreement also governs the rights and obligations of the members. Failure to follow your own governance rules, or doing so inconsistently, can cause confusion and friction between the members. Under those conditions, it's difficult to resolve member disputes because no one knows what the "real rules" are (or, each side knows what it thinks the real rules are). Is the rule what's written in the operating agreement or what the practice has been? Why is a rule that hasn't been enforced consistently in the past being enforced this time? On matters of LLC governance, as with all matters covered by the operating agreement, first follow the provisions of the operating agreement.

In the next section, we discuss the mechanics of governance—how decisions are made and documented.

Meetings, Consents, and the Company Record

As noted above and in the Chapter 6 and Chapter 7 operating agreements, members and managers can take an action by voting at a meeting or by a unanimous written consent in lieu of a meeting. We won't dwell on the mechanics of calling meetings here. Pay attention to any notice and quorum requirements for meetings in the operating agreement. The notice needn't be overly formal—the time, place, invitees, and purpose of the meeting are sufficient—and you can send it by any reasonable means, including email if you know that all invitees regularly check their email.

You don't have to document every little daily decision. You'll be on safe ground if you follow this rule: Any decision worth voting on is worth documenting.

Take Minutes to Document Votes

The easiest way to document the actions (votes) taken at a member of manager meeting is through minutes of the meeting. As with meeting notices, meeting minutes don't need to be super-formal or follow any rigid format.

If the purpose of the minutes is to record the votes taken at the meeting, you can skip the formality and legalese associated with some LLC minutes templates. Your minutes need to provide basic information about the meeting and then describe the votes taken. You don't need to include details like when the meeting was called to order or who chaired the meeting, although you can certainly add that information.

FORMS

A sample minutes of managers' meeting is shown below. A blank meeting minutes form is included in Appendix C and is downloadable from this book's companion page. See Appendix A for the link.

Sample Minutes of Managers' Meeting

A meeting of the managers of 4C Candles LLC was held on May 24, 2024, at 3 p.m. at the company offices and by videoconference.

In attendance: Carly Abelson, Carmen Becerra, Constance Li (remote)

Absent: None

The managers took the following actions at the meeting:

1. The minutes of the February 8, 2024 managers' meeting were approved (3-0 vote).
2. The company will switch its checking account from First Federal Bank to Second National Bank (2-1 vote, with Abelson dissenting).
3. Cash distributions totaling $150,000 will be made to the members, according to their percentage membership interests (3-0 vote).

Minutes prepared by Constance Li and distributed to the members on May 28, 2024.

Making Decisions by Unanimous Written Consent

The alternative to taking a vote at a meeting is to agree on an action by unanimous written consent. We discussed written consents in the relevant operating agreement provisions in Chapter 6 and Chapter 7. Written consents are a great way to handle ownership and management decisions when all the members or manager agree and there's no need to deliberate and vote on a matter in a meeting. And let's face it, that describes a lot of decisions in a small business.

Like minutes, written consents can be simple and devoid of legalese. They need to describe the action being consented to and show that the consent is unanimous and meant to be taken as if a vote at a meeting.

FORMS

A sample unanimous written consent is shown below. A blank unanimous written consent is included in Appendix C and is downloadable from this book's companion page. See Appendix A for the link.

Unanimous Written Consent of Members

The undersigned, being all the Members of 4C Candles LLC, consent to the following action(s) as of the date last signed below; such consent to be taken as if a vote (or votes) at meetings, per the Company's Operating Agreement:

1. Carly Abelson, Carmen Becerra, and Constance Li are reappointed as the Managers of the Company for the upcoming calendar year.
2. The company will elect to be taxed as an S corporation, rather than a partnership, beginning next tax year. The managers are hereby authorized to file all forms and take all other actions necessary to make this election.

_____   Date: _____
Carly Abelson, Member

_____   Date: _____
Carmen Becerra, Member

_____   Date: _____
Constance Li, Member

_____   Date: _____
Chris Williams, Member

P A R T

E

Dissolving Your LLC

Chapter 12—Dissolving Your LLC

Dissolving Your LLC

FORMS IN THIS CHAPTER

Accessing state government forms in this chapter. State government forms used to illustrate particular legal and tax filings are available on your state's appropriate state agency website.

You and your fellow members have decided to end your LLC. Perhaps the business has run its course. Maybe the members aren't getting along and no longer want to work together. Whatever the circumstances that led to the decision to end the LLC, you'll need to go through the process of dissolving the company and winding up its legal, business, and tax affairs.

The focus of the chapter is on voluntary dissolution (dissolution by agreement of the members), but much of the process described here also applies to two other types of dissolutions—fixed-term dissolutions and judicial dissolutions. Voluntary dissolution involves four steps:

1. Agree to dissolve.
2. File final tax returns and obtain tax clearance.
3. File dissolution paperwork with the state.
4. Wind up the business.

One could break up the fourth step (winding up the business) into multiple steps, but the tasks are the same however they're broken down. The following steps take you from the decision to end the company to the final distribution of company assets.

Step 1: Agree to Dissolve

Before you can all proclaim, "It's over!" you should step back and review the dissolution provisions of your operating agreement. Follow those provisions—they indicate the events that trigger dissolution and the process for dissolving (even if not in great detail). If you don't have a written operating agreement, you'll be relying on state law for the terms of your dissolution.

The dissolution clause of the operating agreements in this book (Paragraph 7(a) in each agreement) includes the following events that trigger dissolution:

- **Fixed-term dissolution.** If you specified an expiration date (dissolution date) in your articles, the LLC is dissolved as of that date.

- **Voluntary dissolution by the members.** The members can dissolve the LLC at any time by a unanimous consent or vote of the members, or by a written dissolution agreement entered into by all the members. We discuss consents and dissolution agreements below.
- **Dissolution by judicial decree.** When the members don't agree on dissolution—some want to dissolve the company and some want to continue it—and they can't agree on buyouts or other resolutions, the member(s) favoring dissolution can petition a court to dissolve the LLC by decree.

Paragraph 7(a) of our member-managed operating agreement (Chapter 5) goes on to state that when a dissolution is triggered, "the members will wind up the affairs of the LLC, and take other actions appropriate to complete a dissolution of the LLC in accordance with applicable provisions of state law." In the manager-managed operating agreement, this responsibility is placed on the managers—the members vote to dissolve and then task the managers with making it happen. The winding up requirement above ("the members will…") applies to all three types of dissolutions—fixed-term, voluntary, and judicial.

Our focus in this section is on voluntary dissolutions, but we touch upon fixed-term and judicial dissolutions briefly below.

Voluntary Dissolutions

The operating agreements in this book and most state laws allow LLC members to take unanimous action at any time to dissolve an LLC. Unanimous actions can be taken by a vote at a meeting or by a unanimous consent in lieu of a meeting. A sample unanimous consent and sample meeting minutes for the dissolution of 4C Candles LLC are included below.

Dissolution by Written Consent

A written consent to dissolve 4C Candles LLC might look like this:

Unanimous Written Consent to Dissolve

The undersigned, being all the Members of 4C Candles LLC, consent to the following action(s) as of the date last signed below; such consent to be taken as if a vote (or votes) at meetings, per the Company's Operating Agreement:

1. The Company is to be dissolved and the business is to be wound up in accordance with the provisions of the Operating Agreement, any relevant provisions of the California Revised Uniform Limited Liability Company Act, and any relevant requirements of the IRS and other taxing authorities.

2. Constance Li is designated as the Member in charge of the dissolution and winding up process. The other Members agree to provide whatever support and assistance is needed from them to accomplish the dissolution of the Company and the winding up of its business.

_____   Date: _____
Carly Abelson, Member

_____   Date: _____
Carmen Becerra, Member

_____   Date: _____
Constance Li, Member

_____   Date: _____
Chris Williams, Member

Dissolution by Vote at a Meeting

If the members of 4C Candles had met and voted instead of acting by unanimous written consent, the minutes for the meeting might read as follows. As you can see, the substance is identical to the written consent in lieu of a meeting.

Minutes of Members' Meeting to Vote on Dissolution

A meeting of the managers of 4C Candles LLC was held on September 22, 2024, at 3 p.m. at the company offices and by videoconference.

In attendance: Carly Abelson, Carmen Becerra, Constance Li (remote), Chris Williams

Absent: None

The members voted unanimously in favor of each of the following actions:

1. The Company is to be dissolved and the business is to be wound up in accordance with the provisions of the Operating Agreement, any relevant provisions of the California Revised Uniform Limited Liability Company Act, and any relevant requirements of the IRS and other taxing authorities.

2. Constance Li is designated as the member in charge of the dissolution and winding up process. The other members agree to provide whatever support and assistance is needed from them to accomplish the dissolution of the Company and the winding up of its business.

I have read the above minutes and attest that they constitute a true and accurate record of votes taken at the meeting.

_____ Date: _____
Carly Abelson, Member

_____ Date: _____
Carmen Becerra, Member

_____ Date: _____
Constance Li, Member

_____ Date: _____
Chris Williams, Member

In your written consent or meeting votes, take care to spell out the actions to be taken (Paragraphs 1 and 2 in the example above) in the degree of detail you require for your dissolution. The specificity and number of required actions depend on the complexity of the dissolution and the status of the relationships among the members. Complex dissolutions and adversarial dissolutions probably merit more detail than simple, amicable dissolutions. For example, you could provide that all creditors will be notified of the dissolution (an optional step in a dissolution, as discussed below), or that particular assets are to be sold to particular buyers. In the sample meeting minutes below, the 4C Candles members omitted any such details.

Dissolution Agreements

If your dissolution is complicated (financially, legally, or emotionally), you could create a separate dissolution agreement (also known as a termination agreement) to govern the dissolution process. If you have an operating agreement but need a separate dissolution agreement due to the complexity of your situation, consider consulting with a business attorney to help with the agreement.

An LLC without an operating agreement should have a written dissolution agreement—if not to spell out the details of the dissolution, then at least to put a legal framework around it. A sample dissolution agreement for an LLC without an operating agreement is included below. The dissolution agreement is light on specifics, but it documents the decision to dissolve the LLC and places responsibility for winding up the company on the members. And because the company has no operating agreement providing for indemnification of members, it also contains an indemnification clause. The clause included here is the same indemnification clause as is found in the operating agreements in this book. In this case, it means that if a member incurs a liability to a third party as a result of the member's activities in dissolving and winding up the company, the company will reimburse the member for the loss.

Sample Dissolution Agreement for an LLC Without an Operating Agreement

This Dissolution Agreement ("Agreement") is effective as of [*date*] and is made by [*name of member*] and [*name of member*] (each a "Member" and collectively the "Members"), who are all the Members of [*company name*], a [*state of organization*] limited liability company (the "Company").

The Members wish to dissolve the Company pursuant to the terms of this Agreement. Therefore, the Members agree as follows:

1. **Vote to Dissolve.** The Company is to be dissolved and the business is to be wound up in accordance with the provisions of the [*state*] Limited Liability Company Act, and any relevant requirements of the IRS and other taxing and administrative authorities.

2. **Winding Up.** The Members will wind up the business, legal, and tax affairs of the Company. The Members will file all documents and take all other actions necessary to liquidate and terminate the Company.

3. **Distribution of Remaining Assets.** Any assets left in the Company after all Company obligations have been met will be distributed to the Members according to their capital interests.

4. **Indemnification of Members.** The Company will indemnify a Member for any debt, obligation, or other liability, including reasonable attorneys' fees, incurred in the course of the Member's performance of duties on behalf of the Company under this Agreement, as long as the Member complied with the duties of loyalty and care when incurring the debt, obligation, or other liability. This provision does not in any way limit the indemnification the Member would be entitled to under applicable state law. The indemnification provided shall inure to the benefit of successors and assigns of any such Member.

The Members execute this Agreement as of the date and year first above written.

By: _____
    [*Member name*], Member

By: _____
    [*Member name*], Member

EXAMPLE: As part of its winding up process, a company terminates a contract with a supplier. The supplier sues the members personally for breach of contract, arguing that the termination was unlawful. The supplier wins the suit and the members are forced to pay damages. The company would be obligated to indemnify (reimburse) the members for the damages paid, as long as the members acted in accordance with their duties of loyalty and care in terminating the contract.

FORMS

A sample dissolution agreement is shown above. A blank dissolution agreement is included in Appendix C and is downloadable from this book's companion page. See Appendix A for the link.

Fixed-Term and Judicial Dissolutions

In addition to voluntary dissolutions, an LLC can be ended by way of a fixed-term or judicial dissolution.

Fixed-term dissolution. States vary in terms of how they treat fixed-term dissolutions. In some states, dissolution is automatic as of the expiration date. Other states allow members to choose to extend or renew the LLC beyond the stated term. Check your state's rules on fixed-term dissolutions. If you want to dissolve the LLC at the end of the fixed term and aren't sure whether the dissolution is automatic, take a member vote to dissolve as of that date to be safe.

Judicial dissolution. A judicial dissolution does not require a member vote to dissolve, because a judge is doing that job for you. But judicial dissolutions are not to be undertaken lightly. They're expensive to get and they can produce unwanted results. In many cases, a judicial dissolution includes the appointment of a receiver (a third-party custodian) to wind up the company. When a receiver is appointed, the members lose control over the winding up process and they incur (or the company incurs) the expense of the receiver's fee. The receiver's fee, of course, is on top of the costs of the lawsuit to obtain in the dissolution decree). A judicial dissolution is a drastic action that should be a last resort for warring LLC members.

Step 2: File Final Tax Returns and Close Tax Accounts

File your final state tax returns with state and federal tax agencies. For federal taxes, and in many states, you will file the same annual return that a partnership files every year, and you will mark it as "final" in the appropriate space.

If your LLC had employees, deposit your final payroll taxes and file employment tax paperwork. If you paid any other taxes, such as sales tax or transient occupancy tax, notify the relevant agencies to cancel your tax certificates and file final returns.

Cancel all tax accounts and identification numbers, including your federal employer identification number (EIN) and your state tax accounts. You must file all of your final tax returns before you can cancel your tax accounts.

RESOURCE

The IRS provides step-by-step instructions for closing a business tax-wise. On the IRS website (www.irs.gov), type "closing a business" or "closing a partnership" in the search box on any page of the site.

Step 3: File Dissolution Paperwork With the State

In most states, a vote to dissolve an LLC does not terminate the legal entity. To end the legal entity, you must file dissolution paperwork with the state, generally in the form of articles of dissolution (also known as a certificate of dissolution, a certificate of cancellation, or a similar name). Some states require more than one form. Check with your secretary of state's office for the appropriate form(s) and guidance on filing.

In all or most states, you can terminate an LLC without filing articles of dissolution. If you don't file your annual report or pay your annual fee (or franchise tax) for a certain number of consecutive years (in some cases as few as two years), the state will administratively dissolve your LLC. So why bother filing dissolution paperwork? Why not simply shut down the business and let the state dissolve the legal entity in a couple of years? You could do that. Many LLCs do. But when you dissolve voluntarily, you wrap up the legal, tax, and business affairs of the company at the same time, in a coordinated manner. It's clear when the company was dissolved and when you entered the winding up phase. When you rely on administrative dissolution in the future, you leave yourself open to a claim that an action you took at a particular time was inappropriate for a company either continuing to operate or winding up (whichever is being claimed). In other words, you can cloud the limited liability picture if you don't have a clear dissolution date while you're closing your business.

The time and expense involved in filing dissolution paperwork are minimal. We recommend observing the formality and filing paperwork rather than leaving it to the state to dissolve your LLC administratively.

Articles of dissolution forms are generally straightforward. The main page of the New York form included below is a good example. It asks only for the name of the LLC, the date on which it was organized, and the event that triggered dissolution.

When to File Your Dissolution Paperwork

In some states, you need to file dissolution paperwork before you begin winding things up. Other states require that you file the dissolution form only after you've finished winding up your business—that is, after you've paid your debts, distributed your assets, and closed any business accounts, registrations, licenses, and permits. Some states require that you receive tax clearance (confirmation that the LLC is fully caught up on its tax obligations) from your state's department of revenue (or similar taxing authority). We discuss tax clearance in Step 4 below.

New York Articles of Dissolution

 **Division of Corporations, State Records and Uniform Commercial Code**

New York State
Department of State
DIVISION OF CORPORATIONS,
STATE RECORDS AND
UNIFORM COMMERCIAL CODE
One Commerce Plaza
99 Washington Ave.
Albany, NY 12231-0001
https://dos.ny.gov

ARTICLES OF DISSOLUTION
OF

_____
(Insert name of Domestic Limited Liability Company)
Under Section 705 of the Limited Liability Company Law

FIRST: The name of the limited liability company is:

_____.

If the name of the limited liability company has been changed, the name under which it was organized is:_____.

SECOND: The date of filing of the articles of organization is:_____.

THIRD: The event giving rise to the filing of the articles of dissolution is:
(Check appropriate statement)

☐ The vote or written consent of a majority in interest of the members of the limited liability company.

☐ There are no members of the limited liability company.

☐ Pursuant to the dissolution date set forth in the articles of organization or operating agreement of the limited liability company.

☐ The following event, as specified in the operating agreement:

_____.

☐ The entry of a decree of judicial dissolution.

X_____
(Signature)

_____
(Type or print name)

Capacity of Signer *(Check appropriate box)*:

☐ Member

☐ Manager

☐ Authorized Person

TIP

Don't forget to cancel registrations in other states. If you registered to do business in other states as a foreign LLC, you'll need to cancel those registrations as well as your home state registration.

Step 4: Wind Up the Business

Once you've taken the legal and tax steps outlined above, your next and final task is to wind up the business affairs of the company. Be thorough when you close the business. Make sure all company debts are paid and that any remaining assets are distributed properly. Inform anyone who needs to know, including employees, customers, and suppliers, that the business is closing. When you conduct an orderly closing, you avoid loose ends that you might have to deal with personally, as former members of the LLC. No unpaid creditors. No unfulfilled contract obligations. No undistributed net assets.

A proper closing also protects your limited liability status. You're not giving ammunition to anyone who would seek to pierce the limited liability veil and go after your personal assets.

Send Notifications and Cancel Business Registrations

Within a reasonable time after the members vote to dissolve the business (or the business is dissolved by an expiration date or judicial decree), notify your employees and be sure to resolve all employment-related matters. Alert your vendors and suppliers, and review any existing contracts to address outstanding obligations, such as payments and work in progress. Do the same with your customers—notify them and review outstanding contracts, orders, accounts receivable, refunds, etc.

Notifying Creditors of Your LLC's Dissolution

At the time you announce your dissolution, you might have creditors on the line—people or businesses that claim you owe them money. Most states don't require you to notify creditors of your LLC's dissolution, but it's a good idea to provide notice. Once a creditor has received notice that your LLC is closing, they have a reasonable period of time to provide you with any new claims (obligations that you are not yet aware of). If no creditors come forward with claims, especially if you gave a deadline for doing so, you can feel more confident that your LLC has no hidden liabilities and that you can safely distribute remaining assets to members at the end of the winding up process.

Liquidate Assets, Pay Debts, and Distribute the Remainder

Almost all states require that you first pay creditors before you distribute your assets to anyone else (including LLC members). If you have more debts than assets, you'll need to prioritize your business debts and try to negotiate settlements with your creditors. If you can do so without infringing on the rights of other creditors, pay any debts that your members might be personally liable for first (such as a debt that you personally guaranteed). If you have any secured debt, you can either return the secured property or sell it and pay off the remaining balance on your business loan. If your secured property is worth more than the money you owe on the property's loan, you should sell it.

If assets are left after all company debts have been paid, the remainder can be distributed to the members according to the formula in your operating agreement (or under state law if you don't have an operating agreement).

After the Fall

When you've completed all four steps described above, are you out from under the responsibilities and risks of your now-former LLC? If someone is injured by a product you manufactured or sold, or a vendor who'd been notified of the closing sends a new invoice long past the reasonable time to have done so, could you be personally on the hook for the liability? The injured party or the vendor in these examples would still need to pierce the LLC veil, even though the LLC no longer exists, in order to go after your personal assets. They would need to show that while the LLC was in existence, including during the winding up period, you did something that caused the forfeiture of your limited liability protection. You didn't maintain proper separation between the owners and the business. Or you acted so negligently or egregiously that you shouldn't be allowed to hide behind your limited liability. As stated above, don't do anything during the dissolution and winding up of the company that would give ammunition to someone looking to pierce the veil and reach your personal assets.

Using the Downloadable Forms on the Nolo Website

This book comes with eforms that you can access online at **www.nolo.com/back-of-book/LLCH.html**

To use the files, your computer must have specific software programs installed. Here is a list of types of files provided by this book, as well as the software programs you'll need to access them:

- **RTF.** You can open, edit, print, and save these form files with most word processing programs such as Microsoft *Word*, Windows *WordPad*, and recent versions of *WordPerfect*. On a Mac, you can use Apple *TextEdit* or Apple *Pages*. You can also work with the forms through a word processing app such as Google *Docs*.
- **PDF.** You can view these files with Adobe *Reader*, free software from www.adobe.com.

Editing RTFs

Here are some general instructions about editing RTF forms in your word processing program:

- **Underlines.** Underlines indicate where to enter information. After filling in the needed text, delete the underline. In most word processing programs you can do this by highlighting the underlined portion and typing CTRL-U.
- **Bracketed text.** Bracketed text indicates instructions. Be sure to remove all instructional text before you finalize your document.
- **Signature lines.** Signature lines should appear on a page with at least some text from the document itself.

Every word processing program uses different commands to open, format, save, and print documents, so refer to your software's help documents for help using your program. Nolo cannot provide technical support for questions about how to use your computer or your software.

CAUTION

In accordance with U.S. copyright laws, the forms provided by this book are for your personal use only.

List of Forms Available on the Nolo Website

To access these forms, go to: **www.nolo.com/back-of-book/LLCH.html**

Form Title	File Name
Member-Managed LLC Operating Agreement	Member-ManagedLLCOperating Agreement.rtf
Manager-Managed LLC Operating Agreement	Manager-ManagedLLCOperating Agreement.rtf
LLC Buyout Agreement	LLCBuyoutAgreement.rtf
LLC Interest Purchase Agreement	LLCInterestPurchaseAgreement.rtf
Assignment of LLC Interest	AssignmentofLLCInterest.rtf
Meeting Minutes	MeetingMinutes.rtf
Unanimous Written Consent	UnanimousWrittenConsent.rtf
LLC Dissolution Agreement	LLCDissolutionAgreement.rtf

Sample Agreements

FORMS

The sample forms in this appendix are downloadable as blank versions on this book's companion page. See Appendix A for the link.

Sample Member-Managed LLC Operating Agreement

Operating Agreement of 4C Candles LLC
A California Limited Liability Company

1. Preliminary Provisions

a. Effective Date

This operating agreement of 4C Candles, LLC (the "LLC"), effective as of June 5, 2023, is adopted by the members whose signatures appear at the end of this agreement.

b. Formation

This limited liability company (LLC) was formed by filing its articles of organization with the California Secretary of State. The legal existence of the LLC commenced on the date of such filing. A copy of this organizational document will be placed in the LLC's records book.

c. Name

The formal name of the LLC is as stated above. However, the LLC may do business under a different name by complying with California's fictitious or assumed business name statutes and procedures.

d. Registered Office and Registered Agent

The registered office and registered agent are as indicated in the articles of organization. The LLC may change its registered office and/or agent from time to time by filing a change of registered agent or office statement with the California Secretary of State.

e. Business Purpose

The purpose of the limited liability company is to engage in any lawful act or activity for which a limited liability company may be organized under the California Revised Uniform Limited Liability Company Act.

Sample Member-Managed LLC Operating Agreement (continued)

f. Duration of LLC

The duration of the LLC is perpetual. However, the LLC will terminate when a proposal to dissolve the LLC is adopted according to the terms of this agreement or when the LLC is otherwise terminated in accordance with law.

2. Membership Provisions

a. Nonliability of Members

No member will be personally liable for the expenses, debts, obligations, or liabilities of the LLC or for claims made against it.

b. Reimbursement of Expenses

Members are entitled to reimbursement by the LLC for reasonable expenses incurred on behalf of the LLC, including expenses incurred in the formation, dissolution, and liquidation of the LLC.

c. Compensation

A member will not be paid for performing any duties associated with membership, including management of the LLC. Members may be paid, however, for services rendered in another capacity for the LLC, as allowed by law and as approved by a majority vote of the members.

d. Other Business by Members

A member may engage in any business activity without the other members' consent, so long as the business activity does not directly compete with the LLC.

e. Members' Percentage interests

A member's membership interest is computed as a percentage of total membership interests, as shown on Exhibit A.

Sample Member-Managed LLC Operating Agreement (continued)

f. Membership Voting

Except as otherwise may be required by the articles of organization, other provisions of this operating agreement, or under the laws of this state, each member will vote in proportion to the member's percentage interest. Further, unless otherwise stated in another provision of this operating agreement, the phrase "majority of members" means a majority of percentage interests.

g. Members' Meetings and Actions Taken by Written Consent

The LLC is not required to hold regular members' meetings. However, one or more members can call a meeting at any time. The member calling the meeting will provide notice of the business to be transacted at the meeting, but other business may be discussed and conducted at the meeting with the consent of all members present. A quorum consists of all members, unless members who cannot attend consent in writing for the meeting to take place in their absence. Except as otherwise provided in this agreement, a vote of the majority of members present at a meeting of the members is required to approve any action taken at the meeting.

Any action required or permitted by this agreement to be taken at a meeting of the members may be taken without a meeting, without prior notice, by unanimous written consent of the members.

h. Admission of New Members

Except as otherwise provided in this agreement, a person or entity will not be admitted into membership unless each member consents in writing to the admission of the new member.

3. Management Provisions

a. Management by Members

This LLC will be managed exclusively by all of its members.

Sample Member-Managed LLC Operating Agreement (continued)

b. Indemnification of Members

A member will be indemnified by the LLC for any debt, obligation, or other liability, including reasonable attorneys' fees, incurred in the course of the member's activities or performance of duties on behalf of the LLC as long as the member complied with the duties of loyalty and care when incurring the debt, obligation, or other liability. This provision does not in any way limit the indemnification the member would be entitled to under applicable state law. The indemnification provided will inure to the benefit of successors and assigns of any such member.

4. Tax and Financial Provisions

a. Tax Classification of LLC

The LLC will be initially classified as a partnership for federal and, if applicable, state income tax purposes. The LLC may change its tax treatment with the consent of all members and by filing the necessary election with the IRS and, if applicable, the state tax department.

b. Tax Year and Accounting Method

The tax year of the LLC will end on the last day of the month of December. The LLC will use the accrual method of accounting.

The tax year and the accounting method of the LLC may each be changed with the consent of all members.

c. Title to Assets

All personal and real property of the LLC will be held in the name of the LLC, not in the name of any individual member.

d. Bank Accounts

All funds of the Company will be deposited in one or more separate bank accounts, using such banks or trust companies as the

Sample Member-Managed LLC Operating Agreement (continued)

members may designate. Withdrawals from such bank accounts are to be made upon such signature or signatures as the members may designate. The funds of the LLC, however and wherever deposited or invested, will not be commingled with the personal funds of any member of the LLC.

e. Tax Matters Partner

If required under Internal Revenue Code provisions or regulations, the LLC will designate a member as its "tax matters partner" in accordance with Internal Revenue Code Section 6231(a)(7) and corresponding regulations, who will fulfill this role by being the spokesperson for the LLC in dealings with the IRS and performing such other duties as required under the Internal Revenue Code and Regulations.

f. Annual Income Tax Returns and Reports

Within 60 days after the end of each tax year, a copy of the LLC's state and federal income tax returns for the preceding tax year will be mailed or otherwise provided to each member, together with any additional information and forms necessary for each member to complete their individual state and federal income tax returns. Along with the necessary tax information and forms, the LLC will also provide a financial report that includes a balance sheet and profit and loss statement for the year.

5. Capital Provisions

a. Capital Contributions

Members have made initial contributions of cash, property, or services as specified in Exhibit A.

b. No Interest on Capital Contributions

No interest will be paid on capital contributions or on capital account balances.

Sample Member-Managed LLC Operating Agreement (continued)

c. Capital Account Bookkeeping

A capital account will be set up and maintained on the books of the LLC for each member. It will reflect each member's capital contribution, increased by any additional contributions by the member and by the member's share of LLC profits, decreased by any distributions to the member and by the member's share of LLC losses, and adjusted as required in accordance with applicable provisions of the Internal Revenue Code and corresponding income tax regulations. Upon a valid transfer of a member's membership interest, the member's capital account will carry over to the new owner.

d. Additional Contributions

The members may agree, from time to time, by unanimous vote, to require the payment of additional capital contributions by the members.

e. Allocations of Profits and Losses

The profits and losses of the LLC, and all items of its income, gain, loss, deduction, and credit will be allocated to members in accordance with the member's percentage interest.

f. Capital Withdrawals

Members will not be allowed to withdraw any part of their capital contributions or to receive distributions, whether in property or cash, except as otherwise allowed by this agreement. A capital withdrawal requires the written consent of all members.

g. Distributions of Cash

Cash from business operations, as well as cash from a sale or other disposition of LLC capital assets, may be allocated and distributed from time to time to members in accordance with each member's percentage interest in the LLC, as may be decided by a majority of members. However, the member(s) will direct distributions to be made each year in an amount sufficient to cover any member's tax liability that may arise based on the allocation of LLC income, gains, losses, or deductions.

Sample Member-Managed LLC Operating Agreement (continued)

h. Allocation of Noncash Proceeds

If proceeds consist of property other than cash, the members will decide the value of the property and allocate such value among the members in accordance with each member's percentage interest in the LLC.

i. Allocation and Distribution of Liquidation Proceeds

Regardless of any other provision in this agreement, if there is a distribution in liquidation of the LLC, or when a member's interest is liquidated, all items of income and loss will be allocated to a member's capital account, and all appropriate credits and deductions will then be made to the capital account before any final distribution is made. A final distribution will be made to members only to the extent of, and in proportion to, any positive balance in a member's capital account.

6. Membership Withdrawal and Transfer Provisions

a. Withdrawal of Members

A member may withdraw from the LLC by giving written notice to all other members at least three months before the date the withdrawal is to be effective. In the event of such withdrawal, the LLC will pay the departing member the fair value of their LLC interest, less any amounts owed by the member to the LLC. The departing and remaining members will agree at the time of departure on the fair value of the departing member's interest and the schedule of payments to be made by the LLC to the departing member, who will receive payment for their interest within a reasonable time after departure from the LLC. If the departing and remaining members cannot agree on the value of departing member's interest, they will select an appraiser, who will determine the current value of the departing member's interest. This appraised amount will be fair value of the departing member's interest and will form the basis of the amount to be paid to the departing member.

Sample Member-Managed LLC Operating Agreement (continued)

b. Restrictions on the Transfer of Membership

Notwithstanding any other provision of this agreement, a member will not transfer their membership in the LLC unless all of the nontransferring members first agree in writing to approve the admission of the transferee into the LLC. Further, no member may encumber a part or all of their membership in the LLC by mortgage, pledge, granting of a security interest, lien, or otherwise, unless the encumbrance has first been approved in writing by all other members of the LLC.

Notwithstanding the above provision, any member will be allowed to assign an economic interest in their membership to another person without the approval of the other members. Any assignment of economic interest will not include a transfer of the member's voting or management rights, and the assignee will not become a member except as provided elsewhere in this agreement.

7. Dissolution Provisions

a. Events That Trigger Dissolution of the LLC

The following events will trigger a dissolution of the LLC:

   i. **Expiration of LLC Term.** The expiration of the term of existence of the LLC, if such term is specified in the articles of organization or this operating agreement, will cause the dissolution of the LLC.

   ii. **Written Agreement or Consent to Dissolve.** The written agreement of all members to dissolve the LLC will cause a dissolution of the LLC.

   iii. **Entry of Decree.** The entry of a decree of dissolution of the LLC under state law will cause a dissolution of the LLC.

If the LLC is to dissolve according to any of the above provisions, the members will wind up the affairs of the LLC, and take other actions appropriate to complete a dissolution of the LLC in accordance with applicable provisions of state law.

Sample Member-Managed LLC Operating Agreement (continued)

b. Dissociation of a Member

The dissociation of a member, which means the death, incapacity, bankruptcy, retirement, resignation, or expulsion of a member, or any other event that terminates the continued membership of a member, will not cause a dissolution of the LLC. The LLC will continue its existence and business following such dissociation of a member.

8. General Provisions

a. Officers

The LLC may designate one or more officers, such as a President, Vice President, Secretary, and Treasurer. Persons who fill these positions need not be members of the LLC. Such positions may be compensated or noncompensated according to the nature and extent of the services rendered as a part of the duties of each office.

b. Records

The LLC will keep at its principal business address a copy of all proceedings of membership meetings and resolutions, as well as books of account of financial transactions. A list of the names and addresses of the current membership also will be maintained at this address, with notations on any transfers of members' interests to nonmembers or persons being admitted into membership.

The LLC's articles of organization, a signed copy of this operating agreement, the LLC's tax returns for the preceding three tax years, and written records of votes taken at member meetings or by unanimous consent, will be kept at its principal business address.

Any member may inspect any and all records maintained by the LLC upon reasonable notice.

c. All Necessary Acts

The members and officers (if any) of the LLC are authorized to perform all acts necessary to perfect the organization of the LLC and to carry out its business operations expeditiously and efficiently as authorized by this agreement and by law.

Sample Member-Managed LLC Operating Agreement (continued)

d. Severability

If any provision of this agreement is determined by a court or arbitrator to be invalid, unenforceable, or otherwise ineffective, that provision will be severed from the rest of this agreement, and the remaining provisions will remain in effect and enforceable.

e. Mediation and Arbitration of Disputes Among Members

In any dispute over the provisions of this operating agreement and in other disputes among the members, if the members cannot resolve the dispute to their mutual satisfaction, the matter will be submitted to mediation. The terms and procedure for mediation will be arranged by the parties to the dispute.

If good-faith mediation of a dispute proves impossible or if an agreed-upon mediation outcome cannot be obtained by the members who are parties to the dispute, the dispute will be submitted to binding arbitration in accordance with the rules of the American Arbitration Association. Any party may commence arbitration of the dispute by sending a written request for arbitration to all other parties to the dispute. The request will state the nature of the dispute to be resolved by arbitration, and, if all parties to the dispute agree to arbitration, arbitration will be commenced as soon as practical after such parties receive a copy of the written request.

All parties will initially share the cost of arbitration, but the prevailing party or parties may be awarded attorneys' fees, costs, and other expenses of arbitration at the discretion of the arbitrator. All arbitration decisions will be final, binding, and conclusive on all the parties to arbitration, and legal judgment may be entered based upon such decision in accordance with applicable law in any court having jurisdiction to do so.

f. Entire Agreement and Amendment

This operating agreement represents the entire agreement among the members, and replaces and supersedes all prior written and

Sample Member-Managed LLC Operating Agreement (continued)

oral agreements among them. This agreement will not be amended, modified, or replaced except by written agreement of all members.

The members sign and adopt this agreement as the operating agreement of the LLC and agree to abide by its terms.

Date: _____

Signature: _____

Name of member: Carly Abelson

Date: _____

Signature: _____

Name of member: Carmen Becerra

Date: _____

Signature: _____

Name of member: Constance Li

Date: _____

Signature: _____

Name of member: Chris Williams

Sample Member-Managed LLC Operating Agreement (continued)

Exhibit A
Members; Initial Contributions; Interests; Other Information

Members

Member Name	Initial Contribution	Interest
Carly Abelson	$10,000	20%
Carmen Becerra	$10,000	20%
Constance Li	$20,000	40%
Chris Williams	$10,000	20%

Officers

None.

Sample Manager-Managed LLC Operating Agreement

Operating Agreement of 4C Candles LLC
A California Limited Liability Company

1. Preliminary Provisions

a. Effective Date

This operating agreement of 4C Candles, LLC (the "LLC"), effective as of June 5, 2023, is adopted by the members whose signatures appear at the end of this agreement.

b. Formation

This limited liability company (LLC) was formed by filing its articles of organization with the California Secretary of State. The legal existence of the LLC commenced on the date of such filing. A copy of this organizational document will be placed in the LLC's records book.

c. Name

The formal name of the LLC is as stated above. However, the LLC may do business under a different name by complying with California's fictitious or assumed business name statutes and procedures.

d. Registered Office and Registered Agent

The registered office and registered agent are as indicated in the articles of organization. The LLC may change its registered office and/or agent from time to time by filing a change of registered agent or office statement with the California Secretary of State.

e. Business Purpose

The purpose of the limited liability company is to engage in any lawful act or activity for which a limited liability company may be organized under the California Revised Uniform Limited Liability Company Act.

Sample Manager-Managed LLC Operating Agreement (continued)

f. Duration of LLC

The duration of the LLC is perpetual. However, the LLC will terminate when a proposal to dissolve the LLC is adopted according to the terms of this agreement or when the LLC is otherwise terminated in accordance with law.

2. Membership Provisions

a. Nonliability of Members

No member will be personally liable for the expenses, debts, obligations, or liabilities of the LLC or for claims made against it.

b. Reimbursement of Expenses

Members are entitled to reimbursement by the LLC for reasonable expenses incurred on behalf of the LLC, including expenses incurred in the formation, dissolution, and liquidation of the LLC.

c. Compensation

A member will not be paid for performing any duties associated with membership, including management of the LLC. Members may be paid, however, for services rendered in any other capacity for the LLC, as allowed by law and as approved by a majority vote of the managers.

d. Other Business by Members

A member may engage in any business activity without the other members' consent, so long as the business activity does not directly compete with the LLC.

e. Members' Percentage interests

A member's membership interest is computed as a percentage of total membership interests, as shown on Exhibit A.

f. Membership Voting

Except as otherwise may be required by the articles of organization, other provisions of this operating agreement; or under the laws of this state, each member will vote on any matter provided for in this

Sample Manager-Managed LLC Operating Agreement (continued)

agreement and any matter submitted to the membership for their approval by the managers in proportion to the member's percentage interest. Further, unless otherwise stated in another provision of this operating agreement, the phrase "majority of members" means a majority of percentage interests.

g. Members' Meetings and Actions Taken by Written Consent

The LLC is not required to hold regular members' meetings. However, one or more members can call a meeting at any time. The member calling the meeting will provide notice of the business to be transacted at the meeting, but other business may be discussed and conducted at the meeting with the consent of all members present. A quorum consists of all members, unless members who cannot attend consent in writing for the meeting to take place in their absence. Except as otherwise provided in this agreement, a vote of the majority of members present at a meeting of the members is required to approve any action taken at the meeting.

Any action required or permitted by this agreement to be taken at a meeting of the members may be taken without a meeting, without prior notice, by unanimous written consent of the members.

h. Admission of New Members

Except as otherwise provided in this agreement, a person or entity will not be admitted into membership unless each member consents in writing to the admission of the new member.

3. Management Provisions

a. Management by Manager(s)

The LLC will be managed by one or more managers. The current managers are listed in Exhibit A.

b. Nonliability of Manager(s)

No manager of the LLC will be personally liable for the expenses, debts, obligations, or liabilities of the LLC, or for claims made against it.

Sample Manager-Managed LLC Operating Agreement (continued)

c. Authority and Votes of Manager(s)

Except as otherwise set forth in this agreement, the articles of organization, or under the laws of this state, all management decisions
relating to the LLC's business will be made by its manager(s).
If there is more than one manager, management decisions will be
approved by a majority vote of the managers, with each manager
entitled to cast one vote for or against any matter submitted to the
managers for a decision.

d. Appointment, Removal, and Term of Manager(s)

The members will have the exclusive right to set the number of
managers and to appoint the manager(s), who will be responsible
for the day-to-day management of the business of the LLC. The
manager(s) will be appointed by a majority of members.

A manager may be removed at any time by a vote of the majority
of the members. In addition, each manager will cease to serve upon
any of the following events:

- the manager becomes disabled, dies, retires, or otherwise
  withdraws from management, or
- the manager's term expires, if a term has been designated in
  other provisions of this agreement.

Upon the occurrence of any of these events, a new manager may
be appointed to replace the departing manager by a majority vote
of the members.

e. Manager Commitment to LLC

Each manager will conduct the affairs of the LLC in good faith and
in the best interests of the LLC. Each manager will devote time to
the LLC as the business requires.

f. Compensation of Manager(s)

No manager is entitled to any fee for managing the operations of
the LLC unless such compensation is approved by a majority vote
of the members.

Sample Manager-Managed LLC Operating Agreement (continued)

g. Indemnification of Manager(s)

A manager will be indemnified by the LLC for any debt, obligation, or other liability, including reasonable attorneys' fees, incurred in the course of the manager's activities or performance of duties on behalf of the LLC as long as the manager complied with the duties of loyalty and care when incurring the debt, obligation, or other liability. This provision does not in any way limit the indemnification the manager would be entitled to under applicable state law. The indemnification provided will inure to the benefit of successors and assigns of any such manager.

h. Management Meetings and Actions Taken by Written Consents

Meetings of the managers will be held on five (5) days' notice or on such shorter notice as may be mutually agreeable to the managers, on the call of any one or more managers. Members will be provided with a written notice of the time and place of each meeting, along with a description of the purpose of the meeting. The presence of a majority of managers constitutes a quorum. Except as otherwise provided in this agreement, the vote of a majority of the managers present at any managers' meeting is required to approve any action taken at the meeting.

Any action required or permitted by this agreement to be taken at a meeting of the managers may be taken without a meeting, without prior notice, by unanimous written consent of the managers.

4. Tax and Financial Provisions

a. Tax Classification of LLC

The LLC will be initially classified as a partnership for federal and, if applicable, state income tax purposes. The LLC may change its tax treatment with the consent of all members and by filing the necessary election with the IRS and, if applicable, the state tax department.

Sample Manager-Managed LLC Operating Agreement (continued)

b. Tax Year and Accounting Method

The tax year of the LLC will end on the last day of the month of December. The LLC will use the accrual method of accounting. The tax year and the accounting method of the LLC may each be changed with the consent of all members.

c. Title to Assets

All personal and real property of the LLC will be held in the name of the LLC, not in the name of any individual member.

d. Bank Accounts

All funds of the Company will be deposited in one or more separate bank accounts, using such banks or trust companies as the members may designate. Withdrawals from such bank accounts are to be made upon such signature or signatures as the members may designate. The funds of the LLC, however and wherever deposited or invested, will not be commingled with the personal funds of any member of the LLC.

e. Tax Matters Partner

If required under Internal Revenue Code provisions or regulations, the LLC will designate a member as its "tax matters partner" in accordance with Internal Revenue Code Section 6231(a)(7) and corresponding regulations, who will fulfill this role by being the spokesperson for the LLC in dealings with the IRS and performing such other duties as required under the Internal Revenue Code and Regulations.

f. Annual Income Tax Returns and Reports

Within 60 days after the end of each tax year of the LLC, a copy of the LLC's state and federal income tax returns for the preceding tax year will be mailed or otherwise provided to each member of the LLC, together with any additional information and forms necessary for each member to complete their individual state and federal

Sample Manager-Managed LLC Operating Agreement (continued)

income tax returns. Along with the necessary tax infor-mation and forms, the LLC will also provide a financial report that includes a balance sheet and profit and loss statement for the year.

5. Capital Provisions

a. Capital Contributions

Members have made initial contributions of cash, property, or services as specified in Exhibit A.

b. No Interest on Capital Contributions

No interest will be paid on capital contributions or on capital account balances.

c. Capital Account Bookkeeping

A capital account will be set up and maintained on the books of the LLC for each member. It will reflect each member's capital contribution, increased by any additional contributions by the member and by the member's share of LLC profits, decreased by any distributions to the member and by the member's share of LLC losses, and adjusted as required in accordance with applicable provisions of the Internal Revenue Code and corresponding income tax regulations. Upon a valid transfer of a member's membership interest, the member's capital account will carry over to the new owner.

d. Additional Contributions

The members may agree, from time to time, by unanimous vote, to require the payment of additional capital contributions by the members.

e. Allocations of Profits and Losses

The profits and losses of the LLC, and all items of its income, gain, loss, deduction, and credit will be allocated to members in accordance with the member's percentage interest.

Sample Manager-Managed LLC Operating Agreement (continued)

f. Capital Withdrawals

Members will not be allowed to withdraw any part of their capital contributions or to receive distributions, whether in property or cash, except as otherwise allowed by this agreement. A capital withdrawal requires the written consent of all members.

g. Distributions of Cash

Cash from business operations, as well as cash from a sale or other disposition of LLC capital assets, may be allocated and distributed from time to time to members in accordance with each member's percentage interest in the LLC, as may be decided by a majority of managers. However, the managers will direct distributions to be made each year in an amount sufficient to cover any member's tax liability that may arise based on the allocation of LLC income, gains, losses or deductions.

h. Allocation of Noncash Proceeds

If proceeds consist of property other than cash, the members will decide the value of the property and allocate such value among the members in accordance with each member's percentage interest in the LLC.

i. Allocation and Distribution of Liquidation Proceeds

Regardless of any other provision in this agreement, if there is a distribution in liquidation of the LLC, or when a member's interest is liquidated, all items of income and loss will be allocated to a member's capital account, and all appropriate credits and deductions will then be made to the capital account before any final distribution is made. A final distribution will be made to members only to the extent of, and in proportion to, any positive balance in a member's capital account.

Sample Manager-Managed LLC Operating Agreement (continued)

6. Membership Withdrawal and Transfer Provisions

a. Withdrawal of Members

A member may withdraw from the LLC by giving written notice to all other members at least three months before the date the withdrawal is to be effective. In the event of such withdrawal, the LLC will pay the departing member the fair value of their LLC interest, less any amounts owed by the member to the LLC. The departing and remaining members will agree at the time of departure on the fair value of the departing member's interest and the schedule of payments to be made by the LLC to the departing member, who will receive payment for their interest within a reasonable time after departure from the LLC. If the departing and remaining members cannot agree on the value of departing member's interest, they will select an appraiser, who will determine the current value of the departing member's interest. This appraised amount will be fair value of the departing member's interest and will form the basis of the amount to be paid to the departing member.

b. Restrictions on the Transfer of Membership

Notwithstanding any other provision of this agreement, a member will not transfer their membership in the LLC unless all of the non-transferring members first agree in writing to approve the admission of the transferee into the LLC. Further, no member may encumber a part or all of their membership in the LLC by mortgage, pledge, granting of a security interest, lien, or otherwise, unless the encumbrance has first been approved in writing by all other members of the LLC.

Notwithstanding the above provision, any member will be allowed to assign an economic interest in their membership to another person without the approval of the other members. Any assignment of economic interest will not include a transfer of the member's voting or management rights, and the assignee will not become a member except as provided elsewhere in this agreement.

Sample Manager-Managed LLC Operating Agreement (continued)

7. Dissolution Provisions

a. Events That Trigger Dissolution of the LLC

The following events will trigger a dissolution of the LLC:

i. **Expiration of LLC Term.** The expiration of the term of existence of the LLC, if such term is specified in the articles of organization or this operating agreement, will cause the dissolution of the LLC.

ii. **Written Agreement or Consent to Dissolve.** The written agreement of all members to dissolve the LLC will cause a dissolution of the LLC.

iii. **Entry of Decree.** The entry of a decree of dissolution of the LLC under state law will cause a dissolution of the LLC.

If the LLC is to dissolve according to any of the above provisions, the manager(s) will wind up the affairs of the LLC, and take other actions appropriate to complete a dissolution of the LLC in accordance with applicable provisions of state law.

b. Dissociation of a Member

The dissociation of a member, which means the death, incapacity, bankruptcy, retirement, resignation, or expulsion of a member, or any other event that terminates the continued membership of a member, will not cause a dissolution of the LLC. The LLC will continue its existence and business following such dissociation of a member.

8. General Provisions

a. Officers

The LLC may designate one or more officers, such as a President, Vice President, Secretary, and Treasurer. Persons who fill these positions need not be members of the LLC. Such positions may be compensated or noncompensated according to the nature and extent of the services rendered as a part of the duties of each office.

Sample Manager-Managed LLC Operating Agreement (continued)

b. Records

The LLC will keep at its principal business address a copy of all pro-ceedings of membership meetings and resolutions, as well as books of account of financial transactions. A list of the names and addresses of the current membership also will be maintained at this address, with notations on any transfers of members' interests to nonmembers or persons being admitted into membership.

The LLC's articles of organization, a signed copy of this operating agreement, the LLC's tax returns for the preceding three tax years, and written records of votes taken at member and manager meetings or by unanimous consent, will be kept at its principal business address.

Any member may inspect any and all records maintained by the LLC upon reasonable notice.

c. All Necessary Acts

The members, managers, and officers (if any) of the LLC are authorized to perform all acts necessary to perfect the organization of the LLC and to carry out its business operations expeditiously and efficiently.

d. Severability

If any provision of this agreement is determined by a court or arbitrator to be invalid, unenforceable, or otherwise ineffective, that provision will be severed from the rest of this agreement, and the remaining provisions will remain in effect and enforceable.

e. Mediation and Arbitration of Disputes Among Members

In any dispute over the provisions of this operating agreement and in other disputes among the members, if the members cannot resolve the dispute to their mutual satisfaction, the matter will be submitted to mediation. The terms and procedure for mediation will be arranged by the parties to the dispute.

Sample Manager-Managed LLC Operating Agreement (continued)

If good-faith mediation of a dispute proves impossible or if an agreed-upon mediation outcome cannot be obtained by the members who are parties to the dispute, the dispute will be submitted to binding arbitration in accordance with the rules of the American Arbitration Association. Any party may commence arbitration of the dispute by sending a written request for arbitration to all other parties to the dispute. The request will state the nature of the dispute to be resolved by arbitration, and, if all parties to the dispute agree to arbitration, arbitration will be commenced as soon as practical after such parties receive a copy of the written request.

All parties will initially share the cost of arbitration, but the prevailing party or parties may be awarded attorneys' fees, costs, and other expenses of arbitration at the discretion of the arbitrator. All arbitration decisions will be final, binding, and conclusive on all the parties to arbitration, and legal judgment may be entered based upon such decision in accordance with applicable law in any court having jurisdiction to do so.

f. Entire Agreement and Amendment

This operating agreement represents the entire agreement among the members, and replaces and supersedes all prior written and oral agreements among the members. This agreement will not be amended, modified, or replaced except by written agreement of all members.

The members and managers of the LLC sign and adopt this agreement as the operating agreement of the LLC and agree to abide by its terms.

Sample Manager-Managed LLC Operating Agreement (continued)

Members

Date: _____

Signature: _____

Name of member: Carly Abelson

Date: _____

Signature: _____

Name of member: Carmen Becerra

Date: _____

Signature: _____

Name of member: Constance Li

Date: _____

Signature: _____

Name of member: Chris Williams

Managers

Date: _____

Signature: _____

Name of member: Carly Abelson

Date: _____

Signature: _____

Name of member: Carmen Becerra

Date: _____

Signature: _____

Name of member: Constance Li

Sample Manager-Managed LLC Operating Agreement (continued)

Exhibit A
Members, Managers; Initial Contributions; Interests;
Other Information

Members

Member Name	Initial Contribution	Interest
Carly Abelson	$10,000	20%
Carmen Becerra	$10,000	20%
Constance Li	$20,000	40%
Chris Williams	$10,000	20%

Managers

Carly Abelson
Carmen Becerra
Constance Li

Officers

None.

Sample LLC Buyout Agreement

LLC Buyout Agreement
4C Candles LLC

This Buyout Agreement ("Agreement") is made as of March 1, 2024 (the "Effective Date"), by and among Carly Abelson, Carmen Becerra, Constance Li, and Chris Williams (collectively "Members" and each a "Member"), and 4C Candles LLC (the "LLC") (each individually a "party" and collectively the "parties").

The Members own all of the ownership interests of the LLC ("Interests") and are parties to the Operating Agreement of the LLC. The Members seek to place certain controls on the transfer of Interests. The LLC is interested in facilitating the implementation of those controls. The parties therefore agree as follows:

1. Restrictions on Transfers and Permitted Transfers

a. While this Agreement is in effect, Members will not, except as provided below, have any right to transfer, encumber or otherwise dispose of their Interests. Transfers made in violation of this Agreement will be invalid and will not be recognized on the books of the LLC.

b. Provided that the transferee duly executes and delivers to the LLC a written agreement to be bound as a Member by the provisions of this Buyout Agreement and the Operating Agreement of the LLC, the following transfers are permitted and may be made without complying with the provisions of Paragraphs 2 and 3 below:

i. Transfers of an Interest to a revocable trust of which the Member is the grantor and primary beneficiary;

ii. Transfers of the Interest of a deceased Member to the executor, administrator, or other legal representative of the estate of the deceased Member; or

Sample LLC Buyout Agreement (continued)

iii. Transfers to the other Members of the LLC provided that such transfers must be in the same proportion that the Interest of each such other Member bears to the total of all Interests.

2. Death of a Member

a. LLC Option to Purchase

Upon receipt of notice by the LLC that a legal representative of the estate of the deceased Member has been appointed, the LLC will have the right for ninety (90) days to agree to purchase all or part of the deceased Member's Interest for the price and on the terms provided in this Agreement. If the LLC elects not to exercise its purchase option, it will notify the surviving Members of this decision before the expiration of the 90-day option period.

b. Surviving Members' Option to Purchase

Upon receipt by the surviving Members of notice that the LLC is not exercising its purchase rights under Paragraph 2(a), the surviving Members, acting together, will have the right for thirty (30) days following such notice to agree to purchase all or a part of the deceased Member's Interest in the proportion that each surviving Member's Interest bears to the total Interests owned by all of the surviving Members, for the price and on the terms provided in this Agreement.

3. Lifetime Transfers

a. Voluntary Transfers

i. **Lock-in period.** The Members agree that no voluntary transfers will be allowed in the first three (3) years of the existence of the LLC, beginning with the Effective Date of the First Operating Agreement of the LLC, without the prior consent of the other Member(s). During this lock-in period, any

Sample LLC Buyout Agreement (continued)

attempted voluntary transfer will be a violation of the Agreement and will be null and void.

ii. **Notification.** After the lock-in period, when a Member intends to transfer any part of their Interest to a third party other than as provided in Paragraph 1(b), the Member will give written notice to the LLC of the proposed transfer, including the identity of the proposed transferee, the purchase price, and other terms of the deal.

iii. **LLC Right of First Refusal.** The LLC has a right to purchase the Interest proposed to be transferred for the same price and at the same terms as the proposed transfer to the third party. The LLC may exercise this right for sixty (60) days following receipt of the notice provided for in Paragraph 3(a)(ii).

b. **Involuntary Transfers**

i. **Involuntary Transfers and Purchase Rights.** Any involuntary transfer made by operation of law or pursuant to a court order, other than by the death of a Member, including but not limited to transfers to a bankruptcy trustee, a creditor pursuant to a court judgment, a guardian or conservator of an incapacitated member, or a spouse or former spouse pursuant to a separation agreement or divorce decree, will be subject to the purchase rights described below.

ii. **LLC Purchase Option.** Upon being notified of an involuntary transfer, the LLC will have sixty (60) days to exercise a purchase option on the Interest in question for the price and on the terms provided in this Agreement.

4. Closing

The closing for any purchase described in Paragraph 2 or 3 will take place not more than sixty (60) days from the notification by the purchasing party or parties of the intent to exercise the purchase right.

Sample LLC Buyout Agreement (continued)

5. Purchase Price

a. **Purchase Price to Be Negotiated.** The purchase price for a purchase under Paragraph 2 or Paragraph 3(b) will be negotiated by the parties at the time of the purchase.

The purchase price will be determined as of the last day of the month immediately preceding (i) the date of death in the case of a purchase under Paragraph 2, or (ii) the effective date of the required notice in the case of a purchase under Paragraph 3(b).

b. **Purchase Price Determined by Appraisal.** If the selling Members and the purchaser(s) (the LLC or the other Members) are unable to agree on a purchase price, the parties will mutually select a qualified business appraiser. The seller will pay one-half the cost of the appraisal and the purchaser(s) (the LLC or the other individual members) will pay the other half. If either party contests the valuation of the appraiser, that party can engage another qualified appraiser, at their own expense, to conduct a separate appraisal. In that event, the purchase price will be the average of the two valuations.

c. **Life Insurance Proceeds.** In the case of the death of a Member, the amount of any life insurance proceeds received by the LLC on account of such Member's death will not be considered in determining the purchase price to be paid for the deceased Member's Interest.

6. Payment of Purchase Price

a. **Payment for a Deceased Member's Interest.** In the event of a purchase following the death of a Member, the purchase price will be due and payable on the date of the closing but only to the extent that there are life insurance proceeds available to pay said purchase price. The balance of the purchase price, if any, will be paid by means of a promissory note ("Note") payable in sixty (60) consecutive equal monthly payments of principal, with interest at the

Sample LLC Buyout Agreement (continued)

applicable federal rate as provided under Section 1274 of the Code, determined as of the Closing Date. The Note will be secured by a pledge of the purchased Interest.

b. **Payment for a Purchase Made Pursuant to an Involuntary Transfer.** The purchase price will be paid with a promissory note ("Note") payable in sixty (60) consecutive equal monthly payments of principal, with interest at the applicable federal rate as provided under Section 1274 of the Code, determined as of the Closing Date. The Note will be secured by a pledge of the purchased Interest.

c. **Prepayment of Note.** The purchasing party will have the right at any time or times to prepay the Note in whole or in part without penalty, provided that any such prepayments will be applied first to any interest then due and the balance to principal.

7. **Life Insurance**

a. **Purchase of Life Insurance.** The LLC may, but is not required to, purchase and be the owner and beneficiary of life insurance policies on the life of one or more of the Members.

b. **Life Insurance Claims.** Upon the death of a Member, the LLC will promptly file a claim to collect any insurance death benefit in one lump sum on each policy covering the life of the deceased Member.

c. **Balance of Life Insurance Proceeds.** The LLC will retain the balance of any insurance proceeds in excess of the purchase price for the deceased Member's Interest.

d. **Sale of Policy to a Withdrawing Member.** The LLC may, but is not required to, offer to sell a life insurance policy on a withdrawing Member to the applicable Member. The purchase price for any such policy will be its cash surrender value minus any outstanding indebtedness on the policy. If the applicable Member declines to purchase the policy, the policy will no longer be subject to this Agreement, and the LLC may retain or dispose of the policy.

Sample LLC Buyout Agreement (continued)

8. Termination

This Agreement will terminate and the Interests subject to this Agreement will be released from the terms of this Agreement on the occurrence of any of the following events:

a. The LLC is dissolved

b. A single Member becomes the sole owner of all the Interests in the LLC; or

c. All Members agree in writing to terminate this Agreement.

9. General Provisions

a. Notices. Any and all notices, including exercises of rights, designations, consents, offers, acceptances or any other communications under this Agreement will be made in writing, by registered or certified mail, return receipt requested, express courier, or by secure email if the parties agree. Notices to the LLC will be addressed to its principal place of business or to an email address designated by the LLC. Notices to Members will be addressed to their personal residences or to an email address designated by the Member. The effective date of a mailed notice will be the date on which it is mailed. The effective date of an email notice will be the date on which it is sent.

b. Amendment and Revocation. This Agreement can be modified, amended or revoked only by a writing signed by the LLC and all of the Members.

c. Binding Effect. This Agreement is binding upon the parties, their heirs, legal representatives, successors, and assigns. This Agreement will also be binding upon any person to whom any Interest is transferred in accordance with or in violation of the provisions of this Agreement.

Sample LLC Buyout Agreement (continued)

d. Specific Performance. The parties agree that they will be irrevocably damaged in the event that this Agreement is not specifically enforced. Accordingly, if the LLC or any person defaults on an obligation to give a notice, make an offer, sell an Interest, or close a sale as specified above, the LLC or any Member may bring an action to compel specific performance by the defaulting party.

e. Severability. If any term or provision of this Agreement is held to be invalid or unenforceable, the remainder of this Agreement will remain valid and be enforceable to the fullest extent permitted by law.

f. Counterparts. This Agreement may be executed in any number of counterparts each of which, when duly executed, will constitute an original.

g. Governing Law. This Agreement will be governed and interpreted according to the laws of California.

On behalf of the LLC and themselves individually, the Members hereby execute this Agreement, which is effective as of the date first written above.

By: _____   By: _____
    Name: Carly Abelson   Name: Carmen Becerra

By: _____   By: _____
    Name: Constance Li   Name: Chris Williams

Sample LLC Membership Interest Purchase Agreement

LLC Membership Interest Purchase Agreement

THIS MEMBERSHIP INTEREST PURCHASE AGREEMENT (this "Agreement") is entered into as of May 15, 2025 (the "Effective Date") between Carmen Becerra, with an address of 567 Spencer Lane, Hayward, CA 94540 ("Seller"), and 4C Candles LLC, with an address of 1234 Sequoia Ave., Pleasanton, CA 94588 ("Purchaser").

Seller presently owns 40% of the membership interests in 4C Candles LLC, a California limited liability company (the "Company").

Seller desires to sell and Purchaser desires to purchase all of Seller's membership interests in the Company. The parties therefore agree as follows:

1. **Sale of Membership Interests.** Subject to the terms and conditions of this Agreement, Seller agrees to sell and Purchaser agrees to purchase all of Seller's membership interests in the Company (the "Membership Interests"), including all rights and privileges associated with the Membership Interests.

2. **Transfer Restrictions.** The parties acknowledge that the Membership Interests are subject to the terms and restrictions of the Company's Operating Agreement and a Buyout Agreement between the members and the Company, and stipulate that the purchase being made under this Agreement does not violate any provision of the Operating Agreement, Buyout Agreement, or applicable law.

3. **Consideration.** The purchase price to be paid by Purchaser for the Membership Interests is $200,000 (the "Purchase Price"), payable as follows: $50,000 upon closing and $150,000 in the form of a 5-year, 5% promissory note payable in annual installments beginning one year from closing.

Sample LLC Membership Interest Purchase Agreement (continued)

4. **Closing.** The closing of the transaction contemplated by this **Agreement** (the "Closing") will take place on a date (the "Closing **Date**") and at a place to be agreed by the parties, but not later than June 30, 2025 without the consent of both parties. The Closing may be conducted simultaneously (in-person or virtually), or by exchange of documents of documents and payments electronically or by overnight courier. The parties agree and acknowledge that no certificate or certificates are necessary to evidence the Transferred Membership Interest that is being transferred under this Agreement, and that the transfer will occur automatically upon the execution of an assignment by the Seller at the Closing.

5. **Representations and Warranties of Seller; Indemnification and Release.** Seller hereby represents and warrants that the following statements are true and correct as of the date of this Agreement and will be true and correct as of the Closing Date. Seller will notify Purchaser promptly if Seller learns between the date of this Agreement and the Closing that any representation made here has ceased to be true.

   a. **Authority; Capacity.** Seller has full power, authority, and capacity to execute and deliver, and to perform its duties and obligations under this Agreement.

   b. **Title.** Seller is the lawful owner of, and has good and marketable title to, the Membership Interests, free any and all liens, restrictions, or claims of any kind, except for restrictions contained in the Operating Agreement and Buyout Agreement of the Company.

   c. **Indemnification and Release by Seller.** Seller agrees to indemnify and release Purchaser from and against any liabilities arising from or caused by a breach of any representation or warranty made by Seller in this Agreement, and any liability related to or involving the Membership Interests, including any tax liability, arising or incurred on or prior to the Closing Date.

Sample LLC Membership Interest Purchase Agreement (continued)

6. **Representations and Warranties of Purchaser; Indemnification by Purchaser.** Purchaser hereby represents and warrants to Seller that the following statements are true and correct as of the date of this Agreement and will be true and correct as of the Closing Date.

   a. **Authority; Capacity.** Purchaser has full power and authority to enter into this Agreement, including any necessary consents from the members of the company, and to perform its obligations under this Agreement.

   b. **Indemnification and Release by Purchaser.** Purchaser agrees to indemnify and release Seller from and against any liabilities arising from or caused by a breach of any representation or warranty made by Purchaser in this Agreement, and any liability related to or involving the Membership Interests, including any tax liability, arising or incurred after the Closing Date.

7. **Entire Agreement.** This Agreement constitutes the entire agreement and understanding between Purchaser and Seller with respect to the subject matter of this Agreement and supersedes all prior understandings, agreements or communications between the parties related to the subject matter of this Agreement.

8. **Binding Effect.** This Agreement is be binding upon, and shall inure to the benefit of, Purchaser, Seller, and their respective heirs, legal representatives, successors, and permitted assigns.

9. **Assignment.** Neither party will assign any of its rights under this Agreement without the prior written consent of the other party.

10. **Multiple Counterparts.** This Agreement may be executed in one or more counterparts, each of which shall be deemed an original but all of which together will constitute one instrument.

11. **Notices.** Any notices or communications required or permitted to be given by this Agreement must be given in writing, and be personally delivered or sent by certified mail, express shipment, or electronically

Sample LLC Membership Interest Purchase Agreement (continued)

with receipt confirmed. A notice is to be sent to the addresses of the receiving party as written above, or to an email address provided by the receiving party.

12. **Amendments.** This Agreement may be amended only by a writing signed by both parties.

13. **Severability.** If any provision of is determined by a court or arbitrator to be invalid, unenforceable, or otherwise ineffective, that provision will be severed from the rest of this Agreement shall for any reason be held to be invalid or unenforceable in any respect, the remaining provisions will continue to be in effect and enforceable.

14. **Governing Law.** This Agreement is to be governed and interpreted according to the law of the state of California.

So Agreed:

Carmen Becerra (Seller):

By: _____

Name:

4C Candles LLC (Purchaser):

By: _____

Name: Constance Li, for 4C
         Candles LLC

Title: Member/Manager

Sample Assignment of LLC Interest

Assignment of LLC Interest

This ASSIGNMENT OF LLC INTEREST ("Assignment") is made by Carmen Becerra ("Assignor") to 4C Candles LLC ("Assignee") as of June 20, 2025 (the "Effective Date").

1. **Assignment.** Pursuant to a Membership Interest Purchase Agreement between the parties, dated May 15, 2025 (the "Purchase Agreement"), and in return for the Purchase Price and other valuable consideration set forth in the Purchase Agreement, the receipt of which Assignor hereby acknowledges, the Assignor irrevocably and unconditionally assigns a 40% Membership Interest (the "Assigned Interest") in 4C Candles LLC, a limited liability company (the "LLC") to Assignee.

2. **Representations and Warranties.** The parties reaffirm the representations and warranties made in the Purchase Agreement.

3. **LLC Consent.** If the LLC is not the Assignee, the LLC approves the transfer of the Assigned Interest from Assignor to Assignee.

4. **Releases.** The Assignor releases the Assignee from all liabilities and claims arising from the Assigned Interest prior to the date of this Assignment. The Assignee releases the Assignor from all liabilities and claims arising from the Assigned Interest on or after the date of this Assignment. The Assignor and the LLC release each other from all liabilities and claims arising under the LLC and Assignor's ownership interest therein.

So Agreed:

Carmen Becerra (Assignor):   4C Candles LLC (Assignee):

By: _____   By: _____

Name: Carmen Becerra   Name: Constance Li, for 4C
                                                        Candles LLC
                                          Title: Member/Manager

Blank Forms

FORMS
The forms in this appendix are downloadable from this book's companion page. See Appendix A for the link.

Member-Managed LLC Operating Agreement

Operating Agreement of
_____ [*Company name*]_____

A __[*State of Organization*]__ Limited Liability Company

1. Preliminary Provisions

a. Effective Date

This operating agreement of _____ [*company name*]_____ (the "LLC"), effective as of _____[*date*]_____, is adopted by the members whose signatures appear at the end of this agreement.

b. Formation

This limited liability company (LLC) was formed by filing its articles of organization with the [___*state of organization*____ Secretary of State. The legal existence of the LLC commenced on the date of such filing. A copy of this organizational document will be placed in the LLC's records book.

c. Name

The formal name of the LLC is as stated above. However, the LLC may do business under a different name by complying with the fictitious or assumed business name statutes and procedures of _____[*state of organization*]_____.

d. Registered Office and Registered Agent

The registered office and registered agent are as indicated in the articles of organization. The LLC may change its registered office and/or agent from time to time by filing a change of registered agent or office statement with the _____[*state of organization*]_____ Secretary of State.

Member-Managed LLC Operating Agreement (continued)

e. Business Purpose

Select one:

Option 1

The purpose of the limited liability company is to engage in any lawful act or activity for which a limited liability company may be organized under the _____[*state of organization*]_____ Limited Liability Company Act.

Option 2

The purpose of the limited liability company is to _____[*state the specific business purpose*]_____, as well as to engage in any lawful act or activity for which a limited liability company may be organized under the _____[*state of organization*]_____ Limited Liability Company Act.

f. Duration of LLC

Select one:

Option 1

The duration of the LLC is perpetual. However, the LLC will terminate when a proposal to dissolve the LLC is adopted according to the terms of this agreement or when the LLC is otherwise terminated in accordance with law.

Option 2

The duration of the LLC will end on _[*fixed dissolution date*]_, unless terminated sooner by the members according to the terms of this agreement or otherwise in accordance with law.

2. Membership Provisions

a. Nonliability of Members

No member will be personally liable for the expenses, debts, obligations, or liabilities of the LLC or for claims made against it.

Member-Managed LLC Operating Agreement (continued)

b. Reimbursement of Expenses

Members are entitled to reimbursement by the LLC for reasonable expenses incurred on behalf of the LLC, including expenses incurred in the formation, dissolution, and liquidation of the LLC.

c. Compensation

A member will not be paid for performing any duties associated with membership, including management of the LLC. Members may be paid, however, for services rendered in another capacity for the LLC, as allowed by law and as approved by a majority vote of the members.

d. Other Business by Members

A member may engage in any business activity without the other members' consent, so long as the business activity does not directly compete with the LLC.

e. Members' Percentage interests

A member's membership interest is computed as a percentage of total membership interests, as shown on Exhibit A.

f. Membership Voting

Except as otherwise may be required by the articles of organization, other provisions of this operating agreement; or under the laws of this state, each member will vote in proportion to the member's percentage interest. Further, unless otherwise stated in another provision of this operating agreement, the phrase "majority of members" means a majority of percentage interests.

g. Members' Meetings and Actions Taken by Written Consent

The LLC is not required to hold regular members' meetings. However, one or more members can call a meeting at any time. The member calling the meeting will provide notice of the business to be transacted at the meeting, but other business may be discussed and conducted at the meeting with the consent of all members present. A quorum consists of all members, unless members who cannot

Member-Managed LLC Operating Agreement (continued)

attend consent in writing for the meeting to take place in their absence. Except as otherwise provided in this agreement, a vote of the majority of members present at a meeting of the members is required to approve any action taken at the meeting.

Any action required or permitted by this agreement to be taken at a meeting of the members may be taken without a meeting, without prior notice, by unanimous written consent of the members.

h. Admission of New Members

Except as otherwise provided in this agreement, a person or entity will not be admitted into membership unless each member consents in writing to the admission of the new member.

3. Management Provisions

a. Management by Members

This LLC will be managed exclusively by all of its members.

b. Indemnification of Members

A member will be indemnified by the LLC for any debt, obligation, or other liability, including reasonable attorneys' fees, incurred in the course of the member's activities or performance of duties on behalf of the LLC as long as the member complied with the duties of loyalty and care when incurring the debt, obligation, or other liability. This provision does not in any way limit the indemnification the member would be entitled to under applicable state law. The indemnification provided will inure to the benefit of successors and assigns of any such member.

4. Tax and Financial Provisions

a. Tax Classification of LLC

The LLC will be initially classified as a ____ [*specify the tax entity— partnership or S corporation*] _____ for federal and, if applicable, state income tax purposes. The LLC may change its tax treatment

Member-Managed LLC Operating Agreement (continued)

with the consent of all members and by filing the necessary election with the IRS and, if applicable, the state tax department.

b. Tax Year and Accounting Method

The tax year of the LLC will end on the last day of the month of ____ [*month—almost always December*]___. The LLC will use the ____ [*specify the accrual method or cash method*]____ of accounting.

   The tax year and the accounting method of the LLC may each be changed with the consent of all members.

c. Title to Assets

All personal and real property of the LLC will be held in the name of the LLC, not in the name of any individual member.

d. Bank Accounts

All funds of the Company will be deposited in one or more separate bank accounts, using such banks or trust companies as the members may designate. Withdrawals from such bank accounts are to be made upon such signature or signatures as the members may designate. The funds of the LLC, however and wherever deposited or invested, will not be commingled with the personal funds of any member of the LLC.

e. Tax Matters Partner

If required under Internal Revenue Code provisions or regulations, the LLC will designate a member as its "tax matters partner" in accordance with Internal Revenue Code Section 6231(a)(7) and corresponding regulations, who will fulfill this role by being the spokesperson for the LLC in dealings with the IRS and performing such other duties as required under the Internal Revenue Code and Regulations.

f. Annual Income Tax Returns and Reports

Within 60 days after the end of each tax year, a copy of the LLC's state and federal income tax returns for the preceding tax year will

Member-Managed LLC Operating Agreement (continued)

be mailed or otherwise provided to each member, together with any additional information and forms necessary for each member to complete their individual state and federal income tax returns. Along with the necessary tax information and forms, the LLC will also provide a financial report that includes a balance sheet and profit and loss statement for the year.

5. Capital Provisions

a. Capital Contributions

Members have made initial contributions of cash, property, or services as specified in Exhibit A.

b. No Interest on Capital Contributions

No interest will be paid on capital contributions or on capital account balances.

c. Capital Account Bookkeeping

A capital account will be set up and maintained on the books of the LLC for each member. It will reflect each member's capital contribution, increased by any additional contributions by the member and by the member's share of LLC profits, decreased by any distributions to the member and by the member's share of LLC losses, and adjusted as required in accordance with applicable provisions of the Internal Revenue Code and corresponding income tax regulations. Upon a valid transfer of a member's membership interest, the member's capital account will carry over to the new owner.

d. Additional Contributions

The members may agree, from time to time, by unanimous vote, to require the payment of additional capital contributions by the members. **[Optional additional language]** If a member fails to make a required capital contribution, that member may be expelled from the LLC by a unanimous vote of the remaining members.

Member-Managed LLC Operating Agreement (continued)

e. Allocations of Profits and Losses

Select one:

Option 1

The profits and losses of the LLC, and all items of its income, gain, loss, deduction, and credit will be allocated to members in accordance with the member's percentage interest.

Option 2

The profits and losses of the LLC, and all items of its income, gain, loss, deduction, and credit will be allocated to members as follows: ____[*state the allocation formula*]___.

f. Capital Withdrawals

Members will not be allowed to withdraw any part of their capital contributions or to receive distributions, whether in property or cash, except as otherwise allowed by this agreement. A capital withdrawal requires the written consent of all members.

g. Distributions of Cash

Select one:

Option 1

Cash from business operations, as well as cash from a sale or other disposition of LLC capital assets, may be allocated and distributed from time to time to members in accordance with each member's percentage interest in the LLC, as may be decided by a majority of members. However, the member(s) will direct distributions to be made each year in an amount sufficient to cover any member's tax liability that may arise based on the allocation of LLC income, gains, losses, or deductions.

Option 2

Cash from business operations, as well as cash from a sale or other disposition of LLC capital assets, may be allocated and distributed

Member-Managed LLC Operating Agreement (continued)

from time to time to members in accordance with the following each member's percentage interest in the LLC, as may be decided by a majority of members. However, the member(s) will direct distributions to be made each year in an amount sufficient to cover any member's tax liability that may arise based on the allocation of LLC income, gains, losses, or deductions.

h. Allocation of Noncash Proceeds

If proceeds consist of property other than cash, the members will decide the value of the property and allocate such value among the members in accordance with each member's percentage interest in the LLC.

i. Allocation and Distribution of Liquidation Proceeds

Regardless of any other provision in this agreement, if there is a distribution in liquidation of the LLC, or when a member's interest is liquidated, all items of income and loss will be allocated to a member's capital account, and all appropriate credits and deductions will then be made to the capital account before any final distribution is made. A final distribution will be made to members only to the extent of, and in proportion to, any positive balance in a member's capital account.

6. Membership Withdrawal and Transfer Provisions

a. Withdrawal of Members

[Optional clause] No member may withdraw from the LLC until __*[number of months]*__ months from the effective date of this agreement.

A member may withdraw from the LLC by giving written notice to all other members at least ____*[number of months]*____ months before the date the withdrawal is to be effective. In the event of such withdrawal, the LLC will pay the departing member the fair value of their LLC interest, less any amounts owed by the member to the LLC.

Member-Managed LLC Operating Agreement (continued)

Select one:

Option 1

The departing and remaining members will agree at the time of departure on the fair value of the departing member's interest and the schedule of payments to be made by the LLC to the departing member, who will receive payment for their interest within a reasonable time after departure from the LLC. If the departing and remaining members cannot agree on the value of departing member's interest, they will select an appraiser, who will determine the current value of the departing member's interest. This appraised amount will be fair value of the departing member's interest and will form the basis of the amount to be paid to the departing member.

Option 2

The fair value of the departing members will be determined as follows: _[*state valuation formula, such as book value or a multiple of profits*]_ .

b. Restrictions on the Transfer of Membership

Notwithstanding any other provision of this agreement, a member will not transfer their membership in the LLC unless all of the nontransferring members first agree in writing to approve the admission of the transferee into the LLC. Further, no member may encumber a part or all of their membership in the LLC by mortgage, pledge, granting of a security interest, lien, or otherwise, unless the encumbrance has first been approved in writing by all other members of the LLC.

Notwithstanding the above provision, any member will be allowed to assign an economic interest in their membership to another person without the approval of the other members. Any assignment of economic interest will not include a transfer of the member's voting or management rights, and the assignee will not become a member except as provided elsewhere in this agreement.

Member-Managed LLC Operating Agreement (continued)

7. Dissolution Provisions

a. Events That Trigger Dissolution of the LLC

The following events will trigger a dissolution of the LLC:

i. **Expiration of LLC term.** The expiration of the term of existence of the LLC, if such term is specified in the articles of organization or this operating agreement, will cause the dissolution of the LLC.

ii. **Written agreement or consent to dissolve.** The written agreement of all members to dissolve the LLC will cause a dissolution of the LLC.

iii. **Entry of decree.** The entry of a decree of dissolution of the LLC under state law will cause a dissolution of the LLC.

If the LLC is to dissolve according to any of the above provisions, the members will wind up the affairs of the LLC, and take other actions appropriate to complete a dissolution of the LLC in accordance with applicable provisions of state law.

b. Dissociation of a Member

The dissociation of a member, which means the death, incapacity, bankruptcy, retirement, resignation, or expulsion of a member, or any other event that terminates the continued membership of a member, will not cause a dissolution of the LLC. The LLC will continue its existence and business following such dissociation of a member.

8. General Provisions

a. Officers

The LLC may designate one or more officers, such as a President, Vice President, Secretary, and Treasurer. Persons who fill these positions need not be members of the LLC. Such positions may be compensated or uncompensated according to the nature and extent of the services rendered as a part of the duties of each office.

Member-Managed LLC Operating Agreement (continued)

b. Records

The LLC will keep at its principal business address a copy of all proceedings of membership meetings and resolutions, as well as books of account of financial transactions. A list of the names and addresses of the current membership also will be maintained at this address, with notations on any transfers of members' interests to nonmembers or persons being admitted into membership.

The LLC's articles of organization, a signed copy of this operating agreement, the LLC's tax returns for the preceding three tax years, and written records of votes taken at member meetings or by unanimous consent, will be kept at its principal business address.

Any member may inspect any and all records maintained by the LLC upon reasonable notice.

c. All Necessary Acts

The members and officers (if any) of the LLC are authorized to perform all acts necessary to perfect the organization of the LLC and to carry out its business operations expeditiously and efficiently as authorized by this agreement and by law.

d. Severability

If any provision of this agreement is determined by a court or arbitrator to be invalid, unenforceable, or otherwise ineffective, that provision will be severed from the rest of this agreement, and the remaining provisions will remain in effect and enforceable.

e. [Optional clause] Mediation and Arbitration of Disputes Among Members

In any dispute over the provisions of this operating agreement and in other disputes among the members, if the members cannot resolve the dispute to their mutual satisfaction, the matter will be submitted to mediation. The terms and procedure for mediation will be arranged by the parties to the dispute.

Member-Managed LLC Operating Agreement (continued)

If good-faith mediation of a dispute proves impossible or if an agreed-upon mediation outcome cannot be obtained by the members who are parties to the dispute, the dispute will be submitted to binding arbitration in accordance with the rules of the American Arbitration Association. Any party may commence arbitration of the dispute by sending a written request for arbitration to all other parties to the dispute. The request will state the nature of the dispute to be resolved by arbitration, and, if all parties to the dispute agree to arbitration, arbitration will be commenced as soon as practical after such parties receive a copy of the written request.

All parties will initially share the cost of arbitration, but the prevailing party or parties may be awarded attorneys' fees, costs, and other expenses of arbitration at the discretion of the arbitrator. All arbitration decisions will be final, binding, and conclusive on all the parties to arbitration, and legal judgment may be entered based upon such decision in accordance with applicable law in any court having jurisdiction to do so.

f. Entire Agreement and Amendment

This operating agreement represents the entire agreement among the members, and replaces and supersedes all prior written and oral agreements among them. This agreement will not be amended, modified, or replaced except by written agreement of all members.

Member-Managed LLC Operating Agreement (continued)

The members sign and adopt this agreement as the operating agreement of the LLC and agree to abide by its terms.

Date: _____

Signature: _____

Name of member: _____

Date: _____

Signature: _____

Name of member: _____

Date: _____

Signature: _____

Name of member: _____

Date: _____

Signature: _____

Name of member: _____

Member-Managed LLC Operating Agreement (continued)

Exhibit A

Members; Initial Contributions; Interests; Other Information

Members

Member Name	Initial Contribution	Interest
_____	_____	_____
_____	_____	_____
_____	_____	_____
_____	_____	_____

Officers

_____

_____

_____

_____

Manager-Managed LLC Operating Agreement

Operating Agreement of
_____[Company name]_____

A __[State of Organization]__ Limited Liability Company

1. Preliminary Provisions

a. Effective Date

This operating agreement of _____[company name]_____
(the "LLC"), effective as of ___[date]___, is adopted by the members
whose signatures appear at the end of this agreement.

b. Formation

This limited liability company (LLC) was formed by filing its articles
of organization with the _____[state of organization]_____ Secretary
of State. The legal existence of the LLC commenced on the date of
such filing. A copy of this organizational document will be placed
in the LLC's records book.

c. Name

The formal name of the LLC is as stated above. However, the
LLC may do business under a different name by complying with
the fictitious or assumed business name statutes and procedures
of _____[state of organization]_____.

d. Registered Office and Registered Agent

The registered office and registered agent are as indicated in the
articles of organization. The LLC may change its registered office
and/or agent from time to time by filing a change of registered
agent or office statement with the _____[state of organization]____
Secretary of State.

Manager-Managed LLC Operating Agreement (continued)

e. **Business Purpose**

Select one:

Option 1

The purpose of the limited liability company is to engage in any lawful act or activity for which a limited liability company may be organized under the ____*[state of organization]*____ Limited Liability Company Act.

Option 2

The purpose of the limited liability company is to ____*[state the specific business purpose]*____, as well as to engage in any lawful act or activity for which a limited liability company may be organized under the ____*[state of organization]*____ Limited Liability Company Act.

f. **Duration of LLC**

Select one:

Option 1

The duration of the LLC is perpetual. However, the LLC will terminate when a proposal to dissolve the LLC is adopted according to the terms of this agreement or when the LLC is otherwise terminated in accordance with law.

Option 2

The duration of the LLC will end on ___*[fixed dissolution date]*___, unless terminated sooner by the members according to the terms of this agreement or otherwise in accordance with law.

2. **Membership Provisions**

a. **Nonliability of Members**

No member will be personally liable for the expenses, debts, obligations, or liabilities of the LLC or for claims made against it.

Manager-Managed LLC Operating Agreement (continued)

b. Reimbursement of Expenses

Members are entitled to reimbursement by the LLC for reasonable expenses incurred on behalf of the LLC, including expenses incurred in the formation, dissolution, and liquidation of the LLC.

c. Compensation

A member will not be paid for performing any duties associated with membership, including management of the LLC. Members may be paid, however, for services rendered in any other capacity for the LLC, as allowed by law and as approved by a majority vote of the managers.

d. Other Business by Members

A member may engage in any business activity without the other members' consent, so long as the business activity does not directly compete with the LLC.

e. Members' Percentage interests

A member's membership interest is computed as a percentage of total membership interests, as shown on Exhibit A.

f. Membership Voting

Except as otherwise may be required by the articles of organization, other provisions of this operating agreement; or under the laws of this state, each member will vote on any matter provided for in this agreement and any matter submitted to the membership for their approval by the managers in proportion to the member's percentage interest. Further, unless otherwise stated in another provision of this operating agreement, the phrase "majority of members" means a majority of percentage interests.

g. Members' Meetings and Actions Taken by Written Consent

The LLC is not required to hold regular members' meetings. However, one or more members can call a meeting at any time. The

Manager-Managed LLC Operating Agreement (continued)

member calling the meeting will provide notice of the business to be transacted at the meeting, but other business may be discussed and conducted at the meeting with the consent of all members present. A quorum consists of all members, unless members who cannot attend consent in writing for the meeting to take place in their absence. Except as otherwise provided in this agreement, a vote of the majority of members present at a meeting of the members is required to approve any action taken at the meeting.

Any action required or permitted by this agreement to be taken at a meeting of the members may be taken without a meeting, without prior notice, by unanimous written consent of the this agreement, a person or entity will not be admitted into membership unless each member consents in writing to the admission of the new member.

3. Management Provisions

a. Management by Manager(s)

The LLC will be managed by one or more managers. The current managers are listed in Exhibit A.

b. Nonliability of Manager(s)

No manager of the LLC will be personally liable for the expenses, debts, obligations, or liabilities of the LLC, or for claims made against it.

c. Authority and Votes of Manager(s)

Except as otherwise set forth in this agreement, the articles of organization, or under the laws of this state, all management decisions relating to the LLC's business will be made by its manager(s). If there is more than one manager, management decisions will be approved by a majority vote of the managers, with each manager entitled to cast one vote for or against any matter submitted to the managers for a decision.

Manager-Managed LLC Operating Agreement (continued)

d. Appointment, Removal, and Term of Manager(s)

The members will have the exclusive right to set the number of managers and to appoint the manager(s), who will be responsible for the day-to-day management of the business of the LLC. The manager(s) will be appointed by a majority of members.

A manager may be removed at any time by a vote of the majority of the members. In addition, each manager will cease to serve upon any of the following events:

- the manager becomes disabled, dies, retires, or otherwise withdraws from management, or
- the manager's term expires, if a term has been designated in other provisions of this agreement.

Upon the occurrence of any of these events, a new manager may be appointed to replace the departing manager by a majority vote of the members.

e. Manager Commitment to LLC

Each manager will conduct the affairs of the LLC in good faith and in the best interests of the LLC. Each manager will devote time to the LLC as the business requires.

f. Compensation of Manager(s)

No manager is entitled to any fee for managing the operations of the LLC unless such compensation is approved by a majority vote of the members.

g. Indemnification of Manager(s)

A manager will be indemnified by the LLC for any debt, obligation, or other liability, including reasonable attorneys' fees, incurred in the course of the manager's activities or performance of duties on behalf of the LLC as long as the manager complied with the duties of loyalty and care when incurring the debt, obligation, or other

Manager-Managed LLC Operating Agreement (continue *)*

liability. This provision does not in any way limit the indemnification the manager would be entitled to under applicable state law. The indemnification provided will inure to the benefit of successors and assigns of any such manager.

h. Management Meetings and Actions Taken by Written Consents

Meetings of the managers will be held on five (5) days' notice or on such shorter notice as may be mutually agreeable to the managers, on the call of any one or more managers. Members will be provided with a written notice of the time and place of each meeting, along with a description of the purpose of the meeting. The presence of a majority of managers constitutes a quorum. Except as otherwise provided in this agreement, the vote of a majority of the managers present at any managers' meeting is required to approve any action taken at the meeting.

Any action required or permitted by this agreement to be taken at a meeting of the managers may be taken without a meeting, without prior notice, by unanimous written consent of the managers.

4. Tax and Financial Provisions

a. Tax Classification of LLC

The LLC will be initially classified as a ___*[specify the tax entity—* *partnership or S corporation]*___ partnership for federal and, if applicable, state income tax purposes. The LLC may change its tax treatment with the consent of all members and by filing the necessary election with the IRS and, if applicable, the state tax department.

b. Tax Year and Accounting Method

The tax year of the LLC will end on the last day of the month of ___*[month—almost always December]*___. The LLC will use the ___*[specify the accrual method or cash method]*___ of accounting.

Manager-Managed LLC Operating Agreement (continued)

The tax year and the accounting method of the LLC may each be changed with the consent of all members.

c. Title to Assets

All personal and real property of the LLC will be held in the name of the LLC, not in the name of any individual member.

d. Bank Accounts

All funds of the Company will be deposited in one or more separate bank accounts, using such banks or trust companies as the managers may designate. Withdrawals from such bank accounts are to be made upon such signature or signatures as the managers may designate. The funds of the LLC, however and wherever deposited or invested, will not be commingled with the personal funds of any member of the LLC.

e. Tax Matters Partner

If required under Internal Revenue Code provisions or regulations, the LLC will designate a member as its "tax matters partner" in accordance with Internal Revenue Code Section 6231(a)(7) and corresponding regulations, who will fulfill this role by being the spokesperson for the LLC in dealings with the IRS and performing such other duties as required under the Internal Revenue Code and Regulations.

f. Annual Income Tax Returns and Reports

Within 60 days after the end of each tax year of the LLC, a copy of the LLC's state and federal income tax returns for the preceding tax year will be mailed or otherwise provided to each member of the LLC, together with any additional information and forms necessary for each member to complete their individual state and federal income tax returns. Along with the necessary tax information and forms, the LLC will also provide a financial report that includes a balance sheet and profit and loss statement for the year.

Manager-Managed LLC Operating Agreement (continued)

5. Capital Provisions

a. Capital Contributions

Members have made initial contributions of cash, property, or services as specified in Exhibit A.

b. No Interest on Capital Contributions

No interest will be paid on capital contributions or on capital account balances.

c. Capital Account Bookkeeping

A capital account will be set up and maintained on the books of the LLC for each member. It will reflect each member's capital contribution, increased by any additional contributions by the member and by the member's share of LLC profits, decreased by any distributions to the member and by the member's share of LLC losses, and adjusted as required in accordance with applicable provisions of the Internal Revenue Code and corresponding income tax regulations. Upon a valid transfer of a member's membership interest, the member's capital account will carry over to the new owner.

d. Additional Contributions

The members may agree, from time to time, by unanimous vote, to require the payment of additional capital contributions by the members.

[Optional additional language] If a member fails to make a required capital contribution, that member may be expelled from the LLC by a unanimous vote of the remaining members.

e. Allocations of Profits and Losses

Select one:

Option 1

The profits and losses of the LLC, and all items of its income, gain, loss, deduction, and credit will be allocated to members in accordance with the member's percentage interest.

Manager-Managed LLC Operating Agreement (continued)

Option 2

The profits and losses of the LLC, and all items of its income, gain, loss, deduction, and credit will be allocated to members as follows: ___[*state the allocation formula*]___.

f. Capital Withdrawals

Members will not be allowed to withdraw any part of their capital contributions or to receive distributions, whether in property or cash, except as otherwise allowed by this agreement. A capital withdrawal requires the written consent of all members.

g. Distributions of Cash

Select one:

Option 1

Cash from business operations, as well as cash from a sale or other disposition of LLC capital assets, may be allocated and distributed from time to time to members in accordance with each member's percentage interest in the LLC, as may be decided by a majority of managers. However, the managers will direct distributions to be made each year in an amount sufficient to cover any member's tax liability that may arise based on the allocation of LLC income, gains, losses, or deductions.

Option 2

Cash from business operations, as well as cash from a sale or other disposition of LLC capital assets, may be allocated and distributed from time to time to members in accordance with the following each member's percentage interest in the LLC, as may be decided by a majority of managers. However, the managers will direct distributions to be made each year in an amount sufficient to cover any member's tax liability that may arise based on the allocation of LLC income, gains, losses, or deductions.

Manager-Managed LLC Operating Agreement (continued)

h. Allocation of Noncash Proceeds

If proceeds consist of property other than cash, the members will decide the value of the property and allocate such value among the members in accordance with each member's percentage interest in the LLC.

i. Allocation and Distribution of Liquidation Proceeds

Regardless of any other provision in this agreement, if there is a distribution in liquidation of the LLC, or when a member's interest is liquidated, all items of income and loss will be allocated to a member's capital account, and all appropriate credits and deductions will then be made to the capital account before any final distribution is made. A final distribution will be made to members only to the extent of, and in proportion to, any positive balance in a member's capital account.

6. Membership Withdrawal and Transfer Provisions

a. Withdrawal of Members

[**Optional clause**] No member may withdraw from the LLC until ____[*number of months*]__ months from the effective date of this agreement. A member may withdraw from the LLC by giving written notice to all other members at least __[*number of months*]__ months before the date the withdrawal is to be effective. In the event of such withdrawal, the LLC will pay the departing member the fair value of their LLC interest, less any amounts owed by the member to the LLC.

Select one:

Option 1

The departing and remaining members will agree at the time of departure on the fair value of the departing member's interest and

Manager-Managed LLC Operating Agreement (continued)

the schedule of payments to be made by the LLC to the departing member, who will receive payment for their interest within a reasonable time after departure from the LLC. If the departing and remaining members cannot agree on the value of departing member's interest, they will select an appraiser, who will determine the current value of the departing member's interest. This appraised amount will be fair value of the departing member's interest and will form the basis of the amount to be paid to the departing member.

Option 2

The fair value of the departing members will be determined as follows: _[*state valuation formula, such as book value or a multiple of profits*]_ .

b. Restrictions on the Transfer of Membership

Notwithstanding any other provision of this agreement, a member will not transfer their membership in the LLC unless all of the nontransferring members first agree in writing to approve the admission of the transferee into the LLC. Further, no member may encumber a part or all of their membership in the LLC by mortgage, pledge, granting of a security interest, lien, or otherwise, unless the encumbrance has first been approved in writing by all other members of the LLC.

Notwithstanding the above provision, any member will be allowed to assign an economic interest in their membership to another person without the approval of the other members. Any assignment of economic interest will not include a transfer of the member's voting or management rights, and the assignee will not become a member except as provided elsewhere in this agreement.

Manager-Managed LLC Operating Agreement (continued)

7. Dissolution Provisions

a. Events That Trigger Dissolution of the LLC

The following events will trigger a dissolution of the LLC:

i. **Expiration of LLC Term.** The expiration of the term of existence of the LLC, if such term is specified in the articles of organization or this operating agreement, will cause the dissolution of the LLC.

ii. **Written Agreement or Consent to Dissolve.** The written agreement of all members to dissolve the LLC will cause a dissolution of the LLC.

iii. **Entry of Decree.** The entry of a decree of dissolution of the LLC under state law will cause a dissolution of the LLC.

If the LLC is to dissolve according to any of the above provisions, the manager(s) will wind up the affairs of the LLC, and take other actions appropriate to complete a dissolution of the LLC in accordance with applicable provisions of state law.

b. Dissociation of a Member

The dissociation of a member, which means the death, incapacity, bankruptcy, retirement, resignation, or expulsion of a member, or any other event that terminates the continued membership of a member, will not cause a dissolution of the LLC. The LLC will continue its existence and business following such dissociation of a member.

8. General Provisions

a. Officers

The LLC may designate one or more officers, such as a President, Vice President, Secretary, and Treasurer. Persons who fill these positions need not be members of the LLC. Such positions may be compensated or noncompensated according to the nature and extent of the services rendered as a part of the duties of each office.

Manager-Managed LLC Operating Agreement (continued)

b. Records

The LLC will keep at its principal business address a copy of all proceedings of membership meetings and resolutions, as well as books of account of financial transactions. A list of the names and addresses of the current membership also will be maintained at this address, with notations on any transfers of members' interests to nonmembers or persons being admitted into membership.

The LLC's articles of organization, a signed copy of this operating agreement, the LLC's tax returns for the preceding three tax years, and written records of votes taken at member and manager meetings or by unanimous consent, will be kept at its principal business address.

Any member may inspect any and all records maintained by the LLC upon reasonable notice.

c. All Necessary Acts

The members, managers, and officers (if any) of the LLC are authorized to perform all acts necessary to perfect the organization of the LLC and to carry out its business operations expeditiously and efficiently.

d. Severability

If any provision of this agreement is determined by a court or arbitrator to be invalid, unenforceable, or otherwise ineffective, that provision will be severed from the rest of this agreement, and the remaining provisions will remain in effect and enforceable.

e. [Optional clause] Mediation and Arbitration of Disputes Among Members

In any dispute over the provisions of this operating agreement and in other disputes among the members, if the members cannot resolve the dispute to their mutual satisfaction, the matter will be submitted to mediation. The terms and procedure for mediation will be arranged by the parties to the dispute.

Manager-Managed LLC Operating Agreement (continued)

If good-faith mediation of a dispute proves impossible or if an agreed-upon mediation outcome cannot be obtained by the members who are parties to the dispute, the dispute will be submitted to binding arbitration in accordance with the rules of the American Arbitration Association. Any party may commence arbitration of the dispute by sending a written request for arbitration to all other parties to the dispute. The request will state the nature of the dispute to be resolved by arbitration, and, if all parties to the dispute agree to arbitration, arbitration will be commenced as soon as practical after such parties receive a copy of the written request.

All parties will initially share the cost of arbitration, but the prevailing party or parties may be awarded attorneys' fees, costs, and other expenses of arbitration at the discretion of the arbitrator. All arbitration decisions will be final, binding, and conclusive on all the parties to arbitration, and legal judgment may be entered based upon such decision in accordance with applicable law in any court having jurisdiction to do so.

f. Entire Agreement and Amendment

This operating agreement represents the entire agreement among the members, and replaces and supersedes all prior written and oral agreements among the members. This agreement will not be amended, modified, or replaced except by written agreement of all members.

The members and managers of the LLC sign and adopt this agreement as the operating agreement of the LLC and agree to abide by its terms.

Manager-Managed LLC Operating Agreement (continued)

Members

Date: _____

Signature: _____

Name of member: _____

Date: _____

Signature: _____

Name of member: _____

Date: _____

Signature: _____

Name of member: _____

Date: _____

Signature: _____

Name of member: _____

Managers

Date: _____

Signature: _____

Name of member: _____

Date: _____

Signature: _____

Name of member: _____

Date: _____

Signature: _____

Name of member: _____

Manager-Managed LLC Operating Agreement (continued)

Exhibit A
Members, Managers; Initial Contributions; Interests; Other Information

Members

Member Name	Initial Contribution	Interest
_____	_____	_____
_____	_____	_____
_____	_____	_____
_____	_____	_____

Managers

_____

_____

_____

_____

Officers

_____

_____

_____

_____

LLC Buyout Agreement

LLC Buyout Agreement
_____[Company name]_____

This Buyout Agreement ("Agreement") made as of ___[*date*]___, by and among the members whose signatures appear at the end of this agreement (collectively "Members" and each a "Member"), as Members of _____[*LLC name*]_____ ("Company"), and between the Members and the Company.

The Members own all of the ownership interests of the Company ("Interests") and agree to the following:

1. Restrictions on Transfers and Permitted Transfers

  a. While this Agreement is in effect, Members will not, except as provided below, have any right to transfer, encumber or otherwise dispose of their Interests.

  b. Provided that the transferee duly executes and delivers to the Company a written agreement to be bound as a Member by the provisions of this Agreement, the following transfers are permitted and may be made without complying with the provisions of Sections 2 and 3 below:

  i. Transfers of an Interest to a revocable trust of which the Member is the grantor and primary beneficiary

  ii. Transfers of the Interest of a deceased Member to the executor, administrator, or other legal representative of the estate of the deceased Member; or

  iii. Transfers to the other Members of the Company provided that such transfers must be in the same proportion that the Interest of each such other Member bears to the total of all Interests.

LLC Buyout Agreement (continued)

2. Death of a Member

a. **Rights of Company.** Upon receipt of notice by the Company that a legal representative of the estate of the deceased Member has been appointed, the Company will have the right for _[number of days]_ days to agree to purchase the deceased Member's Interest for the price and on the terms provided in this Agreement.

b. **Rights of Surviving Members.** If the Company does not exercise the purchase rights provided for in Paragraph 2(a), the surviving Members will have the right to purchase the deceased Member's Interest at the price and on the terms provided in this Agreement. The surviving Members will have _[number of days]_ days from the end of the _[number of days]_ -day period provided for in Paragraph 2(a) to exercise this purchase right. Any purchase made under this provision must be made either in proportion to the surviving Members' individual interests or, if disproportionate, with the consent of all surviving Members.

c. **Closing.** The closing for a purchase under Paragraph 2 will take place within _[number of days]_ after receipt of the notice provided above.

3. Lifetime Transfers

a. **Voluntary Transfers**

  i. **Lock-in period.** The Members agree that no voluntary transfers will be allowed in the first _[number of years]_ of the existence of the Company, beginning with the Effective Date of the First Operating Agreement of the Company, without the prior consent of the other Member(s). During this "lock-in" period, any attempted voluntary transfer will be a violation of the Agreement and will be null and void.

LLC Buyout Agreement (continued)

ii. **Notification.** After the lock-in period, when a Member intends to transfer any part of their Interest to a third party other than as provided in Paragraph 1(b), the Member will give written notice to the Company of the proposed transfer, including the identity of the proposed transferee, the purchase price, and other terms of the deal.

iii. **Company Purchase Rights.** The Company has a right to purchase the Interest proposed to be transferred for the same price and at the same terms as the proposed transfer to the third party. The Company may exercise this right for __[number of days]__ following receipt of the notice provided for in Paragraph 3(a)(ii).

iv. **Other Members' Purchase Rights.** If the Company does not exercise its purchase right under Paragraph 3(a)(iii), the other Members will have the right to purchase the Interest in question at the same terms, provided that the purchase is made in proportion to the other Members' respective Interests in the Company or, if disproportionate, with the unanimous consent of the other Members. The other Members will have __[number of days]__, beginning at the end of the __[number of days]__-day period provided for above, to exercise this purchase right.

b. **Involuntary Transfers**

i. **Involuntary Transfers and Purchase Rights.** Any involuntary transfer made by operation of law or pursuant to a court order, other than by the death of a Member, including but not limited to transfers to a bankruptcy trustee, a creditor pursuant to a court judgment, a guardian or conservator of an incapacitated member, or a spouse or former spouse pursuant to a separation agreement or divorce decree, will be subject to the purchase rights described below.

LLC Buyout Agreement (continued)

    ii. **Company Purchase Rights.** Upon being notified of an involuntary transfer, the Company will have _[number of days]_ to purchase the Interest in question for the price and on the terms provided in this Agreement.

    iii. **Other Members' Purchase Rights.** If the Company does not exercise its purchase right under Paragraph 3(b)(ii), the other Members will have the right to purchase the Interest in question for the price and on the terms provided in this Agreement. The other Members will have _[number of days]_, beginning at the end of the _[number of days]_ -day period provided for above, to exercise this purchase right.

    iv. **Closing.** The closing for a purchase under Paragraph 3 will take place within _[number of days]_ after receipt of the notice provided above.

  c. **Transfers in Violation of Agreement.** Transfers made in violation of this Agreement will be invalid and will not be recognized on the books of the Company.

4. Purchase Price

Select one:

Option 1

a. **Predetermined Purchase Price or Formula.** The purchase price for a purchase under Paragraph 2 or Paragraph 3(b) will be the following price or determined by the following formula _[fill in the price or formula for determining the price]_ .

Option 2

a. **Purchase Price to Be Negotiated.** The purchase price for a purchase under Paragraph 2 or Paragraph 3(b) will be negotiated by the parties at the time of the purchase.

The purchase price will be determined as of the last day of the month immediately preceding (i) the date of death in the case

LLC Buyout Agreement (continued)

of a purchase under Paragraph 2, or (ii) the effective date of the required notice in the case of a purchase under Paragraph 3(b).

b. **Purchase Price Determined by Appraisal.** If the selling Members and the purchaser(s) (the Company or the other Members) are unable to agree on a purchase price, the parties will mutually select a qualified business appraiser. The seller will pay one-half the cost of the appraisal and the purchaser(s) (the Company or the other individual members) will pay the other half. If either party contests the valuation of the appraiser, that party can engage another qualified appraiser, at their own expense, to conduct a separate appraisal. In that event, the purchase price will be the average of the two valuations.

c. **Life Insurance Proceeds.** In the case of the death of a Member, the amount of any life insurance proceeds received by the Company on account of such Member's death will not be considered in determining the purchase price to be paid for the deceased Member's Interest.

5. Payment of Purchase Price

a. **Payment for a Deceased Member's Interest.** In the event of a purchase following the death of a Member, the purchase price will be due and payable on the date of the closing but only to the extent that there are life insurance proceeds available to pay said purchase price. The balance of the purchase price, if any, will be paid by means of a promissory note ("Note") payable in __*[state the number of monthly, quarterly, or annual payments]*__ consecutive equal __*[monthly, quarterly, or annual]*__ payments of principal, with interest at the applicable federal rate as provided under Section 1274 of the Code, determined as of the Closing Date. The Note will be secured by a pledge of the purchased Interest.

LLC Buyout Agreement (continued)

b. **Payment for a Purchase Made Pursuant to an Involuntary Transfer.**
The purchase price will be paid by means of a promissory note
("Note") payable in _____[*state the number of monthly, quarterly,
or annual payments*]_ consecutive equal _[*monthly, quarterly, or
annual*]_ payments of principal, with interest at the applicable
federal rate as provided under Section 1274 of the Code, determined as of the Closing Date. The Note will be secured by a
pledge of the purchased Interest.

c. **Prepayment of Note.** The purchasing party will have the right at
any time or times to prepay the Note in whole or in part without
penalty, provided that any such prepayments will be applied first
to any interest then due and the balance to principal.

6. **Life Insurance**

a. **Purchase of Life Insurance.** The Company may, but is not required
to, purchase and be the owner and beneficiary of life insurance
policies on the life of one or more of the Members.

b. **Life Insurance Claims.** Upon the death of a Member, the Company
will promptly file a claim to collect any insurance death benefit
in one lump sum on each policy covering the life of the deceased
Member.

c. **Balance of Life Insurance Proceeds.** The Company will retain the
balance of any insurance proceeds in excess of the purchase
price for the deceased Member's Interest.

d. **Sale of Policy to a Withdrawing Member.** The Company may, but is not
required to, offer to sell a life insurance policy on a withdrawing
Member to the applicable Member. The purchase price for any
such policy will be its cash surrender value minus any outstanding
indebtedness on the policy. If the applicable Member declines to
purchase the policy, the policy will no longer be subject to this
Agreement, and the Company may retain or dispose of the policy.

LLC Buyout Agreement (continued)

7. Termination

This Agreement will terminate and the Interests subject to this Agreement will be released from the terms of this Agreement on the occurrence of any of the following events:

a. The Company ceases all operations

b. The written consent of all Members to terminate this Agreement

c. Bankruptcy, receivership, or dissolution of the Company; and

d. A single Member becomes the sole owner of all the Interests in the Company.

8. General Provisions

a. **Notices.** Any and all notices, exercise of rights, designations, consents, offers, acceptances, or any other communications provided for herein, will be given in writing, by registered or certified mail, return receipt requested, which will be addressed, in the case of the Company, to its principal place of business and, in the case of a Member, to their personal residence. The effective date of such notice, exercise of right, designation, consent, offer, acceptance or other communication, any law or statute to the contrary, will be deemed to have been given at the time it is duly deposited and registered in any United States Post Office or Branch Post Office.

b. **Amendment and Revocation.** This Agreement can be modified, amended, or revoked only by a writing signed by the Company and all of the Members.

c. **Binding Effect.** This Agreement is binding upon the parties, their heirs, legal representatives, successors, and assigns. This Agreement will also be binding upon any person to whom any Interest is transferred in violation of the provisions of this Agreement.

LLC Buyout Agreement (continued)

d. **Specific Performance.** The parties agree that they will be irrevocably damaged in the event that this Agreement is not specifically enforced. Accordingly, if the Company or any person defaults on an obligation to give a notice, make an offer, sell an Interest, or close a sale as specified above, the Company or any Member may bring an action to compel specific performance by the defaulting party.

e. **Severability.** If any term or provision of this Agreement is held to be invalid or unenforceable, the remainder of this Agreement will remain valid and be enforceable to the fullest extent permitted by law.

f. **Counterparts.** This Agreement may be executed in any number of counterparts each of which, when duly executed, will constitute an original.

g. **Governing Law.** This Agreement will be governed and interpreted according to the laws of ___[state]___.

On behalf of the Company and themselves individually, the Members hereby execute this Agreement, which is effective as of the date first written above.

By: _____   By: _____

Name: _____   Name: _____

By: _____   By: _____

Name: _____   Name: _____

LLC Interest Purchase Agreement

LLC Interest Purchase Agreement

THIS MEMBERSHIP INTEREST PURCHASE AGREEMENT (this "Agreement") is entered into as of __[date]__ (the "Effective Date") between __[name of selling member]__, with an address of __[address of seller]__ ("Seller"), and __[name of purchaser]__, with an address of __[address of purchaser]__ ("Purchaser").

Seller presently owns __[percentage interest]__% of the membership interests in __[name of company]__, a __[state of organization]__ limited liability company (the "Company").

Seller desires to sell and Purchaser desires to purchase all of Seller's membership interests in the Company. The parties therefore agree as follows:

1. **Sale of Membership Interests.** Subject to the terms and conditions of this Agreement, Seller agrees to sell and Purchaser agrees to purchase all of Seller's membership interests in the Company (the "Membership Interests"), including all rights and privileges associated with the Membership Interests.

2. **Transfer Restrictions.** The parties acknowledge that the Membership Interests are subject to the terms and restrictions of the Company's Operating Agreement and a Buyout Agreement between the members and the Company, and stipulate that the purchase being made under this Agreement does not violate any provision of the Operating Agreement, Buyout Agreement, or applicable law.

3. **Consideration.** The purchase price to be paid by Purchaser for the Membership Interests is $__[purchase price]__ (the "Purchase Price"), payable as follows: __[state the payment terms]__.

LLC Interest Purchase Agreement (continued)

4. **Closing.** The closing of the transaction contemplated by this Agreement (the "Closing") will take place on a date (the "Closing Date") and at a place to be agreed by the parties, but not later than __[*latest closing date*]__ without the consent of both parties. The Closing may be conducted simultaneously (in-person or virtually), or by exchange of documents of documents and payments electronically or by overnight courier. The parties agree and acknowledge that no certificate or certificates are necessary to evidence the Transferred Membership Interest that is being transferred under this Agreement, and that the transfer will occur automatically upon the execution of an assignment by the Seller at the Closing.

5. **Representations and Warranties of Seller; Indemnification and Release.** Seller hereby represents and warrants that the following statements are true and correct as of the date of this Agreement and will be true and correct as of the Closing Date. Seller will notify Purchaser promptly if Seller learns between the date of this Agreement and the Closing that any representation made here has ceased to be true.

   a. **Authority.** Seller has full power, authority, and capacity to execute and deliver, and to perform its duties and obligations under this Agreement.

   b. **Title.** Seller is the lawful owner of, and has good and marketable title to, the Membership Interests, free of any and all liens, restrictions, or claims of any kind, except for restrictions contained in the Operating Agreement and Buyout Agreement of the Company.

   c. **Indemnification and Release by Seller.** Seller agrees to indemnify and release Purchaser from and against any liabilities arising from or caused by a breach of any representation or warranty made by Seller in this Agreement, and any liability related to or involving the Membership Interests, including any tax liability, arising or incurred on or prior to the Closing Date.

LLC Interest Purchase Agreement (continued)

6. **Representations and Warranties of Purchaser; Indemnification by Purchaser.** Purchaser hereby represents and warrants to Seller that the following statements are true and correct as of the date of this Agreement and will be true and correct as of the Closing Date.

   a. **Authority; Capacity.** Purchaser has full power and authority to enter into this Agreement, including any necessary consents from the members of the Company, and to perform its obligations under this Agreement.

   b. **Indemnification and Release by Purchaser.** Purchaser agrees to indemnify and release Seller from and against any liabilities arising from or caused by a breach of any representation or warranty made by Purchaser in this Agreement, and any liability related to or involving the Membership Interests, including any tax liability, arising or incurred after the Closing Date.

7. **Entire Agreement.** This Agreement constitutes the entire agreement and understanding between Purchaser and Seller with respect to the subject matter of this Agreement and supersedes all prior understandings, agreements, or communications between the parties related to the subject matter of this Agreement.

8. **Binding Effect.** This Agreement is to be binding upon, and shall inure to the benefit of, Purchaser, Seller, and their respective heirs, legal representatives, successors, and permitted assigns.

9. **Assignment.** Neither party will assign any of its rights under this Agreement without the prior written consent of the other party.

10. **Multiple Counterparts.** This Agreement may be executed in one or more counterparts, each of which shall be deemed an original but all of which together will constitute one instrument.

11. **Notices.** Any notices or communications required or permitted to be given by this Agreement must be given in writing, and be personally delivered or sent by certified mail, express shipment, or electronically

LLC Interest Purchase Agreement (continued)

with receipt confirmed. A notice is to be sent to the addresses of the receiving party as written above, or to an email address provided by the receiving party.

12. **Amendments.** This Agreement may be amended only by a writing signed by both parties.

13. **Severability.** If any provision of is determined by a court or arbitrator to be invalid, unenforceable, or otherwise ineffective, that provision will be severed from the rest of this Agreement shall for any reason be held to be invalid or unenforceable in any respect, the remaining provisions will continue to be in effect and enforceable.

14. **Governing Law.** This Agreement is to be governed and interpreted according to the law of the state of ___[name of state]___.

So Agreed:

___[name of Purchaser]___ (Purchaser):   ___[name of Seller]___ (Seller):

By: _____   By: _____

Name:
Title:

Assignment of LLC Interest

Assignment of LLC Interest

This ASSIGNMENT OF LLC INTEREST ("Assignment") is made by __*[name of seller/assignor]*__ ("Assignor") to __*[name of purchaser/assignee]*__ ("Assignee") as of __*[date]*__ (the "Effective Date").

1. **Assignment.** Pursuant to a Membership Interest Purchase Agreement between the parties, dated __*[date of purchase agreement]*__ (the "Purchase Agreement"), and in return for the Purchase Price and other valuable consideration set forth in the Purchase Agreement, the receipt of which Assignor hereby acknowledges, the Assignor irrevocably and unconditionally assigns a __*[percentage interest]*__% Membership Interest (the "Assigned Interest") in __*[name of company]*__, a __*[state of organization]*__ limited liability company (the "LLC") to Assignee.

2. **Representations and Warranties.** The parties reaffirm the representations and warranties made in the Purchase Agreement.

3. **LLC Consent.** If the LLC is not the Assignee, the LLC approves the transfer of the Assigned Interest from Assignor to Assignee.

4. **Releases.** The Assignor releases the Assignee from all liabilities and claims arising from the Assigned Interest prior to the date of this Assignment. The Assignee releases the Assignor from all liabilities and claims arising from the Assigned Interest on or after the date of this Assignment. The Assignor and the LLC release each other from all liabilities and claims arising under the LLC and Assignor's ownership interest therein.

Assignment of LLC Interest (continued)

So Agreed:

__[*name of Assignor*]__ (Assignor):   __[*name of Assignee*]__ (Assignee):

By: _____   By: _____

                                       Name:
                                       Title:

[*If the Assignee is an individual member, not the LLC, include the following consent and signature*]

The LLC consents to the above assignment.

By: _____

Name:
Title:

Meeting Minutes

Meeting Minutes

A meeting of the _____*[members or managers]*_____ of _____*[company name]*_____ was held on __*[meeting date]*__, at ____*[meeting time]*____ at _____*[meeting location]*_____.

In attendance:

Absent:

The __*[members or managers]*__ took the following actions at the meeting:

1.

2.

3.

Minutes prepared by __*[name of preparer]*__ and distributed to the __*[members or managers]*__ on ___*[date]*___.

Unanimous Written Consent

Unanimous Written Consent

The undersigned, being all the _____[*members or managers*]_____
of _____[*company name*]_____, consent to the following action(s)
as of the date last signed below; such consent to be taken as if a vote
(or votes) at a meeting, per the Company's Operating Agreement:

1.

2.

3.

By: _____ Date: _____
    [*Name of Member or Manager*]

By: _____ Date: _____
    [*Name of Member or Manager*]

By: _____ Date: _____
    [*Name of Member or Manager*]

By: _____ Date:_____
    [*Name of Member or Manager*]

LLC Dissolution Agreement

LLC Dissolution Agreement
_____[Company name]_____

This Dissolution Agreement ("Agreement") is effective as of __[date]__ and is made by the Members whose signatures appear below (each a "Member" and collectively the "Members"), who are all the Members of ___[company name]___, a ___[state of organization]___ limited liability company (the "Company").

The Members wish to dissolve the Company pursuant to the terms of this Agreement. Therefore, the Members agree as follows:

1. **Vote to Dissolve.** The Company is to be dissolved and the business is to be wound up in accordance with the provisions of the ___[state]___ Limited Liability Company Act, and any relevant requirements of the IRS and other taxing and administrative authorities.

2. **Winding Up.** The Members will wind up the business, legal, and tax affairs of the Company. The Members will file all documents and take all other actions necessary to liquidate and terminate the Company.

3. **Distribution of Remaining Assets.** Any assets left in the Company after all Company obligations have been met will be distributed to the Members according to their capital interests.

4. **Indemnification of Members.** The Company will indemnify a Member for any debt, obligation, or other liability, including reasonable attorneys' fees, incurred in the course of the Member's performance of duties on behalf of the Company under this Agreement, as long as the Member complied with the duties of loyalty and care when incurring the debt, obligation, or other liability. This provision does not in any way limit the indemnification the Member would be entitled to under applicable state law. The indemnification provided shall inure to the benefit of successors and assigns of any such Member.

LLC Dissolution Agreement (continued)

The Members execute this Agreement as of the day and year first above written.

_____

[*Member name*], Member

_____

[*Member name*], Member

Index

More from Nolo

Nolo.com offers a large library of legal solutions and forms, created by Nolo's in-house legal editors. These reliable documents can be prepared in minutes.

Create a Document Online

Incorporation. Incorporate your business in any state.

LLC Formation. Gain asset protection and pass-through tax status in any state.

Will. Nolo has helped people make over 2 million wills. Is it time to make or revise yours?

Living Trust (avoid probate). Plan now to save your family the cost, delays, and hassle of probate.

Download Useful Legal Forms

Nolo.com has hundreds of top quality legal forms available for download:

- bill of sale
- promissory note
- nondisclosure agreement
- LLC operating agreement
- corporate minutes
- commercial lease and sublease
- motor vehicle bill of sale
- consignment agreement
- and many more.

www.nolo.com

NOLO

Save 15% *off your next order*

Register your Nolo purchase, and we'll send you a
coupon for 15% off your next Nolo.com order!

Nolo.com/customer-support/productregistration

On Nolo.com you'll also find:

Books & Software

Nolo publishes hundreds of great books and software programs for consumers and
business owners. Order a copy, or download an ebook version instantly, at Nolo.com.

Online Forms

You can quickly and easily make a will or living trust, form an LLC or corporation,
or make hundreds of other forms—online.

Free Legal Information

Thousands of articles answer common questions about everyday legal issues,
including wills, bankruptcy, small business formation, divorce, patents,
employment, and much more.

Plain-English Legal Dictionary

Stumped by jargon? Look it up in America's most up-to-date source for definitions
of legal terms, free at Nolo.com.

Lawyer Directory

Nolo's consumer-friendly lawyer directory provides in-depth profiles of lawyers all
over America. You'll find information you need to choose the right lawyer.

LLCH1